W9-CKI-468

MENUS FOR IMPULSIVE LIVING

MENUS FOR IMPULSIVE LIVING

A Revolutionary Approach to Organizing and Energizing Your Life

KURT LELAND

DOUBLEDAY

New York London Toronto Sydney Auckland

Published by Doubleday, a division of
Bantam Doubleday Dell Publishing Group, Inc.
666 Fifth Avenue, New York, New York 10103

Doubleday and the portrayal of an anchor
with a dolphin are trademarks of Doubleday,
a division of Bantam Doubleday Dell Publishing
Group, Inc.

LIBRARY OF CONGRESS CATALOGING-IN-PUBLICATION DATA

Leland, Kurt.
Menus for impulsive living: a program for self-realization /
by Kurt Leland.—1st ed.
p. cm.
1. Spirit writings. 2. Self-realization—Miscellanea.
3. Impulse—Miscellanea. I. Title.
BF1301.L53 1989 88-31468
133.9'3—dc19 CIP

ISBN 0-385-26013-X
Copyright © 1989 by Kurt Leland

All Rights Reserved
Printed in the United States of America
April 1989
First Edition

BOOK DESIGN BY KATHRYN PARISE

BG

ACKNOWLEDGMENTS

I would like to thank the following people, without whom this book would not have been possible: my parents, for never saying no when I had made up my mind to do something; Andrea Isaacs, and Brian and Judy Galford, for seeing me through the best and worst of times; Alan Goodwin, for his boundless and infectious enthusiasm for Charles, which I have often needed to draw upon for support; Richard Vanstone, for being there a lot at the very beginning; Mark Douglas, fellow first-time author, for the opportunity to learn from each other's triumphs and mistakes; and Nancy Whitely, whose presence and love is felt from no matter how far away.

I'm much obliged to Jim Fitzgerald at Doubleday for a number of suggestions that have shaped the book in important ways; and to Ceci Scott, Jim's assistant, for service above and beyond the call of duty. Barbara Bowen of Eleanor Friede Books has also been enormously helpful at critical moments. As for Eleanor Friede herself, I must say that I'm deeply appreciative of her presence in my life both as editor and human being—wonderfully wise in both realms.

Special recognition goes to the Boston Charles group for their willingness to find out if what Charles says really works; and to Steve Katz and George Corbett, who have given me the precious gift of seeing and understanding so much of who I am.

Finally, to say that I'm eternally grateful for the presence of Charles in my life is probably an understatement. Whoever he is and wherever he comes from, he's the best friend I could ever hope to have.

This book is dedicated to the memory of Jane Roberts and Seth—whom I never met. Without their pioneering work in channeling, I might never have encountered Charles or discovered the Menus system.

FOREWORD

"It always seems to me that so few people live—they just seem to exist—and I don't see any reason why we shouldn't *live always*—till we die physically—why do we do it all in our teens and twenties." Thus the artist Georgia O'Keeffe wrote to one of her close friends shortly before she turned twenty-eight, in 1915. Coming across her words just after I turned thirty, I couldn't help but feel the same way. In fact, for the last few years I have noticed that my friends speak with less and less enthusiasm about living. Their conversations are taken up with concern about their jobs, money, attempts to buy a house, or whether or not to have children. Gone are the fiery debates about life and art, the unbridled passion for new experience, even the simple delight in coincidence. It would seem that as these people grow older, the magic of life is draining away, slowly and insidiously.

A few years ago, as I was completing a portfolio of music compositions to submit for my master's degree at the University of Illinois, I, too, was a victim of this loss of enthusiasm for life. I worked as many as twelve hours a day to get the portfolio finished. Every day seemed so much like the last one that it got harder and harder for me to get out of bed and face it. I felt tired all the time, unmotivated to take even the slightest pleasure in what I was doing or to make time for something more enjoyable. Like so many people these days, I had become a slave of routine, which was mercilessly crushing the will to live.

When I finished the portfolio and turned it in, I found myself in an uncomfortable position. Up to that point in my life, schoolwork of one kind or another had been a significant factor in determining my use of time. Now I was done. Also, I didn't have a job. I had been making a living as a psychic counselor for a number of years, channeling an entity who calls himself Charles. But since I had recently moved to Boston and not many people knew of my work, readings were few and far between. What was I going to do with all this unstructured time? Before, it had been hard to get up because I had too much to do; now it was hard because I had too little.

Luckily Charles came to my rescue. He suggested that I try to let my use of time be guided exclusively by impulses. To make this easier, he offered me the concept of Menus for Impulsive Living. Because I had bought a word processor a few years back, I was familiar with the kind of menu he meant. Many computer programs begin by presenting a list of choices identified with numbers or letters of the alphabet. Each choice directs the computer into a different aspect of the program, responsible for executing a particular task. You simply decide which choice is best for what you need to get done, punch the number or letter, and then off you go. Evidently impulses work something like that. There are several different categories, each one supported by a different state of consciousness. Charles identified these categories with letters of the alphabet and then demonstrated how to use them to schedule a day impulsively. Not only would everything that needed to be accomplished get done, but also productivity and efficiency would increase considerably. There was even a category of impulses that would start to bring the magic back into life!

By applying this system I have regained my enthusiasm for living. As if that weren't enough, I have been able nearly to achieve my ideal body, after years of flabbiness due to unintentional neglect. I get more work done more quickly and have time for more fun. Every aspect of my life has been favorably transformed. But living impulsively isn't necessarily easy. It can be a rigorous discipline at times—especially since our society tends to discount impulses. Since information on the Menus system first came through in 1985, Charles has greatly amplified the system. There are many helpful hints and exercises designed to make it easier to live impulsively. Nearly every aspect of life is covered: home, the office, children, travel, even how to draw a new love relationship into your life. Charles has provided guidelines for anyone caught up in the often difficult circumstances of living in today's world. No matter the demands on your time, you can lead a life motivated primarily by impulses.

Charles claims to speak from the soul's perspective on this world. He often points out that the soul doesn't see things quite the way we do. It has a different set of priorities, involved with learning and growth of a spiritual nature. This agenda often seems to conflict with our own sense of what we need to be doing at any particular time. The Menus system also provides a framework that will allow the soul's agenda for our self-realization to assert itself, but within the context of our daily lives.

Charles demonstrates that a balance can be achieved between the purely physical and material demands that our presence in the world among family, friends, colleagues, and coworkers make upon us, and the spiritual demands of becoming who we truly are. Many spiritual disciplines of the past have sought to impose severely limiting structures upon daily life, as in the case of the charismatic spiritual leader who claims that enlightenment can come only if you leave work and family behind. Charles, however, provides a means whereby the current structure of your life becomes the starting point for the path towards self-realization. Application of his concepts will not cut your ties to the world but will enhance them in deeply fulfilling ways. You may have to make some adjustments, so that the soul's agenda and your own personal priorities do not interfere with one another. But by and large, there is little chance that you will have to give up doing the things you love in order to achieve enlightenment. For, according to Charles, enlightenment is nothing more than knowing what to do next under any given set of circumstances.

Kurt Leland
September 1988

CONTENTS

PART ONE

IMPULSES AND MENUS

PART TWO

FUNCTIONS OF THE MENU A IMPULSES

PART THREE

CREATING AN IMPULSIVE LIFESTYLE

PART FOUR

SPECIAL APPLICATIONS

AUTHOR'S NOTE

Charles uses the pronoun *we* to refer to himself. He does this because he considers our relationship to be a kind of equal partnership, consisting of a nonphysical source of information and a human being who has developed the capacity to translate this information into words. There are only three portions of the book that I have written without his aid—the Foreword; most of Chapter 9, which contains my personal Menus for Impulsive Living as examples; and the Notes at the end.

PART ONE

IMPULSES AND MENUS

CHAPTER 1

What Is an Impulse?

There is something at once both seductive and dangerous about the word *impulse.* Impulse-motivated behavior, it would seem, could lead to a horrible crime as readily as to a pleasant day at the beach. Calling oneself impulsive can be a matter of pride, in which case the word is synonymous with *spontaneous* or *free.* But calling someone else impulsive often carries negative connotations: he or she is somehow not responsible. Regardless of whether the word holds positive or negative connotations, it is always in some sense held up against the idea of dreary routine. Impulses upset routine, whether for better or for worse. And since routine has a mind-numbing effect, people crave to live impulsively.

Without routine, life can become at once mysterious and exciting. Yet everyone has work of some kind to do. An impulsive lifestyle would seem to offer carte blanche to shirk one's duties. But what if it were possible to accomplish that work to the same level of quality in much less time? What if you could not only get that work done but also greet each day with anticipation of the adventures it might bring, rather than with a dread of how much it might seem the same as the last?

This book offers a means of structuring your thinking about time so that you can live impulsively and yet responsibly. You can allow yourself to be seduced by impulses without worrying that you might be putting the security of job or family on the line. Using this system of managing the day, what you or others might require will certainly get accomplished. And simultaneously, life will become an inexhaustible source of wonder.

What is an impulse? In our view, an impulse is a message sent to the ego either from the soul or from the body. This message indicates that a certain action is appropriate at a certain time. When the message comes from the soul, the action will have something to do with the process of self-realization, of becoming who you truly are; when from the body, it will have something to do with physical survival. An example of the soul type of impulse might be to interview for another job if the one you have seems oppressive or dissatisfying. An example of the body type of impulse would be to eat, sleep, or exercise. Since the soul has an investment in your remaining present in physical reality until you have accomplished certain kinds of learning and since the body has an investment in its own survival over time, there is no such thing as a self-destructive impulse. Furthermore, the soul will never send an impulse toward an action that might thwart someone else's process of self-realization. True impulses, therefore, can hardly be called dangerous. They will never encourage destructive behavior.

From our perspective, actions motivated by such powerful emotions as rage or hatred are not *im*pulsively but *com*pulsively motivated. There is a certain neurotic aspect to such behaviors, which indicate a severe misalignment of ego and soul. The same would be true, but to a lesser extent, with individuals who feel the compulsion to shoplift or commit other minor transgressions.

Even so, the soul has a different concept of ethics than that supported by your society. Society might argue that you must go to the office five days a week to make a living. Yet, when you arise on a certain morning, you might feel compelled by an impulse to go the beach. The question is, would pursuing that impulse put you behind? Or would it refresh you sufficiently that you could get much more work accomplished the next day? Some brilliant member of the work force, when faced by a similar dilemma, invented the term *mental health day* in order to justify pursuing such an impulse.

Our point is that from the soul's perspective, anything that you do under the motivation of a true impulse is intended to keep you healthy and to inspire growth. At least eighty years are required for the completion of the lessons chosen by the soul for each lifetime in physical reality. Certainly the body can serve you in health and vigor for that entire period, from start to finish. But you must not abuse the body in any way. You must learn to enter into an active dialogue with both body and soul so that they can assert their needs to the ego with the fullest confidence they will be satisfied. It is through impulses that these needs are made known. *Menus for Impulsive Living* will enable you to become aware of impulses so that you can achieve maximum creativity and productivity in all areas of your life while minimizing wear and tear on the body.

How do you know what a true impulse is? In the case of the body, this is relatively easy: genuine hunger and tiredness constitute impulses toward eating and sleeping. In the case of the soul, however, there are so many aspects of the process of self-realization that an impulse directing you toward a certain action may only come once in a lifetime. These impulses may be more difficult to perceive simply because they are less familiar. Nevertheless, there are certain methods by which you can detect such impulses.

There are two basic kinds of impulses: the first directs you toward a certain activity; the second directs you away from a certain activity. We shall call the first type *impulses for* and the second *impulses against.* The impulse for will manifest as an inner prompting that makes the activity seem highly important or attractive at a given moment. It somehow feels completely appropriate. Unless there are mental obstructions to acting impulsively, you may simply find yourself in the midst of performing this action, without having really considered it. Perhaps you keep thinking about a certain food. The idea of having it seems highly appealing, and eventually you go to the store to get it. There is no question in your mind about how much you will enjoy it. You may even find yourself reaching for it without thinking as you push your cart down the aisle. These are some of the ways an impulse for may express itself.

The impulse against, on the other hand, manifests itself as an aversion to doing something. It feels wrong somehow. Perhaps you have gone to your favorite restaurant and decided that you're tired of what you usually order, that you'd rather try something else for a change. Or perhaps someone has served you a vegetable that you usually like, but on this occasion it doesn't taste good to you. These are some of the ways an impulse against may express itself.

Ideally, impulses for or against would manifest themselves as clearly as in our examples. But there is a stubborn streak in human nature. The ego doesn't like being told what to do. An impulse emanating from the body or the soul might feel like a command that must be obeyed. Sometimes the ego will resist, like a child throwing a temper tantrum. The ego likes to feel that it has supreme control over all aspects of the self. It may thwart the body or the soul by refusing to pursue an impulse for or purposely ignoring an impulse against. Yet the ego came into existence as a result of the soul's nonphysical beingness coming into contact with the physical matter of the body. Thus, the ego represents a special blend of both physical and nonphysical realities, in the same way that an estuary is a special blend of fresh water and ocean. Since the ego represents the interface of soul and body, it is not independent of them. To ignore the needs of either of its two sources will threaten its own survival. It is never appropriate to refuse or ignore impulses.

How can you tell when an impulse is expressing itself if the ego might be refusing or ignoring it? True impulses have a certain persistence about them. They will not vanish from your awareness until they have been acted upon. In order to refuse or ignore them, the ego must talk itself out of noticing and acting upon them. Whenever you try to persuade yourself to do a certain thing, you are ignoring an impulse against. And whenever you try to persuade yourself *not* to do a certain thing, you are ignoring an impulse for. A rather typical technique of persuasion is concealed in the word *should.* Whenever you tell yourself that you should be doing a certain thing, there is always something else that you are trying to talk yourself out of doing. If you say, "I should do X," you are actually suppressing the second part of the sentence: "instead of Y." By reversing your position—doing Y instead of X—you will have acted on the true impulse.

Impulses could perhaps best be described by an analogy from classical physics. When an object is set in motion, it will theoretically continue in the same direction and at the same speed indefinitely unless it is acted upon by another force. That force may approach the object from another direction and may be stronger or weaker than the force that originally set the object in motion. The angle and strength of that force will change the direction and speed of the object. In this way inertia—which in the human world expresses itself as resistance to change—is overcome.

At any given moment, your life is headed in a certain direction that may or may not have as its ultimate goal the becoming of who you truly are. Course adjustments may be required from time to time. Impulses are attempts on the part of the soul to maneuver you onto the easiest and most direct route toward self-realization. The mere act of having been born, of having come into this world with lessons to be learned and work to be accomplished, has set you in motion. Impulses will change your course—your "vector"—to keep you true to the goal of discovering and fulfilling the soul's purposes in this lifetime.

The soul is constantly applying such forces. They may be manifested as outward or as inward events. Yet there is always an impulse that directs an individual to participate. It is only one's resistance to such participation—inertia—that makes life seem difficult or unpleasant. Because many factors have contributed to today's inability to respond to impulses, or even to perceive them, we have evolved a structure within which it becomes possible to recognize and act on impulses on a regular basis. This system will help you overcome inertia.

The idea of living impulsively may sound especially attractive if you crave a life of spontaneity and adventure. Such a life could free you of mind-numbing routine. Perhaps it seems even more appealing now that you know that impulses originate from the soul. For you to develop that sense of adventure would be at the same time to live spiritually. But even if you do not consider yourself a spiritual person, there is something of value to be had from pursuing impulses. We have already mentioned that one purpose of our system is to enable maximum productivity with minimum wear and tear on the body. To live impulsively will not only minimize this wear and tear, but it may even go so far as to arrest or reverse the symptoms of aging.

Perhaps you have experienced the fear of growing old. If you look carefully at this fear, you will discover that it contains an interesting paradox. While you may worry about the seemingly inevitable deterioration of the physical mechanism ("getting older"), at the same time you value growth into ever more full realizations of yourself ("maturation"). One of the keys to life in physical reality is this: *Symbols are a means your consciousness uses to monitor its own development.* There must be some means other than aging through which to acknowledge the degree to which you have become yourself. From the soul's perspective, exhaustion, wrinkles, crow's-feet, sagging breasts, or stiff joints symbolize how much you have *resisted* self-fulfillment. A youthful vibrancy that firms up what has become flabby and smooths out what has become wrinkled would be a much more appropriate expression of becoming more truly yourself.

The Fountain of Youth is not a mythical place; it is an attitude toward life. That attitude consists in nothing more than removing all inner blocks to perceiving and acting upon impulses. Aging is primarily caused by stress, which is itself the result of allowing routine to block recognition of impulses. The Menus for Impulsive Living will tend to break down routine so that these impulses may express themselves.

C H A P T E R 2

Basic Assumptions

While the system of managing time and energy described in this book can be used no matter your lifestyle or belief system, there are certain unconventional assumptions that underlie it. It is not required that you believe all or any of these assumptions in order for the system to work for you. But treating them *as if* they were true for the time being will certainly make it easier to read and absorb what follows. After you have had some success applying the information in this book, you can decide for yourself whether or not to incorporate any of these provisionally true beliefs into your belief system.

We prefer the word *validity* to the word *truth* when it comes to beliefs. If a belief works for you, improving your quality of life and deepening your sense of self, then it is valid. It may, however, be succeeded by other, more useful beliefs. In this case, the former belief is not false but simply no longer valid. *Usefulness* should be the measure of validity, not ultimate truth. All too often people rigidly adopt certain belief systems as "truth," never allowing them to change. Their beliefs are supposedly true now and will therefore be true forevermore. It is utterly impossible to achieve self-realization with this sort of attitude. You don't have to throw out everything you believe to be true in order to read this book; but to make the going easier, you should replace the concept of truth with the concept of validity.

In the previous chapter we asserted that there is a soul guiding you toward self-realization through impulses. No one has ever been able to prove that there is a soul. Some people believe that the existence of the soul is absolutely true; others, that it is a complete fiction. Rather than arguing to support our claim, we would simply like to point out that it is *useful* for us to make this assumption. It explains the origins of impulses. By the end of the book, if you have had the positive experience of feeling happier and more fulfilled through following impulses, it might be useful for you to adopt the belief that impulses emanate from a soul that guides you at every moment toward becoming who you truly are.

The second major assumption that underlies this book is that you have been born into this life in order to learn certain lessons and realize certain goals: you have a *life purpose.* The soul exists outside of time and space, but it learns things through you that can only be learned *within* time and space. In a sense, you and your body are like a rubber glove through which the soul, like a hand, reaches into physical reality. Just as your range of activities would be severely limited if the human species had been created without hands, so would the soul's range of activities be severely limited if it did not have you to learn through.

Often, when different departments of an organization act at cross purposes, people will say: "The right hand doesn't know what the left hand is doing." This makes it sound as if each hand had its own little brain inside, and both were pursuing their own goals independently of each other. In a sense, the ego and the soul often behave in just this fashion. Though you are the rubber glove that the soul works through, the hand inside that glove has a will of its own. Thus, the ego can sometimes thwart the intentions of the soul. Imagine how you would feel if your brain told your hand to write down a response to a test question you absolutely must answer correctly and, instead, the hand drew pictures of flowers. Often the soul is just as frustrated with the behavior of the ego.

You may remember how you felt as a teenager when your parents told you to do something, such as taking out the trash. You might have done everything in your power to avoid it, out of a feeling of rebelliousness. Yet the task may have required a mere five minutes of your time—and far less expenditure of energy than having to deal with the tensions that arose between yourself and your parents because of your resistance. At one time or another, almost everyone behaves this way when it comes to the soul's requirements for self-realization. It is almost as if there were a kind of conspiracy going on, in which people support each other in making sure that nobody (or as few people as possible) become who they truly are. Bullying, disapproval, and rejection of those who seem different because they follow their own, individual inner voices are among the techniques of making sure people don't become who they truly are. But there is also a more subtle aspect of this conspiracy. It is as if the soul were the parent of a teenager who had to be sent upon an important mission. If the teenager were to fail in its mission, the parent would suffer intensely. But instead of accomplishing it, the teenager gathers up a group of friends—all on similar missions—and goes to an amusement park.

We are not saying that fulfilling one's life purpose is as "unpleasant" a task as taking out the trash or that it takes all the fun out of life. Rather, life on earth is as full of distractions as an amusement park, and in a certain sense, humankind is experiencing a kind of adolescence. It rebels against the soul and immerses itself in distraction. Everything that you perceive as problematic in the world—from crime on the streets and corruption in government to sex offenses, war, and starving Third World nations—is a symptom of this adolescence. Mankind can only enter its maturity through each individual's acknowledging and fulfilling his or her life purpose. When every person knows what he or she has come here to learn and works tirelessly to manifest that personal destiny, then all the problems will disappear.

What do we mean by the words *life purpose*, and how does this term relate to your life? There are as many different life purposes as there are people currently present on the planet. A personal life purpose does not consist of just one thing done over and over for as long as you live. You may feel, for example, that you have been called to become a health practitioner. While this may indeed be one aspect of your life purpose, it will not necessarily be the only one. It may be part of your life purpose to have children as well or to write poetry on the side.

We have broken down the concept of life purpose into a number of components so that its true nature might be better understood. The first component could be called *service to the body*. Since your body is the vehicle through which the soul learns its lessons in physical reality, the better shape it's in, the easier it is to learn those lessons. Feeding the body properly and engaging in daily exercise are both part of your life purpose. So is avoiding overuse of substances such as tobacco, drugs, or alcohol, all of which tend to diminish the body's capacity to function efficiently.

The second component of your personal life purpose could be called *service to the soul*. For you to come up with an appropriate response to every situation life has to offer is an actual need of the soul. If you try to avoid facing life, the soul learns nothing. The kinds of situations we mean could be external, as in the case of involvements with other people, or internal, as in the case of psychic experiences or dreams. Reading up on how to handle certain situations (intimate relationships, for example), engaging in therapy sessions, or attending self-development seminars can help you fulfill this aspect of your life purpose.

The third component of your life purpose could be called

service to the Creator. By this we do not mean going to worship services. The Bible says that you were created in the image of God. This means that you have the gift of creativity. Part of your life purpose is to come to an appreciation of the magnificence of creation by becoming a creator yourself in some way. It is therefore essential for you to have a creative outlet. This could take the form of any of the traditional arts —painting, sculpting, choreographing, writing, or composing. Or it could be a craft such as weaving baskets, constructing ship models, throwing pottery, or making jewelry. Cooking and gardening can also be creative acts. Because you were created to fulfill a certain function within the universe, whenever you create something that will fulfill a certain function in your life—whether an expressive function, as in a painting, or a practical one, as in a bookshelf you have designed—you become more capable of sensing how you fit into the cosmos as a whole.

The fourth component of your life purpose could be called *service to the personality.* There is an almost unlimited number of expressive characteristics available to humanity. Part of your life purpose is to realize as much of your humanity as possible, in terms of range and depth of feeling. The development of intellectual and psychic capacities are equally important. The more of these feelings and capacities you explore and incorporate into your life, the richer your personality and your experience of daily living. The wisdom and joy that become possible through the realization of this richness makes it easier to fulfill other aspects of your life purpose.

Creativity can be a means of exploring the expressive characteristics available to humanity and making them your own. But it is not enough simply to create. The expressive potential of any creative act is fully realized only when other people are invited to participate in it in some way. This is accomplished by showing the work to them or performing it for them. Whether this audience is made up of the general public or of your most intimate friends is immaterial. You will never become fully aware of what you have learned about yourself as a human being through any creative act until you have shared it with others. Service to personality can also be accomplished by attending the performances of others. Being moved by how an actor or dancer or musical artist has developed his or her personality means that you are getting in touch with your own larger expressivity.

Your social persona is yet another kind of creation. It is made up of all kinds of feelings and techniques of expression, some invented or discovered within yourself, some borrowed from people you admire. Socializing allows you to perform this creation. Even being "the life of the party" can contribute to fulfilling your life purpose, as long as you're not just trying to call attention to yourself. When performing your social persona, it is rarely appropriate to indulge in histrionics. Yet you should allow yourself to be as expressive of *who you truly are* as possible. This enables other people to get in touch with their own expressivity and helps them enrich their lives.

The fifth component of your life purpose is *service to family.* By "family," we mean not only your blood relatives but also the spiritual family of your closest friends. It is a part of your life purpose to help and guide them toward self-realization. And it is just as important to allow yourself to be helped and guided *by* them. It is not required that you have children to fulfill this aspect of your life purpose. But once you have made that decision, it becomes a part of your life purpose to care for them to the best of your ability.

The sixth component of your life purpose is *service to humanity.* Often your job will be an expression of such service. It isn't necessary to touch the lives of everyone on the planet in order to serve humanity. All that is required is for you to be working in some way toward bettering the physical, emotional, intellectual, or spiritual well-being of humankind—even if "humankind" comprises only a handful of people. If their lives are significantly improved, then they may have more of an inclination to help others in the same way. And these others may themselves reach out to serve some sector of humanity. After several generations have passed, your work may in fact have come to touch the lives of a considerable portion of humankind, no matter how small your accomplishment may have seemed to you at the time.

The seventh component of your life purpose is *service to all life.* Humans constitute but one species on a planet teeming with animal and plant life. Working to improve quality of life for them, as well as for yourselves, is essential. The first step in connecting to this aspect of your life purpose is to explore nature in an unobtrusive and appreciative way, such as hiking or camping out. More in-depth study of the things that interest you—wildflowers, trees, mushrooms, animal tracks, or edible plants, for example—will develop a sense of wonder at, and responsibility for, your presence on this planet. You might then be moved to support ecological organizations, the stewardship of endangered species, wilderness preservation, or the cleanup of the environment. Serving all life runs the gamut from recycling waste to picking up litter, and from lobbying for ecological causes to making contributions of time or money to a museum, a zoo, the Audubon Society, or the Save the Whales campaign. Some people's life purpose may call them to take direct action, while that of others may move them simply to support such work. In this, as in all other areas of your life purpose, it is never appropriate to allow one kind of service to supplant the others. The soul, for example, would not condone an activist's doing something that earns an extended jail sentence if he or she has children who must be cared for.

Our seven-point program for fulfilling your life purpose might seem impossible, given the demands of modern living. Working a job for forty hours a week and raising children the rest of the time may seem like all that anybody could hope to have the time and energy for. The soul knows this. And it sends you impulses chosen and timed in such a way that you can fully realize yourself in *all* the ways it requires of you in the course of a lifetime. You don't have to quit your job or leave your family to become who you truly are.

The third assumption basic to this book concerns the existence of what we call *life force.* After you have eaten, certain digestive processes will convert food into the energy that runs your body. This is not the same thing as life force. It is entirely possible for you to have eaten well and yet feel listless and unmotivated to do anything. What you lack in such a moment is life force, not calories to burn.

Life force originates in the nonphysical reality inhabited by the soul. The soul projects life force into physical reality in order to animate the body. It is made available to you during sleep, in ways we shall explain later. You use it each day to fuel your process of self-realization at the mental and emotional levels. The closer you come to discovering how best to fulfill your life purpose in each of the seven areas mentioned above, the more life force flows through you. You will feel enthusiastic, motivated, happy, satisfied, and youthful. The more you resist fulfilling your life purpose in any of these areas, the less life force flows through you. You will feel unenthusiastic, listless, unhappy, dissatisfied, and old. In a sense, moving toward fulfillment of your life purpose is like the game in which children cry, "You're getting warmer!" You can always tell whether you are moving toward it or away from it by how happy ("warmer") or unhappy ("cooler") you feel in any given moment.

Life force enables you to draw to yourself whatever you might need to fulfill your life purpose. Just as a current flowing through a wire generates a magnetic field around that wire, so do you exude a kind of magnetism when large amounts of life force are flowing through you. This magnetism ensures the satisfaction of every need upon which the process of becoming who you truly are depends—anything from survival needs (food, shelter, clothing) to emotional needs (love, nurturance, support). Without these things, it can become difficult to work toward fulfillment of your life purpose. The mind would be too worried and distracted to entertain thoughts of self-realization. Only in rebelling against the soul or in falling prey to the conspiracy we mentioned above do you block your ability to draw what you need into your life.

The ego is like a self-regulating valve of life-force flow. When the ego acts against the impulses projected by the soul, this self-regulating valve closes down. Less life force flows through the body, which begins to experience a kind of energy starvation. Such energy starvation can lead to physical deterioration if it is prolonged. Symptoms of aging reflect the extent of this deterioration. Just as one feels and looks better after eating when one has gone too long without food, so does the body feel and look better when it is not starved for life force because of ignored impulses. To live impulsively—which is to say, to heed the course adjustments made by the soul on your journey toward self-realization—is just as much a need as to provide the body with food.

It may seem that a major factor prohibiting fulfillment of your life purpose in every area is the amount of time spent working a job. Yet the money made at work contributes to the satisfaction of needs on many levels. Quitting and joining a spiritual community in some remote area may not be the answer. Although you could find a job that allows you to combine several aspects of your life purpose, this is not absolutely necessary as long as your work fulfills at least one. Much more effective is finding a means of encouraging each hour to contribute to fulfillment of your life purpose in some way, both at work and away from it.

If you are deeply dissatisfied with your work or with life in general, it may be that you are not moving toward fulfillment of life purpose. Wholeheartedly applying yourself to any one of the areas of service listed above will tend to bring the others into focus. Simply being creative, for example, can often move you in a new career direction; or working on becoming more expressive could help you get closer to your family. The concepts of life purpose, life force, and happiness are all so closely related that doing whatever satisfies you most deeply is sure to be part of who you truly are. All you need do is create a lifestyle that supports your process of becoming. This book will show you how.

C H A P T E R 3

The Natural Schedule

Impulses can be perceived only against the backdrop of a certain degree of ordinariness. Just as an external force modifies the vector and speed of a moving object, so do impulses modify ordinariness.

If you think back to your childhood, you may remember a time when your day was largely determined by what your mother had to be doing at a given time. Prior to this, *you* determined your mother's schedule with your cries for sustenance, your naps, and your dirty diapers. When you become an adult, purely physical needs such as eating, sleeping, or going to the bathroom do not demand all of your attention. Yet they require satisfaction every single day. These needs establish the fundamental ordinariness of life, against which impulses may be perceived. They create what could be called *the Natural Schedule,* which is quite different from clock time. It is impossible to live an entirely impulse-motivated existence without maintaining an awareness of them.

In the Natural Schedule, each day begins when you awaken and ends when you fall asleep. While this may seem obvious, arising each morning to an alarm clock or retiring at a set hour each night is not natural. More often than not, these times have been arbitrarily chosen by the ego rather than expressed as needs by the body. The criteria for such choices are often based upon beliefs about how much sleep is necessary—and how much one can get away with and still arrive at work on time! Yet there *is* an impulse to awaken, as well as an impulse to fall asleep. To live according to the Natural Schedule requires that you become aware of when these impulses manifest themselves and that you act upon them immediately.

The impulse to fall asleep is quite easy to detect: it becomes increasingly difficult for you to keep your eyes open. Again, this may seem perfectly obvious. Yet how many times have you gone to bed at your appointed hour and lain awake for an extended period, unable to fall asleep? The true sleep impulse had not yet manifested itself. You could have used the time wasted in tossing and turning to accomplish something worthwhile. At some point you would have noticed that your eyelids were getting heavy, and upon going to bed, you would have found yourself falling asleep immediately.

Forcing yourself to stay awake until your usual bedtime, even when your eyelids have become droopy, also serves no useful purpose. Whatever you are trying to accomplish will suffer from your inability to maintain concentration.

The impulse to sleep can also manifest itself in the middle of the day, indicating the importance of a nap. Once again, resisting it will lead to a lack of ability to focus on the project at hand. You may still be able to get something accomplished, but it will take far longer than if you were to allow yourself a nap of perhaps twenty minutes before resuming it.

The impulse to awaken is also easy to detect: it coincides with the need to urinate that gets you out of bed, usually between five and seven o'clock in the morning and often just before dawn. Barring late-night alcohol consumption that may have speeded up the body's purification system and provided that there have been no loud noises in the middle of the night, the first impulse to urinate generally coincides with the body's having had enough sleep. The actual amount of sleep may vary from day to day—from as much as eight hours to as little as five and a half.[1]

You may wish to experiment with staying awake once you have been gotten up by this impulse to urinate—no matter how much before your habitual time of arising it might occur. Give yourself some activity to do, quiet enough so as not to disturb others living with you but fascinating enough that all of your mental faculties can be engaged. Something that stimulates the circulation, such as a walk or run, would be ideal. Greeting the sunrise in this fashion can call forth a sense of well-being the likes of which you may never have known before. You will at last be overcoming the belief that you need more sleep than the body actually requires. When the body's needs are fully respected, your consciousness becomes suffused with contentment. This contentment will accompany your every action throughout the day.

Besides the impulses to awaken and to fall asleep, there is a third impulse of paramount importance to the Natural Schedule: the impulse to urinate. It may seem to you that you simply urinate whenever the bladder is full. But why do you notice occasional changes in the volume of urine discharged —sometimes a large amount, sometimes scarcely a trickle? It would appear that the bladder decides for itself what "full" means and that this amount can vary throughout the day. In reality, however, it is the soul that decides when to trigger the impulse to urinate. The feeling of fullness in the bladder is simply the physical manifestation of that impulse. It manifests itself whenever a change in focus of consciousness is about to take place. The reason urination serves such a function lies in brain chemistry. Any change in the focus of your consciousness initiates a change in the balance of chemicals in your brain. Chemicals in excess of the levels required to maintain the new focus are released into the bloodstream as waste products. Other chemicals, produced by various glands throughout the body, will then begin to support the new focus. If the bladder is full, the processing of waste products cannot take place. Wastes then build up in the system and do not allow the new chemical balance in the brain to assert itself. Confusion or fatigue—an unfocusable consciousness—will be the result. In order to maintain clarity of focus throughout the day, you must urinate upon the urge to do so. We use the word *chemical* in the broadest sense, including anything found in the bloodstream or the cerebrospinal fluid which nurtures the brain, from blood sugars and neurotransmitters to hormones and trace elements. By "change in focus of consciousness," we do not mean merely thinking about something else. Instead, we mean such things as a change from logical to creative thought or a change from strenuous physical activity to reflective thought.

Changes in brain chemistry have an impact on every cell of the body, instructing each one to interact in a certain manner with others. The body is a whole system: it is all brain, it is all biceps, it is all big toe. What happens in one area causes corresponding changes in all other areas. The brain's perception of a threat, for example, tenses all of the muscles, alerting them to the possibility that flight might be necessary. This happens instantly, before the brain even has an opportunity to assess the danger inherent in the situation. The adrenal glands have altered the brain's chemistry. There will be a release of waste products originating in the former balance. A strong impulse to urinate will result from the need of the body to establish a new brain chemistry. This is one of the reasons why the phrase "I almost peed in my pants" is often used with reference to a fearful situation.

The relationship between urination and one's ability to focus consciousness could perhaps best be explained by way of an analogy. A teacher (the ego) stands before a blackboard (consciousness) writing sentences or equations (thoughts). When the board has become cluttered, a fresh writing surface is necessary. As any student knows, the only way to return a blackboard to its pristine clarity of black is to wash it, say, with a sponge and water (the body's purification system).

When the sponge (a urinary-tract organ, such as the liver) becomes full of chalk dust (the excess brain chemicals, to be released as waste), it must be dipped in a pail of water (another organ such as the kidney) until the board has been wiped clean. For the board to be wiped clean yet again, a fresh pail of water must be fetched. This requires emptying the original pail into the sink (bladder), where it runs out through the plumbing (urination). One may then feel an urge to drink some water, which serves to replenish the balance of fluids in the body so that purification can begin again—just as the pail must be refilled in order to cleanse the board once more. Refusal to heed the impulse to urinate can be likened to using an eraser to wipe off the board. The chalk left over from the previous thoughts expressed on the board (waste products) is smeared by the eraser as a fine film of dust over the board's surface, which can make it harder to perceive the next set of expressions to be written (lack of mental clarity). Frequent erasures of the board lead to mounds of chalk dust on the floor—just as the body's waste products tend to settle into the muscles, causing feelings of heaviness and fatigue.

The impulse to urinate will manifest itself at irregular intervals throughout the day. Sometimes as little as twenty minutes or as much as two or three hours will pass between times of urination. In all cases, the impulse will manifest itself either because you have intentionally shifted your focus of consciousness, thus engaging yourself in another activity, or are no longer capable of maintaining concentration on, or interest in, the project at hand.

In the Natural Schedule, the periods between urinations represent units of time that roughly correspond to the hours but are inherently flexible. Time as measured by the clock has no such flexibility. Every hour contains the same number of minutes, and the length of every minute is identical. Yet you can experience one hour as passing quickly and another as dragging on forever. The reason for this anomaly is that the experience of time is primarily psychological, no matter how it has been arbitrarily subdivided by the clock. Trying to fit the flow of your experience—which is also primarily psychological—into such rigid subdivisions greatly reduces your productivity.

In Greek mythology there is a character named Procrustes, an infamous highwayman who offered an iron bed to his "guests." If the guest was too tall for the bed, Procrustes used an ax to lop off as much of the leg as was necessary to make the adjustment. If the guest was too short for the bed, Procrustes stretched him until his body assumed the proper dimensions. An hour is like the bed of Procrustes, always of the same dimensions. Work is like the unfortunate guest, stretched to fill time or hurried (lopped off) in order not to exceed the proscribed hour. By "work," we mean any activity that requires effort, whether physical or mental.

Clearly, if Procrustes had changed the size of the bed rather than the size of his guests, they would have been a lot happier. In our analogy, this would correspond to making the shift from clock time to psychological time, using the flexible time units between urinations instead of the hours. In this way, psychological time can begin to regulate the flow of experience. Time will seem to stretch or contract as the work demands, instead of the other way around.

The secret of the Natural Schedule is to manage your day through heeding the impulse to urinate. All you have to do is perceive the period between urinations as a *flexible time unit* dedicated to the accomplishment of some task. You should devote yourself to that task only until the next impulse to urinate arises. By that time, you may no longer be able to maintain concentration on it. Just acknowledge that a change in focus of consciousness is required, urinate, and then dedicate the next flexible time unit to accomplishing something else.

CHAPTER 4

Menus A, B, and C

The primary reason people have difficulty perceiving impulses is that they value certain activities over others. If an impulse arises toward a less-valued activity, it will frequently be overridden by an intent to pursue a more-valued activity. There may be no impulsive backing for this more-valued activity. Wanting to pursue it will often be motivated by techniques of self-persuasion, such as using the word *should.*

Careers are often the only sources of justifiably pursuable impulses for many people. Impulses arising from the body or the soul toward other kinds of activities, such as exercising or paying attention to one's dreams, are simply ignored. And yet these impulses can represent genuine needs on the part of the body or the soul. Whenever a need goes unsatisfied, one's ability to function efficiently in all other areas of life diminishes. Stimulating the circulation through exercise could easily speed up the completion of a work project, because of the enhanced mental clarity that exercise often brings. Furthermore, one's dreams could point the way toward how to solve some work-related problems. All impulses work toward the benefit of the whole personality and will support, rather than interfere with, one another—unless they are ignored.

Any ignored impulse produces stress. Stress could be described as the state of being in need of something that you purposefully deny to yourself—by telling yourself that something else is more important. To live impulsively requires that you get rid of the system of values that supports this kind of thinking. At the same time, you will be freeing yourself of the tendency to accumulate stress. The medical profession has begun to acknowledge that stress is one of the major factors contributing to illnesses of all kinds. Ridding yourself of stress by following your impulses will guarantee a long and happy life, relatively free of illness and accidental injury.

To make it easier to perceive impulses—and to break down the value system that favors certain ones over others—we have devised the Menus for Impulsive Living. In computer terminology, the term *menu* is applied to a set of choices that appears on the screen when one has just started up a program. Each choice will lead to a different portion of the program, responsible for the execution of a specific task. These choices are frequently listed next to letters of the alphabet, which identify the keys to be pressed to set the program in motion. There are seven broad categories of impulses that one is likely to perceive in the course of a day, and we have labeled them in a similar fashion:

FIGURE 1

THE MENUS FOR IMPULSIVE LIVING

MENU A—The Natural Schedule

MENU B—Physical Focus

MENU C—Self-Awareness

MENU D—Work

MENU E—Play

MENU F—Cycles

MENU G—Surprises

Menu A consists of the same set of impulses for everybody. But Menus B through F must be constructed by each individual according to his or her needs or tastes for certain kinds of activities. Menu G, like Menu A, is the same for everyone.

You are already familiar with the Menu A impulses to awaken, to sleep, and to urinate, since they make up the Natural Schedule. Menu A also contains three further impulses: to quench thirst, to eat, and to defecate.

Even though many states of consciousness originate in the soul's intentions for your growth and self-realization, the capacity to maintain each state of consciousness derives from bodily functions, such as the impulse to urinate. With Menu A we have sought to maximize these maintenance capacities by bringing your attention to actions you have performed for years without a second thought. Any sense of well-being—as well as the very continuity of life itself—depends upon a daily reiteration of choices from Menu A. Every Menu A impulse signals the importance of making a shift from one focus of consciousness to another, such as from wakeful activity to sleeping. Besides providing the fundamental ordinariness of living against which impulses may be more easily perceived, Menu A also allows you to replace arbitrary time with psychological time, based on the capacities of the body to maintain states of consciousness.

Efficiency in managing time and energy requires recognition of the different states of consciousness initiated by the soul. It also requires that you honor the body's fluctuating capacity to maintain these states of consciousness by knowing when to enter or leave them. Equally important is the ability to recognize which efforts are best suited to which states of consciousness. To achieve maximum productivity and minimum wear and tear on the body, you must learn to avoid mismatching activities and states of consciousness. The Menus system will help you do this.

The biological functions of urinating, quenching thirst,

sleeping, awakening, eating, and defecating constitute the most vital of physical needs—the pursuit of which determines your capacity to function not only physically but psychologically. Yet the body's needs are not solely limited to those listed on Menu A. The body also requires exercise in order to achieve maximum efficiency in all areas. The key to achieving such efficiency is the circulation.

The circulation involves not only the heart's pumping action but also the lungs' contribution of oxygen, the digestive tract's provision of nutrients, the urinary tract's removal of waste products, and the lymphatic system's contribution of white corpuscles as immunological agents. The performance of the entire body is affected by the circulation. And if the circulation is sluggish, it becomes difficult to maintain a strong focus of consciousness on the task at hand.

Not only your efficiency but also your sense of well-being is largely determined by the body's capacity to maintain states of consciousness. It is the purpose of Menu B to stimulate the circulation in order to allow these states of consciousness to be maintained for longer periods of time and with greater clarity. Menu B also allows you to develop and maintain muscle tone, increase flexibility and coordination, and encourage the release of tensions. Through Menu B you develop and maintain the presence of the soul in the body. We call this process *physical focus.* So Menu B is the Physical Focus Menu. Along with Menu A, it is the primary way of fulfilling the service-to-the-body aspect of your life purpose.

Everyone who wishes to construct a Menu B will have to do so on his or her own, based upon personal likes and dislikes for certain kinds of physical activity. The important thing is for Menu B to contain a sufficient variety of choices that routine will not set in. The boredom that results from routine—in exercise, as in life—is the opposite of living impulsively.

On your Menu B you will eventually list activities that help you develop:

1. *flexibility* (release from stiffness)
2. *coordination* (harmonious interaction of all body parts)
3. *body image* (growth into the most perfect realization of your body)
4. *presence* (awareness of being within the body)

Specific instructions for constructing menus will be given in a later chapter.

Working on improving the flexibility of the body requires some form of gentle yet persistent stretching, such as yoga. To improve coordination of the body, you might choose to do anything from walking or running to ice-skating or aerobic dancing. Improving the body image requires exercises that reshape some portion of the body, such as sit-ups or weight lifting. Enhancement of presence in the body needs a bit more explanation.

The stiffness or muscular rigidity that results from stress is a sign that awareness has been withdrawn from some portion of the body. The accompanying pain attempts to refocus your attention on that part. Sometimes the pressure of someone else's touch, as in massage, can be effective in drawing awareness back into the affected part. Structural reintegration of the body—through rolfing or the Alexander technique, for example—can also be beneficial, especially when the posture has been severely affected by muscular tension.[2] Awareness has usually been withdrawn because of an unresolved emotional upset that is "stored" in that body part. The ideal bodywork practitioner would seek not only to release the tension in physical terms but also to assist the client in addressing the emotional upset. Once awareness has been fully returned to the affected body part, tension and rigidity will have disappeared. Besides hands-on bodywork, there are also a variety of approaches to movement that enhance presence within the body, such as that developed by Moshe Feldenkrais.[3]

Use of a steam room or a sauna could be listed under this aspect of the Physical Focus Menu. In a steam room or sauna, any body part that is tense will feel hotter than the rest of the body—often uncomfortably so. Directing awareness to the parts of the body that feel hot and then attempting to relax them will make you aware of where you tend to acquire tension. Such awareness can also help you release this tension, because it improves your sense of presence in the body.

The mind and the body are so closely interrelated that physical inflexibility can be a sign of psychological blocks and vice versa. Furthermore, lack of coordination means that not all aspects of the mind are working in tandem. Menu C, the Self-Awareness Menu, offers the possibility of removing these psychological blocks. As you exercise the body through the activities on Menu B, the mind catalogs inflexibilities and problems in coordination. It then sets in motion the processes that will release them. This is where Menu C comes in. The Self-Awareness Menu functions as a means of determining the nature of, and of working toward a release from, mental inflexibilities and problems of coordinating consciousness—specifically, through monitoring and altering beliefs, attitudes, and behaviors. Attention to both the Physical Focus Menu and the Self-Awareness Menu will ensure maximum flexibility and coordination of both conscious awareness and of the body itself. Menu C activities can also help you get in touch with the growth that the soul requires of you at any given time. In this way, you are better equipped to fulfill the service-to-the-soul aspect of your life purpose. Receiving advice or allowing yourself to be guided by members of your physical or spiritual families is also a self-awareness activity and helps to fulfill the service-to-family aspect of your life purpose. An important part of considering such advice is checking to see if it matches or contradicts your understanding of yourself. You may not always have the clearest picture of who you are, and sometimes advice or guidance that seems to contradict your sense of self can midwife new insights and perspectives. It is better to weigh them carefully than to reject them outright.

On Menu C you may record such activities as meditation or dream interpretation.[4] Reading books on psychological, self-help, philosophical, or spiritual themes might also be included. Undertaking exercises in changing beliefs—such as those from the Seth workbook entitled *Create Your Own Reality* or from the *Course in Miracles*—could be chosen as self-awareness activities. So could undertaking journal work along the lines of *The New Diary* or experiments in consciousness alteration, such as those from Jean Houston's *The Possible Human.*[5]

Relationships represent one of the primary areas in which the soul's lessons are learned. Anything that helps you keep your friendships, family connections, intimate involvements, and business or professional associations running smoothly belongs to the Self-Awareness Menu. There are many books, workshops, and seminars designed to provide guidance in these areas. Seeking marriage counseling, seeing a social worker or psychotherapist, or attending group therapy sessions are all valid self-awareness activities.

As you monitor the contents of consciousness and seek to alter them through Menu C, you may become aware of psychic or intuitive abilities with which you were previously unfamiliar. These can include the capacities to develop and maintain presence in an out-of-body state and to channel information from some nonphysical source.[6] Any form of expanded awareness can considerably broaden the relationship with the soul, so that guidance about the nature of the tasks the soul expects of you may become more available. There are many books, workshops, and seminars designed to assist you in getting in touch with your own inner guidance. Whether the words *intuitive* or *psychic* or *subconscious* or *higher self* are used in association with the techniques taught in these forums is immaterial. In our view, they are all methods of gaining more direct access to the soul's perspective on your life.

CHAPTER 5

Menus D and E

THE MENUS FOR IMPULSIVE LIVING

MENU A—The Natural Schedule

MENU B—Physical Focus

MENU C—Self-Awareness

MENU D—Work

MENU E—Play

MENU F—Cycles

MENU G—Surprises

Menu D is the Work Menu. On it, you record everything that you do to increase your level of self-valuation. You accomplish this end through earning money or appreciation. In the case of earning money, every activity that has something to do with your career belongs on Menu D. Appreciation can come from doing volunteer work, doing favors for friends, or placing works of art you have created in front of an audience, whether at a gallery or in a performance hall.

What exactly do we mean when we say "level of self-valuation"? We have mentioned that the closer you come to fulfilling your life purpose, the happier and more satisfied you feel.

You begin to discover your place within the world, your function within humanity. As you come to see that you are making a genuine contribution to the lives of others, you begin to realize that the very fact that you are alive makes a difference. Through perceiving the appreciation of others for what you alone can do, you become aware that you are a unique and invaluable part of humankind. Because you have begun to value yourself for who you truly are, life will come to seem ever more worthwhile. You will feel more deserving of creating special opportunities for yourself in all areas, from leaving behind a relationship or job that isn't satisfying, to taking an exotic and adventuresome vacation. A rise in level of self-valuation occurs with every step you take toward fulfilling your life purpose.

Your level of self-valuation determines the ease with which you are capable of satisfying your needs. The better you feel about yourself, for example, the more likely you are to attract a person of quality with whom to get involved in a love relationship. Some of your fundamental needs—such as for food, shelter, clothing, heat, water, and electricity—require money in order to be satisfied. Your level of self-valuation also determines the ease with which you can draw money to yourself. We mean this both literally and figuratively.

Most jobs that pay the minimum wage usually have little to do with fulfilling a life purpose. A college student could help pay for his or her education by grilling hamburgers at a fast-food restaurant perhaps. But after graduation, his or her sense of self-valuation will have risen. Getting a job that relates in some way to his or her major will often reflect this rise by paying more money. Students who valued themselves enough through school to study hard and get good grades will probably find more opportunities available to them than the ones who didn't care.

Similarly, if you are stuck in a low-paying job or one with intolerable work conditions, telling yourself you're not qualified for anything better indicates problems in self-valuation.

It will be impossible for you to draw more money to yourself through a better paying job until you feel good enough about yourself to try for one.

The connection between level of self-valuation and ability to draw money to oneself becomes even more clear for people who are self-employed or work on commission. Feeling good about yourself means that you will be relaxed with a customer or client, who will be more inclined to like or appreciate you. Most people will choose to take their business to someone they like, regardless of how much better qualified someone else about whom they feel indifferent might be. Conversely, if you are feeling financially desperate, you run the danger of approaching people without regard to their personhood, seeing them only as opportunities to make money, and thus causing potential clients or customers to avoid you. This sort of desperation derives from self-valuation problems.

There are so many factors affecting your ability to value yourself that something seemingly unrelated to work can have an impact on your ability to make money or to hold on to it. Perhaps you are experiencing problems in a love relationship. While you are driving somewhere, angrily muttering to yourself that you're not going to speak to your partner until he or she sees the light, you misjudge a turn and have an accident. Your level of self-valuation was falling, because of your resistance to working things out. This will be reflected in the unexpected expense of having to repair the damage to your car.

The aspects of your life purpose expressed through the Work Menu depend on the type of career you have chosen. If your work in some way betters the emotional, physical, or spiritual well-being of mankind, then the service-to-humanity aspect is involved. If you are a professional artist, choreographer, or composer, then your work brings together service to the Creator and service to humanity. Similarly, if you are a professional performer, then service to the personality and service to humanity have been combined. If you are an environmental activist, whether you are paid for your work or not, you are serving not only humanity but all life. Raising a family can earn appreciation. So the things that you do to help your children realize themselves belong to the Work Menu—such as driving them to and from after-school activities. This kind of work helps you to fulfill the service-to-family aspect of your own life purpose.

The physical inflexibilities and lacks of coordination cataloged in the Physical Focus Menu and the belief obstructions that you attempt to release through the Self-Awareness Menu usually represent resistances of some kind to fulfillment of one's life purpose. Through the Work Menu, you have the opportunity of proving to the soul that such resistances have been released, by applying yourself more diligently to fulfillment of your life purpose. If you have been successful in accomplishing such releases, then your level of self-valuation increases. More money or greater appreciation comes your way as a symbol of that increase. It becomes easier for you to satisfy your needs.

But what exactly is work? The word implies an activity that not only engages you but also causes some tangible product to come into being. This product could be anything from a piece of sculpture to a business contract. Such products are generated using the same techniques of creating reality as those with which you construct your psychological universe, largely unconsciously. Another function of the Work Menu is to make you conscious of these techniques of reality creation.

What you believe about reality *is* reality for you. To change your perspective on reality, therefore, is to change that reality. It is by means of the Work Menu that you monitor how well or poorly you are creating the reality you experience. But why is attention to how you create your own reality important? Because if you are doing it poorly, certain fundamental needs may be going unfulfilled. This could greatly slow down, if not completely stall, your learning the lessons that the soul requires of you.

Certain beliefs about yourself will make it more difficult for you to ensure the satisfaction of your needs than others. For example, a belief that you are somehow inadequate is likely to become a self-fulfilling prophecy. By worrying obsessively about making mistakes, you may very well make yourself so tense that you can hardly help but perform badly on your job. The belief in inadequacy might then create the reality of being fired. At that point, your lack of income will make it increasingly difficult for you to ensure the satisfaction of your needs. Your attention will be primarily focused on mere survival, and the soul's requirements for your growth will be largely ignored. It is through the release of such negative beliefs, accomplished by means of the activities you have listed on the Self-Awareness Menu, that you begin to change your reality. But it may be difficult to sense how much your beliefs have changed. With the Work Menu, you have the opportunity of seeing the impact of these changes immediately: your self-valuation rises, and you are more capable of satisfying your needs.

The Work Menu involves attention not only to your life purpose but also to the interrelationship of the level of self-valuation, the ability to satisfy needs, and the techniques of reality creation. This makes it an intense focus of growth. In their own ways, the Physical Focus Menu and Self-Awareness Menu can be just as demanding. Just as you may sometimes need a break from a demanding work project, so do you sometimes need a break from the rigors of self-realization. Menu E, the Play Menu, can provide such a break. It becomes a means of refreshing yourself whenever interest, ability to concentrate, and endurance begin to flag. Yet play is more than mere refreshment from work: it is an essential source of creativity and spontaneity that, by its very nature, is guided by impulses. No one can force you to play, nor can you force yourself to play. When you feel the urge for recreation, you are following an impulse. To play is to be reminded of the spontaneity and ease that could accompany even the most demanding activities on the Work Menu.

Through Menu E, you can reconnect with the impulsive schedule of childhood. Play can help you recover and refresh the sense of being guided by spontaneity. Whenever you feel overloaded by the sheer amount of things that need to get done, whenever you feel unable to decide what to do next, make time for play. Your ability to perceive impulses will be renewed in other areas.

Anything done for simple enjoyment—such as reading up on a topic of interest unrelated to work or self-awareness—belongs to the Play Menu. Games, too, are an important aspect of play. The point of any game is not so much to win but to submit to a series of challenges that demand creative approaches to be resolved. Many people tend to overemphasize the Work Menu, with the result that they view games as inconsequential. But games exercise the great flexibility of human consciousness. They help that consciousness to learn to adapt itself to any internal or external situation.

Being able to analyze a real-life situation and come up with possible ways to approach it requires the same problem-solving abilities as playing certain games. Chess or backgammon, for example, require the envisioning of possible futures—that is, anticipating the moves your opponent will make and projecting the consequences of your own moves. The game-playing strategies that you come up with are simply means of organizing your perceptions of possible futures. Creative problem-solving in the business world also involves perceiving possible futures. Playing chess or backgammon can therefore have a beneficial impact on the Work Menu: you can take the well-rehearsed process of strategy development directly into the "game" of life.

Games offer a multitude of specific problems and challenges for which the player must come up with solutions. The effect is similar to that of weight-training machines designed to exercise a certain muscle. Each game allows you to exercise a specific skill that involves manipulation of consciousness. An example of what we mean by "manipulation of consciousness" is being able to project and then organize perceptions of possible futures. Just as the entire body can benefit from exposure to a variety of weight-training machines, which can lead to greater overall strength and enhanced performance in other areas, so can your consciousness benefit from the exercise offered by a multitude of games. Such exercise increases the strength of your consciousness—its capacity to deal with the large variety of life situations you are likely to encounter, regardless of their intensity. Strange as it may seem, the greater flexibility of consciousness that develops from game-playing can actually enhance your ability to manage a crisis.

In symbolic terms, a game is a life situation taken out of context. Though the particular life situation may not be immediately apparent, the playing of even the simplest games is far from trivial. For example, a jigsaw puzzle removes a life situation from context: not being able to view the entire pattern of your experience or to picture all the parameters acting upon a specific event. It poses the challenge of putting the pieces of the situation into proper perspective by discovering how they fit together. Through the development of strategies, you meet that challenge. Sorting out and assembling the border pieces first means clearly determining the limits of the situation. Sorting pieces by color means getting a sense of the types of influences acting upon the situation. As the picture on the puzzle pieces begins to emerge, specific strategies of looking at real-life situations are being exercised. If the activity of putting a jigsaw puzzle together has been added to the Play Menu, the soul will generate an impulse toward it whenever these strategies are needed in real life.

This will also be true of card games. In most card games, a hand of cards is dealt to you at the beginning of the game. These cards represent the skills, abilities, or awarenesses that the soul makes available to you at birth or just before you enter a new life situation. Throughout the game you receive more cards. These represent new skills, abilities, or awarenesses made available by the soul at key points in order to enrich your range of possible future actions. The game will consist in making various arrangements of these cards. In some games, such as gin rummy, the goal is to gain the highest number of points. This means to produce the fullest realization of yourself from the skills, abilities, and awarenesses made available by the soul. In other games, such as hearts, the goal is to gain the lowest number of points. This means to avoid making decisions that would *prevent* the fullest realization of yourself. Winning the game means that of all the players, you have succeeded best in exercising your inherent flexibility of consciousness. In the case of virtually all card games, the life situation taken out of context is "to make the most of what you have," and the challenge is to recognize and respond to opportunities for advancement toward self-realization.

The plot of a movie, novel, or play is yet another type of game. Specific, usually problematic life situations have been removed from the context of life itself. The unfolding of the plot shows you how the characters respond to the challenges that confront them. As a witness to the consequences of their decisions, you are able to perceive the usefulness or ineffectuality of certain strategies or approaches to these problems.

In a similar way, the emotions that come up while listening to music are also taken out of the context of life. The challenge to be met here is to lower any social or personal inhibitions that have been placed on the expression of emotion. As you listen and are moved, your ability to express emotion is being rehearsed. The range of feeling embraced by the music will then become available whenever a real-life situation requires a similar response.

Attending an art exhibition exercises observational abilities by removing them from the context of living. The challenge is to overcome habits of perception that result in not really seeing the power, intensity, beauty, or order of the interior or exterior universes. This is accomplished by submitting to the manipulations of consciousness undertaken by the artist in fashioning his or her work—the use of color, the methods of organization, and the stylistic approach.

Going to a dance concert will have a similar effect. Movement has been removed from the context of living. The challenge to be met is that of releasing the social or personal inhibitions placed on expressive movement. The myriad movement possibilities of the human body are rehearsed in front of you by the performer. Some of them might encourage you to be more expressive in your own movement, contributing a certain elegance to the sweep of your hands while talking or a certain gracefulness to your gait.

Even going on a roller coaster can have a beneficial effect upon your consciousness. In this case, the life situation taken out of context is the intensity of change—with all of its ups and downs, and feelings of being tossed about helplessly from one crisis to another. The challenge is learning to submit to internal or external changes, by coming to trust that the soul will not allow you to "fly off the handle" (or be thrown from the ride).

If you have added several games to your Menu E, the soul will time the broadcasting of impulses toward them for whenever the skills, abilities, or awarenesses exercised by them might be required by the life situation through which you happen to be passing. The function of the Play Menu is to make sure that the capacities of human consciousness not drawn upon at any given time by the other menus remain fresh, well rehearsed, and easily accessible when required. Thus, the proverb "All work and no play makes Jack a dull boy" has a much wider range of implications than you might think. The pressures of attempting to raise the level of self-valuation through work can often cause you to favor certain kinds of consciousness manipulations and neglect others. The

Play Menu prevents the vast storehouse of human capabilities from atrophying under such conditions.

Even though the Play Menu can allow you to take a break from the rigors of self-realization, it is one of the primary areas in which the service-to-the-personality aspect of your life purpose can be fulfilled. If you pursue a creative hobby or practice an art for your own private enjoyment, then the service-to-the-Creator aspect is also involved. Examples would be model-building or gardening. If you have a young family, playing games with your children can be a way of fulfilling service to family as well.

C H A P T E R 6

Menus F and G

THE MENUS FOR IMPULSIVE LIVING

MENU A—The Natural Schedule

MENU B—Physical Focus

MENU C—Self-Awareness

MENU D—Work

MENU E—Play

MENU F—Cycles

MENU G—Surprises

The Work and Play menus allow for the acting out of the whole personality in all of its possible expressions—both those of immediate use in fulfilling your life purpose and those which might atrophy without periodic exercise. Menu F, the Cycles Menu, allows you to become aware of the changes that have occurred in the sense of self as a result of going back and forth between work and play. It also enables you to perceive how you have been affected by the reorganization of belief structures accomplished through the Self-Awareness Menu and by the increased flexibility, coordination, and shapeliness of the body accomplished through the Physical Focus Menu.

The Cycles Menu contains a variety of activities, each of which is repeated on a more or less regular basis. The average duration between repetitions will tend to differ for each activity. Yet they will all pertain in some way to the upkeep of one's image and to the opening and closing of a cycle of growth, whether of a single day or a decade. Menu F should include such activities as showering, shaving, clipping nails, getting a haircut, putting on or taking off makeup, and cleaning house.

We purposefully use the term *cycles* instead of *habits*. The important thing about the Cycles Menu is not the repetitiousness of the activities but rather the sense of self you leave behind by accomplishing them. Everything on this menu, no matter how humble, acts as a symbol of transformation. Spring-cleaning, for example, clears out the gloom of winter. Rearranging furniture signifies a new perspective on your living situation. Laundering clothes allows you to freshen up your self-image, which may have become soiled or rumpled during a hectic workweek. The purpose of the Cycles Menu is to provide a release from accumulated experience, which can pile up like dust or dirty laundry, in order to make way for new experiences. The result is a continual renewal of self-image.

Self-image has a variety of forms. The first is purely personal and involves such activities as showering and shaving, clipping fingernails or toenails, or getting a haircut. Another type of self-image has to do with how you take care of the things that you own and your surroundings: buying or mending clothes, watering the houseplants, picking up after yourself, housecleaning, or undertaking home repairs, for example. A third type of self-image is emotional. This has to do with keeping your friends posted, in letters, phone calls, or conversations, on the developments that have taken place in your life since the last such contact. The next type of self-image is intellectual. It comes up whenever you are placed in a position of demonstrating something you have learned in the areas of information, skills, or techniques. Taking an oral or written examination involves this type of self-image, whether you are completing a college course or going for certification as a scuba diver.

Yet another type of self-image is financial, which allows you to gauge changing levels of self-valuation. The associated activities are paying bills, balancing your checkbook, and visiting the bank. Again, your level of self-valuation fluctuates according to your progress in learning the lessons of the soul. When self-valuation has risen, it becomes easier to make money and to satisfy your needs. The opposite is true when your level of self-valuation falls. Keeping track of your accounts can be one way of monitoring your spiritual growth. Clearly, to neglect your bookkeeping will indicate a neglect of the soul's agenda for your self-realization. On the other hand, being obsessive about making money is just as inappropriate.

Because Cycles Menu activities have to do with self-image, they can help you fulfill the service-to-the-personality aspect of life purpose. This will be especially true whenever you buy clothes, colognes, or cosmetics that express something of who you are. It will also be true anytime you select an item for the home not just because you need it but because the style or design suits your character. Whenever you go shopping to replace things that have worn out or things that you have grown tired of wearing or seeing so frequently, you are leaving behind an old self and ushering in a new one.

Service to family may also be fulfilled by certain special Cycles Menu events, such as a birthday, engagement party, baby shower, wedding, bar or bas mitzvah, anniversary, or funeral. Attending each of these events provides support for the blood relatives or spiritual family members who are leaving behind one self in favor of a new one—the single self for the married self, the newlywed self for the parent self, or the married self for the widowed self, for example. These occasions often provide opportunities for you to catch up with relatives or friends you rarely see. Your conversations will help you see how much you have grown since the last time the family gathered.

Another component of your life purpose that can be fulfilled by certain Cycles Menu activities is service to all life. Periodic trips to a recycling center to drop off newspapers or glass bottles and jars is related to housecleaning, in that you are ridding yourself symbolically of accumulated experience in order to make room for more. Sometimes the glass will break as you toss your bottles and jars into storage bins. This can have a highly therapeutic effect, helping you to release pent-up anger or frustration. Picking up litter in your environment can also fulfill service to all life. We mentioned that the physical aspect of self-image includes your immediate surroundings. You will feel better about yourself in a clean and orderly environment than in a messy one, whether this environment exists within the house or out-of-doors.

Making financial contributions to environmental organizations belongs to the Cycles Menu. In this case, your financial self-image is involved. Again, you will feel better about yourself for having made such contributions. Your level of self-valuation will rise, because you are leaving behind an ignorant or apathetic self and beginning to take some responsibility for the stewardship of the planet. In a similar fashion, financial contributions to charities allow you to fulfill the service-to-humanity aspect of your life purpose. Giving clothes, appliances, or furniture that you no longer use to charitable causes is yet another means of serving humanity through the Cycles Menu.

While engaged in any Cycles Menu activity, you should reflect on the growth accomplished since the last time you did the same thing. Think about the self you have left behind, and see if you can get a fix on the new self that is emerging. Generally speaking, this will be easier for longer cycles than for shorter ones. But even during an evening shower, for example, you can reflect on the day just finished. A morning shower could allow you to ponder the previous night's dreams. Shaving can demonstrate quite literally that growth is a daily matter. Think about any of the problems you were able to resolve since the last time you shaved. As the stubble washes down the drain, you are releasing the worries or cares that had been connected to these problems.

Try not to perform the most often repeated Menu F activities—such as showering, shaving, doing the dishes—every day or always at the same hour, if you can help it. Skip a day occasionally or shift a morning activity to the evening, or vice versa, in order to freshen up your concept of time. The Cycles Menu helps to break down dependency on arbitrary time by substituting more-extended versions of Menu A's flexible time units. Thus, a day does not necessarily have to comprise twenty-four hours; it can be measured as the flexible time unit between showers or shaves. Other time periods of flexible length, all determined by the frequency of Menu F impulses, can substitute for weeks and months. Some periods will be longer, and some shorter, than the standards. But all of them will be spontaneously and impulsively determined. The periods between nail-clippings, haircuts, housecleanings, laundry days, car washes, or piano tunings are examples of larger units of psychological growth. The soul times these activities in such a way that you may look back over the period between the last manifestation of the impulse and the current one in order to determine how that growth has progressed.

We mentioned that there is a means of determining how much you have matured without accumulating symptoms of aging. In Menu F the cycles of growth are not measured in terms of how many days, weeks, months, or years older you are but by the soul's astute timing of impulses. It is possible for you to view your life as a multitude of layers of such cycles, some coinciding with others, as when you take a shower, shave after two days, and clip your nails after three weeks, all within a few minutes of each other. Perhaps you have also decided to commence spring-cleaning on this day and have an appointment for a piano tuning. Thus, two larger cycles—the former pertaining to the seasons, the latter to a period of half a year or more—would also coincide with the shorter ones. Each of these cycles represents a unit of growth. Your awareness of the growth accomplished during it helps you determine the extent to which you have become yourself—that is, how much you have matured.

Thinking back to the way you used to be actually encourages the cells of the body to rejuvenate. All you have to do is use the Cycles Menu as a means of meditating on the growth you have accomplished between successive repetitions of the same activity. You should not only think about the self you have become but also about the self you were at the beginning of the cycle. This encourages the cells to return to former states of functioning, in spite of what the calendar might tell you about how much older you are. Such meditations permit you to acknowledge maturation while allowing you to throw off the ravages of time. Rejuvenation can occur no matter how stressful the period of growth just ended may have been—and no matter how much your face or figure shows such stress. In order to ensure maximum benefit from this rejuvenation effect, though you must release yourself from the tendency to accumulate stress—by following each and every impulse. You must also be able to remember exactly what it felt like to be the self you were before the stressful period of growth began.

Although Menu F activities can provide the beneficial rejuvenation effect just described, this effect depends entirely on how much mental presence you maintain in accomplishing them. Because some of them need to be repeated so very often, it is easy to become bored and make them into habits or routines. In fact, routine could be defined as "lack of mindfulness." If you mindlessly repeat your Cycles Menu activities, you won't have a clear idea of who you are, who you have been, or who you are becoming. This lack of mental presence will begin to affect the other menus as an increasing inability to perceive impulses. As routine swallows up more and more of your life, boredom and world-weariness will set in. Symptoms of aging will begin to appear, symbolizing the stress you are accumulating through lack of full participation in the process of maturation. This will be even more true if you tell yourself that you don't have time for Cycles Menu activities and then let them pile up. During periods of difficult growth, there can be nothing more soothing than putting your living space or the financial aspects of your life in order. This will actually help clear your mind to focus on the growth being accomplished in the emotional area.

The more demanding your life is, the easier it can be to lose mindfulness of what you are doing and who you are becoming to force of habit. Yet there is a category of impulses specifically designed to break down routine and renew joie de vivre: Menu G, the Surprise Menu. While you are responsible for making up Menus B through F yourself, Menu G, like Menu A, is the same for everyone. The Menu G impulses may take any of the following forms: coincidences, synchronicities, unusual occurrences, unexpected happenings, magical or miraculous events.

Menu G impulses always interrupt your involvement in some other activity. They represent a direct intervention on the part of the soul, intended to guide you out of an activity not appropriate for the moment into another one that is. Just as your relations to the body deteriorate when you ignore the Menu A impulses, so do your relations to the soul deteriorate when you ignore the Menu G impulses. Spiritual malaise and a sense of purposelessness are the results of such an attitude.

The Menu G impulse often manifests itself as an adventure of some sort: your willingness to let it interrupt the project you have been engaged in has broken you out of routine. Or it can manifest itself as an unpleasant surprise: the soul might intervene to catapult you out of a course of action that could lead to dire consequences. If you had your heart set on the previous course of action, you may feel disappointed. But this disappointment pales in comparison to the misery you would have experienced had you persisted. The degree of resistance to being redirected by Menu G determines the vector force the soul will have to apply to change your course of action. It stands to reason that the more willing you are to "go with the flow" of life, the less likely it will be that you will experience unpleasant surprises.

As with Menu A, you do not consciously select a Menu G experience. You merely stand in readiness. You must be fully prepared to drop what you are doing and follow the Menu G impulse to whatever magical, miraculous, or unexpected happenings lie in wait. Generally speaking, you will recognize yourself in the midst of a Menu G activity, rather than consciously select it. Because Menu G surprises will always interrupt things, it is your willingness to allow such interruptions to take place that determines whether or not you will have adventures. The less attached you are to maintaining a preordained schedule, the more free you will be for the release from routine that Menu G supplies.

When the soul has intervened to redirect your life, flowing with it means magic and adventure; resisting it blocks later surprises. If you rarely experience adventures, then you are too much in love with routine. The first requisite of the adventuresome soul, therefore, is to yield to the Menu G impulse—to follow it no matter how strong the attachment to finishing whatever you had been doing up to that point may be. Do so without resistance, hesitation, grumbling, or distrust. Even begrudging participation can inhibit later Menu G surprises.

It is possible to perceive your life as if it were the set of an adventure movie. But first you must become aware of the props, which we call *Menu G vehicles.* A Menu G vehicle is an ordinary aspect of everyday life that suddenly reveals extraordinary and unexpected possibilities as a surprise impulse rides it into your life. *Any* experience, action, activity, event, object, situation, or place can become such a vehicle. Someone you have never met or even a person you know can become a Menu G vehicle. Only your past refusals to pursue Menu G impulses or your begrudging release of interrupted plans have locked such vehicles into banality. Anytime you ignore a Menu G impulse, the vehicle for that impulse undergoes a kind of blacklisting. Resenting the inevitable interruption it will cause tends to block that vehicle from producing another Menu G experience in the future. The extent to which your surroundings appear dull, dreary, and unexciting is the extent to which you have blacklisted them. There is only one way to reverse this blacklisting: you must cease to ignore Menu G impulses. The more vehicles you come to recognize by perceiving their adventure potential—which is accomplished by joyfully allowing them to interrupt your plans—the more free your life will be to produce adventure.

Even so humdrum an object as the telephone or so tedious a situation as running errands can become vehicles for Menu G surprises. As you recognize and allow yourself to be carried away by each new vehicle, you will have added a new prop to the movie set of your life. Eventually this movie set can come to comprise everything you are surrounded with. Magical, indeed, will be the day when you discover yourself transposed entirely from the ordinary to the extraordinary aspects of reality, for then you will be the true hero of a constantly unfolding adventure.

Sudden and unexpected damage or injury constitutes a special category of Menu G vehicles. Any belief, attitude, or behavior that somehow blocks you from fulfilling your life purpose is damaging. The soul has an investment in getting you to release such beliefs, attitudes, or behaviors so that you may realize its master plan for you in this lifetime. Due to resistance on your part, the soul must sometimes use unpleasant surprises to focus your attention on problem areas. Unpleasant surprises run the gamut from something as simple as breaking a shoelace to something as potentially harmful as a car accident. Even the sudden onset of an illness could be considered an unpleasant surprise. The purpose of such surprises is exactly the same as that of any other Menu G occurrence: the soul has intervened to redirect the course of your life. Don't ignore them in favor of the pleasant ones just because you don't enjoy them. As you will see, this approach can be dangerous.

Whenever damage occurs, it is of paramount importance that you immediately try to trace it to the damaging beliefs, attitudes, or behaviors that lurk behind it. Otherwise the soul will consider that you have not gotten the message. It may feel it must increase the degree of damage in order to get through to you.

Ultimately, the soul is responsible for the brief moments of inattentiveness that place you in dangerous or vulnerable positions with respect to others, or that lead to careless acts of your own. Each such moment, and the damage that results from it, is an omen of warning. The greater the degree of resistance to moving toward fulfillment of your life purpose, the greater the degree of damage you are likely to draw to yourself. Yet there is not a single life-threatening accident that has not been preceded by a multitude of smaller warnings, such as broken dishes. Damage tends to manifest itself first in your environment. Things that you don't have a great deal of personal attachment to will be affected. If the message behind the damage is ignored or misinterpreted, then things with ever-increasing degrees of personal value will be affected. Losing something or discovering that it has been stolen can also indicate the presence of damaging beliefs. If you do not heed these messages, the damage will get even closer. It will begin to affect the body—at first in minor ways, such as a broken fingernail. Not paying attention will again cause the damage to escalate. You may cut or scrape yourself, pull a muscle, sprain an ankle, break a bone, or become ill.

Acute resistance can lead to more-serious accidents. If the damaging beliefs, attitudes, or behaviors strike at the very root of your true identity and completely block the soul's ability to learn its lessons through you, there's a chance the damage could become life-threatening. Indeed, most cases of premature death are the result of a supremely stubborn refusal to become who one truly is. Damage shouldn't have to go this far to get your attention. A lot of misery could have been avoided if you had traced that broken shoelace to the damaging beliefs, attitudes, or behaviors behind it.

You are responsible for damage that occurs to anything you own, even if someone else has caused it. He or she has simply become a Menu G vehicle, pointing out the presence of damaging approaches to life. Such a person may have his or her own damaging beliefs, attitudes, or behaviors to deal with. Because the damage has affected something you own, it will have to do with how he or she views your relationship. In your case, however, the damage will have more to do with what the object itself represents to you.

Carelessness and neglect are the two primary causes of damage. When damage is the result of carelessness, clearly there is something careless about your overall approach to life. When damage is the result of neglect, there is something important about yourself you have not been attending to.

Figuring out which of your beliefs, attitudes, or behaviors have been responsible for damage requires a certain amount of mental agility. Usually the thoughts you were having at the moment the damage occurred—or the moment you finally noticed damage that had occurred earlier, at an unknown time—will provide important clues. Also, the soul will often try to convey the nature of a damaging belief, attitude, or behavior to you symbolically, through the type of damage and what it affects. You can use the same principles that apply to dream interpretation to figure out the internal cause of the damage.

Here's an example of how to interpret real-life events as if they were dream images: Your car overheats on the highway. This is the first time it has ever done this. Where were you headed? What were you leaving behind? What were you thinking about? Perhaps you were quite angry about something that had just happened between yourself and someone close to you. Hence, the soul is trying to convey that you will not be able to get on with your life (continue to drive the car) until you stop being so "burned up" (overheated) about this incident. It might seem easier to explain away such an instance by saying the car is old and the radiator had simply sprung a leak. Yet we insist that such things happen *only* when there is a message from the soul about damaging beliefs, attitudes, or behaviors. If this weren't so, then why do difficulties like these always seem to occur at the most inconvenient times? Could this be because you're more likely to pay attention then?

Our example may seem pat. But the soul has an investment in getting across its messages about damaging approaches to life as quickly as possible. It will not play games with you by providing purposely obscure symbols. As a matter of fact, the soul waits until you are doing something that could be a perfect symbol of the psychological damage you are causing yourself. Then it applies gentle vector forces to your thoughts until the problematic approaches to life are uppermost in your mind. At this point, it will cause a momentary lapse of consciousness, which you will experience as the inattentiveness or apparent carelessness that often precedes an accident, causes you to lose something, or opens the way for theft.

All souls collaborate with one another to get their respective charges to learn their lessons in physical reality. Thus, while you are shopping, an unknown person in the parking lot could experience that momentary lapse in consciousness and throw open his or her car door so forcefully that it leaves a dent in yours. Your own soul will try to bring any damaging approaches to life that it wishes you to become aware of to mind just in time for you to discover the dent—either when you return from shopping or at some later time. As cruel as this might seem to someone who has just bought a new car, it is vastly more humane than causing damage to one's person. If there were no such thing as resistance to fulfilling one's life purpose, there would be no such thing as damage.

Here's an example of how the soul produces an unpleasant surprise that involves damage to one's person: When a man shaves his face, he is vulnerable to nicking himself. If the soul has a message to get across about how certain thoughts are damaging his self-image (symbolized by the face), it will nudge these thoughts into his awareness. At the precise moment they are most present in his mind, the soul will cause the lapse of consciousness we mentioned—and the razor will slip. Everything the man needs to know is packed into these few moments—both the thoughts guilty of inflicting the damage and the symbolic nature of the damage itself.

If you are unable to figure out what a particular kind of damage means from the clues that surround its appearance, then your soul will broach the subject in dreams. Dreams can be extremely helpful, because they not only diagnose the reasons for damage but often point out damaging beliefs, attitudes, and behaviors long before real-life damage begins to draw your attention to them. Not remembering dreams is often a sign of a refusal to look at these damaging beliefs, attitudes, and behaviors. Such a refusal usually manifests itself as a belief that dreams are insignificant or meaningless—which is itself a damaging belief. Actual damage in physical reality then becomes the only means whereby the soul can convey the necessity of releasing damaging approaches to life. It should be clear that interpreting dreams is the most powerful preventive medicine when it comes to unpleasant surprises.

How do you release yourself from damaging beliefs, attitudes, and behaviors? Just follow your impulses. All damaging approaches to life result from blocking impulses to fulfill your life purpose. If you catch yourself in the act of arguing for or against pursuing a course of action or telling yourself you should or shouldn't do a certain thing, you are blocking an impulse. Reversing your position unblocks that impulse. Damage will be utterly unnecessary if you simply monitor your thoughts with this in mind.

We have said that impulses will never lead to anything destructive. It may seem contradictory to speak of damage and unpleasant surprises. Yet all impulses perceived within the mind *are* inherently constructive. In the case of Menu G, the adventure or damage manifests itself *before* an impulse is perceived. It seems to happen to you. Afterward, you may perceive an impulse to become involved in some way with the surprise—perhaps by participating in the adventure or by analyzing the symbolism behind the damage. Even in the case of an unpleasant surprise, this impulse will be constructive, because it will help you discover and release a damaging belief, attitude, or behavior. If it were not for the all too human tendency to resist fulfillment of one's life purpose, the soul would have no need of sending such apparently destructive messages. To eliminate the possibility of damage from your life, all you need do is acknowledge and act upon the constructive impulses that the soul is constantly broadcasting to you. Whether you are surprised by adventures or by unexpected difficulties, heeding Menu G impulses helps you fulfill the service-to-the-soul aspect of your life purpose.

CHAPTER 7

How to Construct Your Own Menus

THE MENUS FOR IMPULSIVE LIVING

MENU A—The Natural Schedule

MENU B—Physical Focus

MENU C—Self-Awareness

MENU D—Work

MENU E—Play

MENU F—Cycles

MENU G—Surprises

As a system, the Menus for Impulsive Living is a set of strategies for becoming aware of impulses. We have provided detailed explanations of the seven categories of impulses you are likely to encounter in the course of a day. Yet merely being aware of the different types of impulses is not enough to guarantee an impulsive lifestyle. You must first construct your own set of menus, based on your preferences for certain kinds of activities within these categories. The key to living impulsively is to give yourself permission *in advance* to acknowledge the needfulness of certain activities so that when an impulse arises toward one of them, you will not intentionally or unintentionally ignore it. Ignoring even a single impulse causes the accumulation of stress and therefore contributes to aging. Writing out your own menus is the means of granting this advance permission.

We recommend that you purchase a notebook within which to record the menus and to perform the exercises provided in later chapters. A stenographer's pad—spiral-bound at the top and with a vertical line running down the middle of each page—would be ideal. Whatever kind of notebook you use, it is essential that the paper have lines to write on.

On the first page write "Menu A—the Natural Schedule." Then, on successive lines, record the six Menu A impulses: to urinate, to quench thirst, to sleep, to awaken, to eat, and to defecate. On the next five pages, write the titles of Menus B through F, but for the moment leave the rest of the pages blank. Then, on the seventh page, write "Menu G—Surprises." Record the Menu G impulses on this menu, one per line: coincidences, synchronicities, unusual occurrences, unexpected happenings, magical or miraculous events.

It may take you a few days of careful thought to produce Menus B through F. Write only one activity per line, and use as few words as possible to describe that activity. Strive to list as many activities as you can with only a single word. A definite mental impact will derive from seeing each thing that you do so briefly described on its own separate line. The activities that demand the most time will take up no more space than the ones you seem to have so little time for. This begins the process of breaking down the tendency to value certain activities over others.

When working on Menu B, divide the paper into four quadrants, two on each side of the vertical line in the middle. Label these quadrants with the four broad categories of Physical Focus activities: flexibility, coordination, body image, and presence. (See Figure 2.) Eventually you will want to give yourself advance permission to pursue impulses toward all four types of Physical Focus activities by including them on Menu B. But for now, write just the ones you characteristically practice. Even if you can think of only one thing to list, such as running, be completely honest with yourself, and record that single word. Then maintain an openness to trying new things. You may find yourself being guided by subtle inner promptings, such as "I wonder what it would be like to do thus and so." That's an impulse to try it out and see. Menu G may intercede to direct you toward other means of exercise. Joining a health club, of course, will immediately offer a variety of new possibilities, from exercise classes to weight machines, to racquet games or swimming.

FIGURE 2

Menu B—Physical Focus	
Flexibility	**Coordination**
Body image	**Presence**

As you proceed with the other menus, be sure not to pad them with things you used to do or with things you want to do but can't ever seem to find enough time for. If you can think of nothing that corresponds to the menu or category in question, leave the page blank except for the title. At this time you are simply taking stock of your experiential disposition. The soul will certainly be aware of your intention to convert your lifestyle from being motivated by habits to being motivated by impulses. New possibilities will automatically begin to become available. Since reading certain kinds of books can easily go on the Self-Awareness Menu, the mere fact that you are currently absorbed in *this* one can provide the first entry for Menu C. Periodic trips to the psychology, self-help, occult, or philosophical sections of a bookstore will then keep this menu fed. You might also see if there are places in your hometown that offer self-awareness type seminars or workshops and then participate in the ones that interest you from time to time. If you are able to remember your dreams, then writing them down and interpreting them can also provide you with an appropriate Menu C activity. Consultations with a psychotherapist or psychic counselor are yet other possibilities.

When you come to the Work Menu, try to break your job down into as many smaller tasks as you can. Perhaps it involves phone calls, business meetings, consultations, and work at a computer terminal. Be as specific (and as brief) as possible. But don't go so far as to list specific projects by name. What you want are the generic components of your job that tend to remain the same, even as you apply yourself to particular assignments that come and go. The smaller the components you break your job down into, the easier it will be to detect impulses toward any of these areas. This can greatly increase your efficiency.

As you make up the Play Menu, be sure to include activities that get you out-of-doors. Because the eight-hour workday is so common in this society, nightlife—dining out, dancing, or attending movies, plays, concerts, or bars—may come to mind as Menu E possibilities more readily than outdoor activities. Yet work may keep you indoors for forty or more hours a week, and the Play Menu is supposed to help you counterbalance work with the exercising of unused aspects of consciousness. The kinds of things that can be done outdoors certainly represent unused aspects of consciousness in such a case. Furthermore, some playtime activities are seasonal, such as going to football games or flying kites. These, too, should be included on the Play Menu. Spending too much time inside, where the climate is controlled year-round, tends to emphasize routine because every day seems more or less the same. Participating in seasonal activities that get you outside allows you to break up this sameness through recognition of the daily, weekly, and monthly changes in the angle of the sun's light, the temperature, the prevailing weather conditions, and the life cycles of flowers and trees. It will be easier to sense the larger rhythms of your own becoming against these rhythms of nature than against the usually unchanging interiors of your office and home.

Some seasonal activities, although fun, might better be included on the Physical Focus Menu because of the extent to which they require coordination or bodily exertion. Ice-skating or skiing would be two examples. In actuality, there will always be some impulses traceable to two or more menus. Making a decision about what menu an impulse arises from may seem trivial in such cases. Yet to call playing on a baseball team a Physical Focus activity rather than a Play activity will mean that the primary focus will be on improving hand/eye coordination in pitching, batting, and catching and on getting exercise through running. Enjoyment of the game will increase because of how much better you will then play.

Besides Menus A and G, which are givens, the Cycles Menu will probably be the easiest to come up with. The practices it describes, which involve personal cleanliness, are pretty much held in common throughout your society: showering, shaving, clipping fingernails, haircuts, and so on. When constructing your own menus, you may wish to begin with this one, because it can be produced so easily.

Let your menus evolve over the course of a number of days or weeks rather than attempting to do them all in one sitting. The following review of the seven categories of impulses can get you started:

Menu A—The Natural Schedule

Impulses that divide the day into flexible time units. Service to the body.

Menu B—Physical Focus

Impulses that make you aware of, and help you overcome, inflexibility, coordination problems, and lack of presence in the body, as you move toward realization of your ideal body. Service to the body.

Menu C—Self-Awareness

Impulses that make you aware of, and help you confront, the lessons of the soul, as well as overcome problematic beliefs that block your ability to create your own reality in the manner most conducive to your growth. Service to the soul and/or service to family.

Menu D—Work

Impulses that allow you to increase your level of self-valuation, in terms of earning money or appreciation through career or volunteer work. Service to the Creator, service to the personality, service to family, service to humanity, and/or service to all life.

Menu E—Play

Impulses that allow you to take a break from fulfilling life purpose or to rehearse the vast storehouse of human potentialities to keep them from atrophying, often through playing games. Service to the Creator, service to the personality, and/or service to family.

Menu F—Cycles

Impulses that allow you to see how much you have matured—without symptoms of aging—and that help you perceive the larger rhythms of psychological growth, built up from the flexible time units of Menu A into longer periods akin to days, weeks, months, and years. Service to the personality, service to family, service to humanity, and/or service to all life.

Menu G—Surprises

Impulses which redirect your projected course of action by interrupting your plans—leading to adventures or to warnings of the presence of damaging beliefs, attitudes, or behaviors—and preventing you from succumbing to routine and world-weariness. Service to the soul.

CHAPTER 8

Sorting Things Out

It would be a monumental task to try to identify what menu everything you could possibly do belongs on. Furthermore, from the soul's perspective, it is the *intent* with which you perform an activity that often determines its menu affiliation. Playing a baseball game could be a Play Menu or a Physical Focus Menu activity, depending on your emphasis: are you playing more for fun or for exercise? For a professional player, it would be a Work Menu activity. The charts in this chapter will help you sort your activities into menus, based on the intent with which you perform them.

Just as there are seven types of impulse, there are also eight broad *categories of experience* into which everything that you do can be sorted. They are as follows:

1. *thinking*—from daydreaming to problem-solving
2. *moving*—from running or walking to skiing or horseback riding
3. *participating*—group involvement, from political or volunteer work to going to church
4. *communicating*—from phone calls or giving a lecture to writing a letter or a book
5. *learning*—from reading to attending a class

6. *creating*—artistic expression, from composing music to inventing a new recipe
7. *lovemaking*—from masturbation to intercourse
8. *healing and maintenance*—any form of response to damage, potential or actual

These categories of experience are not governed by any particular menu. They may apply to any one of the Menus B through F. Their exact form of expression will change, depending on your intent. Intents need not be mutually exclusive. For example, going to a town meeting to speak your piece about an unpopular proposal involves both participating and communicating. Don't worry about all the ways that the categories of experience can blend. The point is simply to use the chart in Figure 3 to help you determine how a change of intent can affect the menu an activity belongs to.

By knowing how the categories of experience apply to each of the menus, you will be much better equipped to sort the things that you do into your own set of menus. Even though everything that you do can be traced to one of these categories, we have made no attempt to be comprehensive. Such an approach would have been too cumbersome to be usable. Instead, we have chosen a number of examples that should help you extrapolate what menus the things that you enjoy doing belong on. Later on, we'll provide a technique you can do on your own to figure out the menu affiliations for anything you're still not sure about.

FIGURE 3

	THINKING[a]	MOVING
MENU B PHYSICAL FOCUS	Directed thought involving exercise or the body: —planning work-outs —body-awareness meditations[b]	Any form of movement done as exercise: —weight lifting —exercise bicycle —aerobic dance class —walking/running —yoga
MENU C SELF AWARENESS	Directed thought involving the psyche or inner growth processes: —meditation —dream interpretation —personal problem-solving	Any form of movement being practiced or rehearsed to overcome physical limitations: —ski lesson —scuba-diving class —practicing a musical instrument[c]
MENU D WORK	Directed thought involving career or work projects: —planning the workday —brainstorming —troubleshooting —decisions on career moves	Any form of movement done professionally or competitively: —ballet —professional sports or athletics —races —tournaments

FIGURE 3 (CONT.)

	THINKING[a]	MOVING
MENU E PLAY	Directed thought involving any form of entertainment or relaxation: —planning vacations —novels or movies —subjects of special interest[c] —daydreaming[d]	Any form of movement done for enjoyment or relaxation:[f] —bicycle riding —horseback riding —ice-skating —waterskiing —ballroom dancing
MENU F CYCLES	Directed thought involving cycles just ended or past events: —going over recent events in one's mind —bringing up old memories	Any form of movement done to regain skills lost or forgotten (this applies only as long as it takes to regain the skills):[g] —from last year or any earlier period

FIGURE 3 (CONT.)

	PARTICIPATING[h]	COMMUNICATING
MENU B PHYSICAL FOCUS	Any form of group involvement in which exercise is the main focus: —training with a partner or other members of a sports team —rough-and-tumble play with one's children	Any form of nonprofessional writing or talking about an exercise or sports training program, such as keeping a record of what one has accomplished and how one feels about it
MENU C SELF AWARENESS	Any form of group involvement in which self-development is the main focus: —going to church —group meditations —experiential workshops —support groups	Any form of talking or writing about the psyche or one's inner growth: —keeping a journal —spirituality/metaphysics —tools for transformation —making new friends[j]
MENU D WORK	Any form of group involvement in which work is the main focus: —staff meetings —political activism —volunteer work —concert rehearsals —doing favors for family or friends[i]	Any form of talking or writing professionally or about one's career: —author —critic —lecturer —teacher —counselor —class assignments[k]

FIGURE 3 (CONT.)

	PARTICIPATING[h]	COMMUNICATING
MENU E **PLAY**	Any form of group involvement in which play is the main focus: —nonprofessional sports —games that require partners or teams —social music making, such as jam sessions	Any form of talking or writing for pleasure or about entertainment: —novels, movies, performances, exhibits —spectator sports —subjects of special interest —anecdotes, jokes[l]
MENU F **CYCLES**	Any form of group involvement which honors the end or beginning of a cycle: —birthdays/graduations —weddings —baby showers/baptisms —bar or bas mitzvahs —funerals	Any form of talking or writing that makes one aware of a cycle of growth just completed: —letters, phone calls to friends —keeping a diary[m] —oral or written examinations

FIGURE 3 (CONT.)

	LEARNING	CREATING
MENU B PHYSICAL FOCUS	Absorbing information about exercise or the practice of a sport by reading or taking a class: —exercise or sports magazines —verbal instruction and demonstrations	Creative expression through movement: —choreography —pantomime —inventing gymnastic routines —free-form dancing
MENU C SELF AWARENESS	Absorbing information about self-development through reading or taking a class: —self-help books —workshops or seminars	The state of high inspiration, in which one becomes attuned to the expressive need of a work of art and possibly its overall form (the details will be worked out in Menu D); artistic expression as therapy
MENU D WORK	Absorbing information about work or one's field through reading or taking a class: —academic instruction —training sessions —professional seminars —specialized publications/research	Creation of works to be placed in front of an audience, whether as a public exhibition or for a circle of intimates; artistic expression as vocation or intensely pursued avocation

FIGURE 3 (CONT.)

	LEARNING	CREATING
MENU E P L A Y	Absorbing information for pleasure:[n] —magazines, newspapers —novels, nonfiction —performances, exhibitions —movies, television —current events —special interests	Use of improvisation to stimulate creativity;[p] artistic expression as a form of recreation
MENU F C Y C L E S	Absorbing information for a second time, after a hiatus:[o] —rereading a book —seeing a movie again —taking a refresher course —studying/review sessions before exams	Setting up retrospective exhibitions of one's art, writing essays or journal entries, or using any other means of placing a work in the context of one's personal and creative growth (such as making a catalog)

FIGURE 3 (CONT.)

	LOVEMAKING[q]	HEALING AND MAINTENANCE[r]
MENU B PHYSICAL FOCUS	Vigorous lovemaking, for exercise and release from tension	Any form of healing or preventive maintenance in which the body is the main focus: —doctor/chiropractor —dentist (cavities)[s] —massage therapist —shopping for athletic equipment
MENU C SELF AWARENESS	Sensitive lovemaking, for exploration of response in oneself and one's partner; exploring new horizons of sensuality	Any form of healing or preventive maintenance in which the mind is the main focus: —therapist/social worker/psychic —therapy group —shopping for self-awareness tools
MENU D WORK	Romantic lovemaking, creating the perfect scenario within which to express how much one values one's partner (candlelight dinner, soft music, subdued lighting, a fire in the fireplace, giving gifts)	Any form of healing or preventive maintenance in which one's job is the main focus: —occupational counseling/job search —union activity —shopping for office supplies/furniture

FIGURE 3 (CONT.)

	LOVEMAKING[q]	HEALING AND MAINTENANCE[r]
MENU E **P L A Y**	Playful, spontaneous lovemaking, involving much laughter and kidding around	Any form of *indirect* healing or preventive maintenance:[t] —music/visual arts —novels or movies with archetypal hero themes[u] —shopping for playthings
MENU F **C Y C L E S**	Lovemaking on special occasions (birthdays, anniversary, holidays), or after a period of separation or abstinence	Any form of repair, replacement, or cleaning: —home repairs —dry cleaning/mending —teeth cleaning —environmental cleanup/recycling —shopping for new selves[v]

a. By "directed thought" we mean keeping yourself focused on a particular topic rather than letting your thoughts wander. An example would be taking a walk in order to think about and work through a personal problem (Self-Awareness Menu).

b. For several excellent body-awareness meditations, see the first two chapters of Jean Houston's *The Possible Human.*

c. By "special interest" we mean fascination with something—Mayan archaeology, astronomy, or wild mushrooms, for example—that has nothing to do with work or self-awareness. Pursuing such special interests can fulfill the service-to-the-personality aspect of your life purpose, as well as provide breaks from the demands of the Work or Self-Awareness menus.

d. Daydreaming is a kind of mental role-playing that allows you to take life situations out of context and improvise various possible outcomes. Hence, it is a type of play. It can also allow you to take a break from the rigors of fulfilling your life purpose, by just letting your mind drift. Such "down time" can be extremely refreshing.

e. Playing a musical instrument provides an excellent example of how an activity can belong to different menus, depending on one's intent. If the intent is to overcome the physical limitations that prevent fluent execution of a passage, then the menu is Self-Awareness (through movement). If one is playing by oneself for fun, then the menu is Play (through movement). If one is taking a lesson on the instrument, the menu is Self-Awareness (through learning). If one is rehearsing with another person or a group for a concert, then the menu is Work (through participation). For social music making, as in jam sessions or sight-reading music for fun, the menu is Play (through participation), but for the actual concert performance it is Work (through communication). If one is *teaching* the instrument, then the menu is Work (through communication).

f. Many kinds of movement allow you to choose between two possible intents: exercise (Physical Focus Menu), or enjoyment or relaxation (Play Menu). Although riding an exercise bicycle will never be anything more than a Menu B activity, riding a real bicycle out-of-doors for exercise can also be highly enjoyable, depending on how intensely it is pursued and how captivating the scenery is. There is nothing wrong with listing such activities as horseback riding, hiking, ice-skating, waterskiing, or ballroom dancing on *both* menus. Your impulses will then tell you whether you want to pursue the activity vigorously enough to call it exercise or casually enough to call it recreational.

g. Whenever you take up a kind of movement that you haven't done for a while, you will probably feel a bit rusty. The intent to regain fluency places you in the Cycles Menu. The amount of time it takes to become fluent again depends on how long it has been since you last performed these movements. If it has been only a few months, you may catch on again quite quickly. If it has been a few decades, however, you'd better take things slowly and methodically rather than jumping in all at once—or you could hurt yourself. If you patiently become aware of the needs of your body throughout the process, never pushing yourself beyond the limits of endurance into pain, there is no reason why you cannot regain a large measure of your former fluency. Once you have regained the lost skill, a different intent takes over. The activity will change menus. Thus, during the first few practices of the new softball season you will be in the Cycles Menu; during later practices you will be in the Physical Focus and/or Play menus, depending on your intent. If you play the games themselves competitively for some kind of award, you will be in the Work Menu.

h. Anything done with one's family belongs to the participating category, from rough-and-tumble play with children (Physical Focus Menu), to attending church together (Self-Awareness Menu), running children to after-school activities (Work Menu), playing games or doing any kind of recreational activities together—such as going to an amusement park (Play Menu), or attending ceremonial occasions—such as a bar or bas mitzvah, a graduation, or a wedding (Cycles Menu).

i. Anytime you do a favor for a family member or a friend you are participating in that person's process of self-realization. This is a form of work because of the appreciation it earns. Running children to after-school activities is just such a favor, which is why we include it on the Work Menu.

j. Making new friends belongs to the Self-Awareness Menu because each person is trying to find the best place in his or her life for the other. A whole new set of possible beliefs, attitudes, and behaviors become available to each individual, as both of them become aware of the needs that the relationship might satisfy, as well as the possible future shape it might take.

k. Homework done for classes—especially writing papers—belongs to the Work Menu (through communication). The research that precedes writing a paper belongs to the Work Menu (through learning). Attending the class itself also belongs to the Work Menu (through learning). But studying or attending a review session for an examination involves the Cycles Menu (through learning). Actually taking the examination also belongs to the Cycles Menu (through communication).

l. Telling stories, anecdotes, or jokes, or bantering and kidding around all belong to the Play Menu (through communication). These are excellent ways of taking a break from fulfilling your life purpose.

m. We make a distinction between keeping a diary (Cycles Menu) and keeping a journal (Self-Awareness Menu). A diary simply records the events of the day; a journal includes thoughts about how these events relate to your growth. Writing down your dreams and interpreting them would be a journal-keeping activity. Recording each day's incidents on a trip to Europe would be a diary-keeping activity. Writing down the details of an unpleasant incident at work would also be a diary-keeping activity—unless your intent was to interpret it in terms of what you learned from it, in which case it would be a journal-keeping activity.

n. It may seem odd that we use the term *information* with respect to novels, performances, exhibitions, and movies. We are not simply referring to information about what a character looks like or does, or what colors or media an artist characteristically uses. We also mean the emotions described, the plots, and the recurrent themes or images. Furthermore, monitoring your *response* to such elements can provide you with information about yourself.

o. Anytime you reread a book, you will become aware of how much you have changed since the last time you read it. The same thing will be true of watching a movie a second time. Taking a refresher course, studying for an examination, or attending a review session all make you aware of how much you have learned over a certain period of time. These occasions help you become aware of the self you were before absorbing this information and of the self you have become through making it a part of you.

p. Improvisation is a form of play because it takes the performance or creation of a work of art out of the context of real life. The artist or performer then has an opportunity to try out various possible approaches to the problems the work poses. Improvisation can also keep all the artist's techniques well rehearsed and ready to be drawn upon by the Work Menu. Improvisation in dance and music are often used as means of overcoming creative blocks. An artist's sketchbook is his or her medium of improvisation, in which solutions to problems of perspective or design are attempted. Some novelists use poetry as a means of keeping their awareness of the possibilities of language well rehearsed. Improvisatory jam sessions help to rehearse the full range of one's performance abilities. Even though jazz played in a concert or recording studio may include elements of improvisation, it actually belongs to the Work Menu, because of the money or appreciation involved.

q. More detailed explanations of how lovemaking relates to each of the menus may be found in Chapter 24.

r. "Healing" here means "making whole," and "maintenance" means "maintaining wholeness." Any need diminishes one's sense of wholeness, so fulfilling your needs is a kind of healing. Since shopping is one of the primary ways of fulfilling needs, it belongs to this category of experience. What menu you are in while shopping depends on what you are shopping for: athletic equipment (Menu B); self-awareness tools, such as self-help books (Menu C); office supplies or furniture (Menu D); things that help you play, from novels to games, to recreational equipment (Menu E); or things that help you enter a new self-image, such as new clothes, or maintain a current self-image, such as replacing a worn-out item (Menu F).

s. We make a distinction between going to the dentist to have cavities filled, teeth crowned, or oral surgery performed, and simply having your teeth cleaned. The latter has to do with upkeep of self-image through preventive maintenance, and so it is a Cycles Menu activity. The other types of dental work represent ways of healing the body and so belong to the Physical Focus Menu. In either case, seeing the dentist is an expression of the service-to-the-body aspect of your life purpose.

t. Many of the arts provide for a kind of indirect healing. Listening to quiet music can have a calming effect when you are upset. Listening to a turbulent piece of music that comes to a harmonious resolution can often lead you through a process of confronting and releasing your own emotional turbulence. The same kind of catharsis can occur through seeing plays or dance concerts, reading novels, or watching movies. Your empathy with the characters portrayed can allow you to prevent psychological damage through discharging unexpressed or repressed emotion. This occurs whenever you feel moved by an artistic experience.

u. Novels and movies with archetypal hero themes (George Lucas's celebrated *Star Wars* trilogy, for example) are about fulfilling one's life purpose, which is felt by the protagonists as a special destiny.[7] The obstacles encountered on the way to fulfilling this destiny represent, in symbolic form, all of the resistances you are likely to encounter on your own quest for self-realization. The emotions that come up as you participate in these fictional journeys can actually help free you from fears and resistances to fulfilling your real-life destiny. The forces of evil represent your own damaging beliefs, attitudes, and behaviors. The feeling of triumph you feel when these forces have been crushed in the end will fortify you in your own inner confrontations. Because of their archetypal nature, such books or movies can provide as much preventive maintenance as dreams in the area of confronting and releasing damaging beliefs, attitudes, and behaviors. This is why we place them in the category of indirect healing.

v. By "shopping for new selves," we mean buying anything that allows you to enter into a new self-image. A higher level of self-valuation can result from wisely spending money on oneself. This higher level of self-valuation can bring with it fresh approaches to problem areas in your life and a greater willingness or self-assurance in dealing with them. Thus, shopping can be an important aspect of the healing process, as anyone who has bought new clothes during times of emotional upset can attest. This is the fundamental truth behind the saying "When the going gets tough, the tough go shopping." House or apartment hunting also allows you to shop for new selves. So does buying a service such as a haircut. Shopping to replace worn out items can reflect your entry into a new self-image, especially if you get something of better quality this time around. We should mention as an aside that buying household products involved in cleaning or repair also belongs on Menu F. A large part of anyone's Cycles Menu will be comprised of such maintenance activities. A more complete list appears in the next chapter.

We did not mention preparing food in either Figure 3 or its notes. Cooking is a special case. It is one of the few activities that can belong to several different categories of experience. When cooking is done informally for family members or close friends, it is a kind of favor that can earn appreciation. Hence, it belongs to the Work Menu (through participating). When it is done formally, as in creating a dinner party involving a number of elaborate dishes, it again belongs to the Work Menu (through creating). In these cases, cooking allows you to fulfill the service-to-the-body and service-to-family aspects of your life purpose.

When cooking is done professionally, it is once again a Work Menu activity. For the master chef it will be Work

Menu through creating. For the other kitchen staff in a restaurant, it will be Work Menu through participating, because of the teamwork involved in mass-producing meals. In these cases, cooking will allow you to fulfill the service-to-humanity aspect of your life purpose.

When you are cooking with a partner, it will be Work Menu through participating (service to the body and service to family). But when you are cooking for yourself alone, it will be Work Menu through creating or through healing and maintenance. The former will be true when you are cooking more involved meals, or altering or inventing recipes. The latter will be true when you are simply throwing something together to satisfy the impulse to eat. When cooking for yourself alone, you are fulfilling the service-to-the-body aspect of your life purpose.

Why does cooking always seem to be associated with the Work Menu? Your ancestors in primitive times hunted, gathered, and grew their own food. A large part of their days was concerned with such tasks, just as a large part of your day is probably concerned with your job. How well they fed themselves was usually determined by how dedicated they were to the work of hunting, gathering, planting, harvesting, preserving, and preparing food. Because survival is a matter of self-valuation, this was their Work Menu. Then as now, if people don't care whether they live or die, they don't value themselves enough to do the work required to survive, whether that means foraging for food or getting a job.

Today, you are able to buy your food instead of spending so much time producing it. But preparing food still belongs to the Work Menu. It might seem more like a Cycles Menu activity, because it must be repeated so often. But how well you feed yourself, family, and friends is usually more a matter of how much you value yourself and them in terms of caring about your collective survival than it is of the self-image you might wish to project. The same is true of making trips to the grocery, which is also a Work Menu activity: what you buy there reflects your level of self-valuation, whether it is junk food or the leanest cuts of beef or the finest seafood. On the other hand, going out to dinner has nothing to do with the Work Menu. The menu you are in will be determined by what you are thinking about if you are alone or the topic of conversation if you are with others.

Growing your own food is Work Menu through creating. After all, you are trying to create an environment in which the plants will flourish and produce the finest harvest. Gardening for recreation, however, is Play Menu through creating. In either case, you are like a god to your little plot of earth. Gardening is not only an art, it is also an excellent metaphor for how you yourself are nurtured by the soul.

From the soul's perspective, the wanton slaughter of animals for sport is not appropriate. It violates the service-to-all-life aspect of your life purpose. However, fishing or hunting wild animals or plants for food is certainly permissible—even if you no longer really need to do so. Because of the combination of strenuous physical activity and finely tuned bodily reactions involved, hunting, gathering, fishing, and cleaning game all derive from the Work Menu, through moving.

When making up your own menus, it is not necessary for you to identify the category of experience along with the menu affiliation, as we have often done in the notes to Figure 3. This was an attempt to demonstrate that there are certain consistencies underlying how we have sorted activities into menus. Without this demonstration, Figure 3 might have seemed wholly arbitrary.

CHAPTER 9

Sample Menus

The Menus system is not meant to be rigidly applied. It is simply a set of strategies for becoming aware of impulses. We hope that it will encourage you to follow any and every impulse you become aware of, whether or not you know what menu a certain activity belongs on.

Constructing your own set of menus is the first step in overcoming the tendency to value certain activities over others. Because overvalued activities will usually screen out impulses toward less-valued ones, making your own menus is essential to the process of becoming aware of impulses. Less-valued activities may satisfy vitally important needs from time to time.

Sorting the activities that you most characteristically pursue into the several categories of impulses can also make you aware of the kinds of impulses you have a tendency to ignore. Some of your menus may have only a few entries or none at all. But the actual process of making them up will help you learn how the intent behind a Self-Awareness Menu activity differs from the intent behind a Work or Play Menu activity. It will then be easier to detect and pursue impulses you may never have previously considered.

Some important background information on the Menu A impulses is necessary before you will be able to create a truly impulsive lifestyle. This material appears in Part II. Then, in Part III, we'll explain how to get the whole system up and running. It might be a good idea to have a first draft of the menus ready by that point.

Now we'll give Kurt the opportunity to provide sample menus and personal commentary on the process of menu construction, based on his own experience with the system. If you find you are having difficulty coming up with appropriate activities for any of the menus, you may wish to try out some of the things on Kurt's lists. Even if it turns out that you don't enjoy a new activity as much as you thought you might, you will have learned something valuable: making up your own menus requires just as much sensitivity to the kinds of activities that aren't right for you as the ones that are.

When I first wrote down my own set of menus, I found it surprisingly difficult to make up Menus B through F. They contained only a few entries at first. I just sat and stared at the nearly empty sheets of paper in shock. Previously I had always felt there were never enough hours in a week—much less a day—for me to do everything I wanted to do. But now it seemed as if there were *many* more hours in the week than activities listed on *all seven pages!* Something within me seemed to implode. I felt the collapse of my former sense of time versus productivity. I had sometimes spent between three and twelve hours a day composing music—and ended up producing only a few measures or pages, with a total duration of perhaps twenty seconds. And now that activity appeared before my eyes as just a couple of words—no longer and no shorter than urinating or going out to a movie, cutting my fingernails or getting a massage! Clearly the Work Menu had been out of control and had at last been placed into perspective.

My first set of menus were not nearly as rich as the ones that follow here. I tried out many activities that I did not find appealing—and none of these are listed. But over the course of several years of impulsive living, I have managed to collect a wide variety of activities that I find rewarding to pursue. As you make up your own set of menus, do not feel obligated to list as many possibilities as you find in these examples. Just let your own menus evolve over the course of time as you become more attuned to the promptings of body and soul.

For purposes of clarity, I have been somewhat more verbose than Charles recommends. I have also listed some of the closely related activities I characteristically pursue on the same line, to save space. In my own stenographer's notebook, however, they each have a separate line, as in his instructions.

MENU A—The Natural Schedule

the impulse to urinate
the impulse to quench thirst
the impulse to sleep
the impulse to awaken
the impulse to eat
the impulse to defecate

MENU B—Physical Focus

Flexibility	*Coordination*
yoga	swimming
stretch and strength class	running
	skipping rope
	ice-skating
	snowshoeing
	riding a bicycle outdoors
	canoeing
	squash
	contact improvisation

Body image	*Presence*
weight lifting (Nautilus equipment)	massage/bodywork
stretch and strength class	steam room
exercise bicycle	contact improvisation
rowing machine	
sit-ups	

Obviously, my Menu B is a personal list. For one thing, although I enjoy dancing, I have never been drawn to take an aerobics class. This doesn't mean that for some reason I don't endorse that sort of physical-focus activity. It's just one of the possibilities I haven't opted to bring into my life—but I could if I ever felt the impulse to.

Because of having been jeered at for my lack of interest in, and aptitude for, team sports when I was growing up, I have tended to shy away from any kind of competitive sport. So I don't list basketball, baseball, or soccer on my Physical Focus Menu. One of my friends is helping me learn to play squash though, but in a noncompetitive way. We just get together and hit the ball around. I'm much more interested in the kinds of coordination involved than in playing for points. Once again, the fact that I have not listed team sports on my Menu B does not indicate any sort of disapproval on my part or Charles's.

You can see that certain kinds of activities may transcend the categories Charles has listed, as with my stretch and strength class. This class is offered by my health club. It includes a period of warm-up stretching at the beginning, for increasing flexibility. It then proceeds to work out each major muscle group in the entire body. Small weights are used for one sequence involving arms and shoulders, and another sequence is involved with toning the abdomen to improve body image.

Another activity that transcends Charles's categories is contact improvisation, a highly expressive form of dance that involves more or less constant contact with one's partner. It can be quiet and graceful, or strong and energetic. In the classes I have taken, various exercises are designed to increase the sense of presence in the body by getting in touch with its several layers—skin, muscle, and bone. When dancing with a partner, one must constantly be aware of the center of gravity from which one moves and of how one's weight is being distributed throughout the body—especially when lifting or carrying one's partner. This, too, increases the sense of presence within the body. Furthermore, the improvisatory quality of the movements poses ever-changing challenges in the area of coordination.

For many people yoga is more a form of meditation than an opportunity to stretch the body. The class I am taking, however, is a very strenuous and athletic variety called Iyengar yoga. This is why I place it on the Physical Focus Menu. In fact, I would differentiate between the yoga practices that emphasize focusing within the body through *asanas* (complex postures held for certain lengths of time) and those that emphasize focusing the mind, as in meditation. The former would be listed on Menu B, while the latter would belong to Menu C.

I find it interesting that Charles has never recommended aerobic exercise, which involves strenuous physical activity that keeps the heartbeat rate above a certain level for a certain length of time. The people at my health club who work out in this fashion are always looking at their watches and pushing themselves harder—and I think this is the key. They don't seem to be paying attention to their own bodies' needs. Their egos have adopted a regimen that ignores signals from the body to quit when it has had enough for the time being. They just keep going until their watches tell them to stop.

When I first began following Charles's advice to pursue a Physical Focus Menu activity once each day, I could barely swim four pool lengths or run a half mile without requiring a rest. I took that rest, even though my workout would not then qualify as aerobic. Once in a while though, I would test my body's limits of endurance, pushing myself beyond what I knew I could do easily—but not so far that I became uncomfortable. I swam those four lengths or ran that half mile as fast as I could or added another four lengths or half mile just to see if I could do it. When I discovered that I could—comfortably—I continued at that level of performance until I felt the next impulse to extend myself in speed or distance.

Never would I compare myself with others and use that as a basis for gauging my own physical focus. Instead, I compared myself to myself—often finding that the mile run felt easier this time than it did a couple of days ago or that I seemed to be swimming faster than usual. Sometimes, for reasons I could never figure out, there might be a day when I just could not run or swim as much, or as quickly, as the last time. I would go with my body rather than with ego-based expectations of my performance. The next time, I would be back to my usual ease and comfort. There were also periods when I did not feel the impulse to run or swim for a number of weeks, and so I engaged in other physical-focus activities instead. When I returned to running or swimming, however, I almost invariably found that my abilities had improved. It seemed to me that my body had gotten bored with running or swimming, and had not been sending me the impulse to do either of these things. I had discovered that even the body dislikes routine.

Through taking this approach to my body—trying to listen to its needs—I have gradually built myself up to the point of being able to swim up to a half mile or run up to three miles. And there may be further increases yet to come, should I feel the impulsive motivation to undertake them. In the meantime, my heart and lungs have certainly strengthened in order to accommodate such activities—at their own rates and without the imposition of the kind of ego expectations I often see associated with aerobic exercise. The reason I have been discussing swimming and running in this context is that whenever I feel the need to get my circulation going, these are what I most often choose to do.

If you enjoy it, chances are your body is enjoying it too—no matter what you're doing for exercise. If you're not enjoying it, then something's wrong. The body is being required to do something it doesn't want to do. Either it's bored with your routine or you're ignoring the signs of its limits on a certain day. I've watched myself gain in muscle mass through shoulders, arms, and chest to the point that some of my old shirts no longer fit me—from using Nautilus equipment for about nine months. Not once did I go beyond the threshold of comfort as I gradually increased the amount of weight used on each machine. Perhaps somebody operating under the "no pain, no gain" paradigm might have achieved the same results in less time. But I am confident that both I and my body have enjoyed this process and that I am not doing damage to myself that will show up years from now. I cringe when I see people's bodies writhing in agony as their ego expectations force them to use weights far in excess of the body's comfort level. Their contorted faces make me think of animals being beaten. All I can think about is that someday the body won't be able to take it anymore. It might just give in, causing more or less permanent damage.

If you have not been doing any type of exercise for a number of years, you might want to consult with a physician before making up your own Menu B. He or she could tell you what kinds of activities would be beneficial, without causing undue strain. Instructors at many health clubs are trained to come up with exercise programs that are tailor-made for an individual's current physical condition. If there are severe inflexibility or coordination problems, then consulting a physical therapist might be in order.

When you make up your own Menu B, the idea is to write down enough activities so that you don't end up doing the same thing every day. But don't make it so large that when it comes time to exercise, you can't decide what to do. My own is so extensive because I like to mix and match Menu B activities to create an endless variety of workouts—doing, say, twenty minutes or so of stretching out, then running a couple miles or riding a stationary bicycle, and then using Nautilus equipment. Sometimes my body needs more than one exercise period in the course of a day. If I didn't have such a large list to choose from, it would be too easy for me to deny later impulses toward the Physical Focus Menu merely because I did not want to repeat myself.

One final point. It's much more important to have a variety of Menu B activities than it is to know for sure whether a certain one belongs to the flexibility, coordination, body image, or presence category. On the other hand, since weight lifting all by itself can decrease the body's flexibility, and not stretching out before running can lead to physical damage, it is important to counterbalance activities in one area with activities in another. As long as you can come up with at least one activity that clearly goes in each category, you'll be fine.

MENU C—Self-Awareness

dream journal
consulting the *I Ching*
receiving trance-written channeling sessions
typing trance-written channeling sessions
recording out-of-body experiences and other psychic adventures
meditation tapes
shamanic rituals
chanting/shamanic drumming
reading books on metaphysical subjects (channeled material, etc.)

attending workshops in spirituality
thinking/talking/writing about what's going on inside me or about Self-Awareness activities
practicing clarinet or piano
making new friends

Receiving personal guidance through intuitive means such as a trance state (as in channeling) is a kind of self-awareness activity. I prefer the term *trance-written* to the more usual *automatic writing.* I'm aware of the words as they come through me, so there is nothing automatic about the process. In this kind of session, Charles answers questions about what's going on in my life.

The *I Ching,* or *Book of Changes,* is an ancient book of Chinese philosophy that can be quite useful in times of crisis or doubt about what decision might be best for one's growth. Through a procedure involving the tossing of coins, a six-line figure called a *hexagram* is derived. There are sixty-four such hexagrams. Each one represents a life situation that a person might encounter at one point or another. The book contains commentaries on these life situations. They can often help one become aware of the soul's perspective on the crisis or the decision. In fact, Charles says that the soul actually influences the tossing of the coins in order to put one in touch with the appropriate guidance in the book. The metaphoric language of the *I Ching* can be a bit obscure at times. The best translation is the Wilhelm-Baynes version.[8]

Shamanism is an ancient method of healing and attunement to the rhythms of nature. I have always been strongly attracted to Native American spirituality, which derives from shamanism to some extent. These symbols and rituals help keep me aware of how mankind is a part of nature and must strive to live in harmony with all other creatures, each of whom performs an invaluable function within the whole. In shamanic practice, drumming and chanting are used as means of achieving a trance state, within which it becomes possible to receive visionary guidance or to conduct healing work.[9]

MENU D—Work

music—composing at the piano
copying scores or parts
adding dynamics, tempos, articulations
copying scores or parts
working with performers
studying scores

poetry—writing/typing/revising
performing in public readings
sending submissions to poetry journals

the Charles material—preparing transcripts of sessions (typing/editing/proofing/printing)

the Charles books—writing/revising

counseling—Charles readings for clients, couples, groups

teaching—the Boston study group (based on the Charles material)

thinking/talking/reading/writing about my Work Menu activities

business correspondence and telephone calls

grocery shopping/cooking

I have yet to make any money as a composer. But applause and reviews of concerts in which my music has been performed, as well as hearing people's comments about it, can help me perceive how well I am valuing myself as a composer. The same is true when I receive letters commenting on Charles material that people have seen in print or when my Boston study group responds to things I have handed out at our meetings.

MENU E—Play

art museums and galleries
orchestra, chamber music, and dance concerts
poetry readings
shopping for records and tapes of classical music
listening to records and tapes of classical music
reading novels or poetry
shopping for books in new or secondhand bookstores
movies
flea markets/antique stores
playing chamber music with friends
thinking/talking about Play Menu activities
stamp collecting
card games (solitaire, gin rummy, hearts, cribbage)
jigsaw puzzles
backgammon
chess
kite flying
sailing
picnics
identifying wild mushrooms
stargazing
Archaeology magazine
newspapers
drawing classes/sketching

Identifying wild mushrooms and stargazing are two hobbies of mine. As hobbies, they are certainly not connected to the Work Menu, no matter how scientifically I might pursue them. As it happens, I simply enjoy the opportunities they offer for getting outdoors. Some mushroom identifications require special chemical agents, which I don't see fit to buy. And I'm not overly concerned about the accuracy of my labelings, since I have no intention of eating any of my finds —even though there are a considerable number of edible wild mushrooms to be found in New England. My telescope is definitely not state-of-the-art, although it is quite adequate for my needs. Wondering at the stars and seeking to label or identify the profusion of life on this planet are certainly aspects of the vast storehouse of human capabilities. Neither of these capacities are emphasized on my Work Menu, and yet the impulses to pursue them remain. So they are clearly Menu E activities.

I used to want to be an archaeologist years ago and actually worked for a number of summers at a dig. The interest has persisted, even though I did not pursue archaeology as a career. Since most of the digs in New England concern the history of European settlement, and not prehistoric Indian occupation—which would be my own personal interest—I must satisfy myself with reading about digs in other parts of the country. Any kind of reading for the simple joy of accumulating information on some topic of interest not related to one's work belongs on the Play Menu. This would also be true of magazines on current events, for example, as well as the daily paper.

I gave up watching television when I was a teenager, because I felt there were better things to do with my life than watch situation comedies, soap operas, and police dramas. I still don't own one, even though my friends insist that I sometimes miss good shows on topics of interest to me. But if I did have my own set, watching it would go on the Play Menu. I've always preferred reading or listening to music. Once again, I hope that my examples have demonstrated that menus can be very personal, if not idiosyncratic.

MENU F—Cycles

showering
shampooing my hair
shaving
trimming my moustache

clipping my fingernails and toenails
getting a haircut
brushing my teeth
visits to the dentist for teeth cleaning
cleaning house
washing windows
home improvements
washing the dishes
putting out the trash
doing laundry
trips to the post office
bank errands
balancing my checkbook
paying bills
bookkeeping (for my counseling practice)
income tax preparation
watering the houseplants
dry cleaning
mending my clothes
having my clothes altered
writing letters
making phone calls to friends
making my bed
getting dressed
picking up yesterday's clothes
getting the piano tuned
washing and waxing the car/vacuuming the interior
trips to the recycling center

My mother would be only too delighted to discover that I have finally realized the importance of making my bed and picking my clothes up off the floor—not to mention taking out the trash. Too bad it took a "higher" (and nonphysical) authority to get the point across! There are other Cycles Menu activities that only come up once in a great while, such as renewing a driver's license or transferring a car title from one state to another. Anything having to do with relocating, since this ends one cycle and begins another, is certainly a Menu F activity.

MENU G—Surprises

- coincidences
- synchronicities
- unusual occurrences
- unexpected happenings
- magical or miraculous events

Here are two examples of Menu G experiences that have happened to me. The first one involves a damaging attitude, and the second, a remarkable coincidence.

Boston drivers are notorious for breaking the rules. They can also be highly creative. For example, I've often seen the familiar "right turn on red" option reinterpreted as "left turn on red from right lane." One day I decided to participate in another favorite Boston pastime—jaywalking. There were two lanes of stopped traffic along my side of the street and one empty lane going in the other direction on the other side. A car had turned into that lane, and I felt that I had enough time to run across before it could reach me. What I hadn't anticipated was that a driver at the end of the long line of traffic on my side would decide to cross the center line and try to get around everyone else, even though there was another car coming right at him. He hit me. I don't know how fast he was going, but I vaulted off his hood and found myself in the air. As I spun around, I saw that his wife had covered her face. I didn't go very high. But when I came down, I was facing in the opposite direction, a couple of feet away. I landed on my feet, went over to the car, and told the guy that he should never cross a double yellow line. Then I walked away. Before I even had enough time to catch my breath, a bum walked up to me and asked if I had any spare change. I noticed that his jeans were torn and covered with blood. Stitches that seemed to run the length of both of his legs showed through the holes. I reached into my pocket and gave him a couple of dollars. As I continued on my way, it suddenly hit me what had happened. That bum had shown me what I would have looked like if the accident had been more serious! Shaken by this, I tried to remember what I had been thinking about as I was crossing the street. My thoughts had centered on an acquaintance who was quite accident-prone. I was wondering whether there was any way I could get him to look at his damaging beliefs. Apparently my soul had given me a warning: I was using him as an excuse not to look at my own!

The second Menu G experience involved my brother Wes, who lives in Colorado. One day he called me on the phone, which was itself an unusual occurrence. He was on Cape Cod, only a few hours away. He wanted me to bring him back to Boston in a couple of days so that he could see where I lived and tour the town. On the appointed day, I drove down to Truro, which is almost on the tip of Cape Cod. The instructions were for me to call him when I got there in order to get directions to the beach cottage where he was staying. Wes can sometimes be a bit unreliable. The whole way down I kept muttering to myself that he'd better be at the number he gave me or I would just turn around and go back to Boston and he would have to find another way to get there.

When I arrived in Truro, the only pay phones I could find were at a combination post office and laundromat. One of the phones was dangling off the hook, and a haggard-looking character was talking on the other. He told me that he had somebody on the other line as well, and that he'd be done soon. Back and forth he went between the two phones. Then he turned around and asked if I was Wes's brother! It turns out that the phone service where Wes was staying had been shut off that very day because the bills had not been paid. The man at the pay phones was the brother of the friend Wes was visiting. Someone he knew had been critically injured in a car accident in New Jersey. He was trying to check on the guy's condition. I got the feeling that if something this serious hadn't come up, he wouldn't have driven into town to use the pay phones. And if he hadn't been using both phones at once, he might never have looked up and recognized me. When he was through, I followed his truck along a back road with many twists and forks, all of them unmarked. By the time we had reached the beach cottage, it was pretty clear that I wouldn't have been able to follow Wes's directions, even if I had been able to call him. Furthermore, if I had taken the directions from him earlier and had gotten lost, there would have been no way to let him know.

The choreography of impulses behind the perfect timing of this event was staggering. My soul had intervened—apparently in collaboration with the soul of the man on the phone and perhaps Wes's as well—to prevent me from leaving Wes behind. It had not occurred to me that he might become unreachable through no fault of his own. We were both saved from a turn of events that might have been damaging to our basically good relationship.

PART TWO

FUNCTIONS OF THE MENU A IMPULSES

CHAPTER 10

The Impulses to Urinate and to Quench Thirst

We have pointed out that the impulse to urinate indicates a need to change focus of consciousness. The descriptions of Menus B through F make it clear that the state of consciousness required for maintaining physical focus through exercise will be different from that required for self-awareness, work, play, or cycles. In fact, each menu represents a different manner of focusing consciousness. The activities listed on any single menu are related to one another by the fact that they all require a similar focus of consciousness. Hence, the impulse to urinate will occur whenever you shift from an activity on one menu to a quite different activity on another.

You may recall that successive impulses to urinate create flexible time units akin to the hours. If each one represents a certain focus of consciousness, then it must be dedicated to the pursuit of activities from a particular menu. For this reason we call the period between urinations a *dedicated time slot.* It represents how long you are capable of maintaining a particular state of consciousness—or presence within a particular menu—with maximum levels of clarity and productivity.

If you limit the amount of time you spend doing something

to the period between urinations and if you move on to an activity from a different menu only after the next impulse to urinate has manifested itself, then you will be operating out of maximum levels of clarity and productivity in *both* periods, no matter how long they might last. It stands to reason that spending a whole day shifting from menu to menu every time you feel the impulse to urinate will allow you to extend these periods of maximum clarity and productivity until they have encompassed all your waking hours.

Generally speaking, people who urinate frequently either are incapable of maintaining certain states of consciousness because of flightiness or emotional stress or are highly creative. Those in the latter group require frequent urinations because of their great flexibility of consciousness. This will certainly also be true of people who are psychically sensitive. On the other hand, people who urinate infrequently either are quite capable of high levels of concentration or are relatively restricted in terms of flexibility of consciousness. They may be stodgy or boring. As a result of applying the Menus for Impulsive Living to your own life, you may find yourself urinating more frequently. This will be a sign of increasing flexibility of consciousness. We mention this fact because medical doctors often ascribe increasing frequency of urination to the onset of some physical disorder.

Because the impulse to urinate is the key to efficient life-force management, it is extremely important that you become sensitized to it. Many people have lost the ability to perceive the genuine impulse to urinate because as children they were faced with parents' or teachers' annoyance at the inconvenience of a child's frequent need to urinate. Yet frequent urination is a natural concomitant of any child's great flexibility of consciousness. Fear of being punished for having to go to the bathroom has caused many a child to lose that flexibility. As a result, almost everyone waits too long before acting on this impulse. During the period of time between when the impulse manifests itself and when it is acted upon, there will be a gradual reduction in productivity and ability to concentrate. The waste products blocked from further processing by the fullness of the bladder will continue to circulate within the system. Their presence causes a reduction in the blood's ability to use oxygen efficiently and consequently a lack of clarity. These waste products will begin to settle into the muscles and joints not in use, especially the legs, which will tend to feel increasingly heavy. By the time this has occurred, both mental and physical fatigue will have taken their toll on whatever you have been doing. Only a brief nap followed by a period of vigorous exercise to clear out the waste chemicals accumulated in the muscles will allow you to reestablish the highest levels of clarity and productivity. It is better for both brain and body that you urinate more, rather than less, frequently.

There are two conditions under which the genuine impulse to urinate will manifest itself. Often you will suddenly become aware of a need to relieve yourself at the exact moment you decide that you are ready to move from one activity to another. You may not have had the slightest hint of this need before the moment you made your decision. This is the genuine impulse to urinate in its purest form. There will be little question in your mind of the appropriateness of acting upon it. For one thing, you would probably prefer not to interrupt whatever you're going to do next by having to go to the bathroom. At other times, you will gradually become aware of a need to urinate that becomes increasingly urgent. In this case, the body is putting you on notice that it will not be able to maintain the current state of consciousness (or brain chemistry) for too much longer. If you persist in ignoring this quiet but persistent tugging at your awareness, it will eventually become more and more insistent until you are incapable of thinking of anything else. It is never a good idea to wait that long, for the reasons mentioned above. Furthermore, during this entire period your ability to focus consciousness will diminish. The best response is to find the most convenient stopping point in whatever you are doing, take a bathroom break, and then return.

The body has a tolerance for the brain's chemical balances that will allow it to support the same one for no more than two periods between urinations. This means that it is possible for you to engage yourself in the same activity or menu for the duration of two dedicated time slots. Beyond that point, the body gets bored with stimulating itself in the same way. And so it will begin to produce a different brain chemistry, despite your intellectual intention to keep at whatever you have been doing. Because the new brain chemistry does not support the activity you are doing, you will experience an inability to concentrate. If you persist, mounting frustration will leak away valuable life force and you will soon end up feeling fatigued. Furthermore, if you do the same thing day in and day out, the body will develop a kind of resistance to that particular brain chemistry. The result will be allergic reactions, especially hay-fever-like symptoms. But the body is not to be blamed for this apparent intolerance of changelessness. The soul itself is actually behind it. Only through developing every aspect of who you are—by engaging in Physical Focus, Self-Awareness, Work, Play, and Cycles menu activities—will you be able to become a well-rounded individual capable of fulfilling every aspect of your life purpose. The soul strongly discourages routine by inciting the body to resist generating the same brain chemistry over and over.

It will certainly not have escaped your attention that public rest rooms usually have a drinking fountain nearby. You may also have noticed that you are usually thirsty after having urinated. The impulse to quench thirst indicates that the body needs water, either to sustain the current brain chemistry or to establish a new one. It is always appropriate to fuel a new focus of consciousness with the intake of some beverage. Any liquid will do. But water is the liquid that will most quickly become available to the system, because of the watery base of the entire physical form. A drink of water will deepen concentration, maintain attention span, and enhance participation and enjoyment within any activity. The impulse to quench thirst should be considered a request by the body or the soul for such enhancements.

Pure water is best. Anything that has been added to it, as in the case of tea or coffee, will affect this new focus of consciousness in unforeseen ways. The same is true of milk, fruit juice, wine, beer, liquor, or soft drinks. If maximum levels of clarity and productivity are your goal, then stick with water. But you may feel impulses upon occasion to drink other beverages, and you should trust that for some reason the body needs you to do so, possibly to sustain a certain kind of brain chemistry. After a tiring and sweaty workout, for example, the brain may need water at the same time as the muscles need to be nurtured with blood sugar in order to relax without cramping. In such a case, fruit juice would be an ideal thirst quencher.

Besides accompanying the entry into a new menu at the point of urination, thirst will also accompany any shift between activities *on the same menu,* even when there is no impulse to urinate. Fluid intake allows some minor adjustments to the prevailing brain chemistry to be made. In this way the prevailing brain chemistry—which need not be changed entirely, as in the case of switching from one menu to another—can better accommodate the new activity.

Having something to drink continuously while working on a project often indicates a certain insecurity about "having what it takes"—in terms of focus of consciousness—to complete it. Frequent sipping has a tendency to dilute the current focus of consciousness. It is best to quench thirst only when you are genuinely thirsty.

In the case of inveterate coffee drinkers, continuous sipping can indicate a complete lack of interest in the project. The mind must be forced into concentration. But the stepped-up ability to concentrate that results from caffeine intake will gradually deteriorate to a level much lower than it was before the coffee had been imbibed. The stupor that is often typical of late mornings or afternoons at work can be the result of having had coffee during breakfast or lunch. This stupor often seems to require further coffee in order to be conquered. An addiction to caffeine generally means that someone's life consists of so many dreary routines that the mind must be forced to take interest in this way. Coffee isn't necessarily bad for you. But using it to support routine—and therefore stress—will certainly lead to symptoms of aging.

The most common reason people drink coffee is because they have trouble feeling fully awake and refreshed in the morning. Even those who are not coffee drinkers can suffer from this malady. The problem usually lies in not paying attention to the impulses to sleep and to awaken, which we shall examine in the next two chapters.

CHAPTER 11

The Impulse to Sleep

It is common knowledge that when you are tired all you need to do is prepare yourself for sleep. When you awaken a while later, you will be refreshed. During that time period your consciousness seems to be turned off, inasmuch as it no longer registers the presence of things in your environment. Even so, upon awakening you may retain a vague awareness that certain inner experiences have taken place. Perhaps you remember a dream or two. Yet, despite the scientific research into what happens during sleep, no one has been able to explain fully why you feel refreshed when you wake up. In this chapter we shall explain why this is so—but from the soul's perspective rather than the scientific or physiological one.

To the soul, everything that you experience in physical reality is as unreal as your dream images seem to you. The soul is not at all concerned with what objects look like or how they are related to one another in space. But the soul is eminently concerned with whether or not you are learning certain lessons while you are focused in a body. These lessons have to do with self-realization and the fulfillment of your life purpose. Yet how does the soul know that you are doing what you need to be doing?

The soul does not simply watch you in every moment like

some kind of omniscient eye, but it does monitor the choices you make in order to assure itself that you are not intentionally or unintentionally thwarting your own growth. It is also available for guidance at every moment, often through the redirective measures of Menu G but also through hunches, intuitions, and, of course, impulses. In the meantime, however, it is primarily focused on its own developmental processes in nonphysical reality. Even though the manner in which you process your daily experience at the ego level is of great interest to the soul, it does not want to interfere with that processing on a moment-by-moment basis. Unless you are about to make some decision that could have devastating consequences for your own or someone else's growth, the soul will wait patiently until you are ready to communicate what you have learned from the events of each day. These communications could be likened to the periodic telephone calls you might make to parents who live far away, in order to tell them the latest happenings in your life. In the case of your relationship with the soul, such communications take place during meditation, naps, and the nightly sleep cycle.

As you speak into a telephone, the sounds of your voice are converted into electrical impulses that will then be translated back into words at the other end. When you are communicating with the soul, a similar translation process occurs. On your end, the information to be communicated comprises how you have made use of your body, all the sense impressions you have received, all the activities you have engaged in, everything you have felt emotionally, and everything you have thought or said in the course of a day. This information must be converted into messages that the soul can understand.

You may have noticed while falling asleep that the muscles of your body sometimes twitch involuntarily. Furthermore, there may be a play of colors or shapes drifting through your awareness. Sometimes you might hear words or fragments of conversations all jumbled up. Flashes of things you saw during the day may appear at random, along with images of things you may not recall ever having seen. Gradually, these disjointed inner perceptions may assemble themselves into a rudimentary plot line, which often seems not to make any sense. Or you may feel swept along by greatly accelerated thought processes that don't leave a trace in your memory. Beyond this point, and often quite a bit earlier, you will probably lose consciousness.

You have been experiencing what psychologists call a *hypnagogic state.* It is more likely to be noticed and remembered after short naps than after the nightly sleep period. The reason is that you don't go quite as deeply into sleep during a nap and may therefore retain more conscious awareness during the entire rest period than is usually true at night. This hypnagogic state allows you to observe the translation process from the language of physical experience to the nonphysical language of the soul.

The first step in this translation process turns sense impressions and feelings into symbolic relationships between shapes and colors. The bodily twitches, snatches of conversations, and imagery from the day's events that surface when you first enter the hypnagogic state indicate that information about the day is being converted into such symbolic relationships. A rushing effect often accompanies this stage in the translation process. It could be likened to listening to a tape recorder with the "fast forward" button pressed down: you know something is going on, but you can't quite grasp what it is.

Next, these fully converted sense impressions and feelings are sorted into categories according to what kind of lessons have been involved. The images that you do not recall having seen in the course of the day are often symbolic representations of these categories. Perhaps a certain behavior on the part of other people often makes you angry. In the course of a particular day, three or four people bring out this reaction in you. These events will all be sorted together into the same category, whether you see the connection or not. Eventually a dream may try to point out this connection to you.

Fragmentary or disjointed plot lines indicate that the sorting stage is coming to a close. In the final stage of the translation process, the categories that have been thus sorted out are placed in the context of your entire life history. They represent the next steps in any of a number of ongoing developmental projects. This stage can occur only during deep sleep, and so you will generally be unaware of it. If, however, you awaken in the morning remembering a dream of epic proportions in which you are a kind of mythological hero confronting a large variety of challenging events, then you are in fact recalling this final stage.

Often the soul has to do a lot of extra work at night, either because you have been insufficiently aware of which experiences go with which lessons during the day or because you have resisted making such connections. Paying attention to the kinds of feelings that come up each day and what seems to inspire them while keeping an eye out for patterns is vitally important. Otherwise you won't have the slightest idea of what your dreams are trying to tell you.

Occasionally you may experience a night in which it seems that you never quite fall asleep, that you have been thinking all night long. In such a case, you have retained consciousness during much of the experiential translation process, whether or not you remember any specific details. In this fashion, the soul lets you know that it has undertaken a massive reorganization of your beliefs, attitudes, and probable behaviors. It is important to realize that even though it might seem that your mind has been active on such a night, you will nevertheless feel refreshed in the morning. You must not assume that since you never actually lost consciousness, you have not gotten the rest that you needed.

One of the reasons you are present in physical reality is to learn how to perform what we call *energy transformations.* Every lesson of this lifetime is either a part or the whole of an energy transformation. The light from the sun results from an energy transformation involving hydrogen atoms. That light allows an apple tree to grow, which is yet another energy transformation. When an apple is picked from the tree and eaten, it feeds you, which is yet a third energy transformation. So it goes with your experience. The soul is like the sun, providing you with life force, and you are like the tree that uses it to grow and produce creative fruit—whether as an artistic project, a loving relationship, a child's well-shaped personality, a flower garden, a comfortable living environment, or a successful business proposition. As you harvest these creative fruits, they feed you. They help you become more of who you truly are. Even though your eating an apple seems to have nothing to do with feeding the energy transformations going on in the sun, your harvesting of creative fruits does feed the soul, which can then continue to provide you with life force. It is during sleep that this process of feeding the soul takes place.

In the nonphysical reality in which the soul resides, thought manifests itself more or less instantly as experience. Physical reality is a greatly slowed-down version of this process of thought manifesting itself as experience. The purpose of this slowdown is to permit you to learn how to purge your energy transformations of randomness of thought. By "randomness of thought," we mean anger, hatred, jealousy, fear, frustration, guilt—all of the so-called "negative" emotions. The purpose of dreams is to point out how you may be inadvertently misappropriating the life force provided by the soul for your learning, by wasting it on these negative emotions. Dreams are messages about how to purge yourself of such randomness of thought. This is why it is so important for you to learn how to interpret your dreams. Besides pointing out how you are affected by randomness of thought, they can also be quite helpful in making you aware of what energy transformations you are currently engaged in.

Meanwhile, the body is busy resting and relaxing itself. All sorts of involuntary shivers and twitches, most of them barely observable, allow the muscles to release accumulated tension. Furthermore, the body's stores of life force will have been used up in the course of the previous day. As the soul is actively engaged in its dream dialogue with the ego, it is also replenishing what we call the *life-force fuel tank* in preparation for the energy transformations to be undertaken in the course of the new day. The combination of muscular relaxation and replenishment of life force is what creates the feeling of being refreshed when you awaken. If you ignore the impulse to sleep in order to stay up as late as possible, the life-force fuel tank may not be as full as usual when you awaken. Some of the energy that would normally be available for the new day will have been used to heal the damage you caused to the body by overextending it. Persisting in ignoring the impulse to sleep for days or weeks on end will result in symptoms of aging. Thus, the full benefits of sleep can only be guaranteed when you pursue the impulse to sleep as soon as it arises. When the body is fully rested, when the previous day's experience has been fully processed, and when the life-force fuel tank has been completely filled, the impulse to urinate will signal "end of process," and you will awaken.

The time required for the several functions of sleep to be accomplished will vary from night to night, depending on the nature and intensity of the previous day's experience. We have mentioned that the impulse to awaken will occur after somewhere between five and a half and eight hours of sleep. The average will be about six. As many as two naps or meditation periods of up to twenty minutes in duration will be required to sustain the highest levels of mental clarity and productivity throughout the day. The timing of these naps will be determined by the impulse to sleep, which expresses itself as an inability to concentrate and a heaviness of the eyelids. Such impulses will tend to occur after six to eight hours of experience have been accumulated, depending on the intensity of focus demanded by the activities you have been engaged in. On relatively undemanding days, only one impulse to take a nap may be perceived, probably occurring in mid to late afternoon.

These naps serve an important purpose. They allow the soul to perform a kind of preliminary processing of the events that have occurred since the last impulse to awaken. This preliminary processing will greatly accelerate the more thorough processing that occurs during the night. Less sleep will then be required at night. Even though six hours of sleep plus two twenty-minute naps will come close to seven hours total, the effect of distributing sleep time in this manner is quite different from taking seven hours all at once. The stiffness, inability to concentrate, and loss of memory capacity that are often associated with growing older will tend to clear up when sleep is redistributed in this way.

It is essential that the naps not exceed twenty minutes or so. A half hour is allowable, but forty minutes is too long. Be careful not to assume that if you don't actually fall asleep, you haven't gotten the rest you need. The most refreshing nap will actually be more like a meditation period focused on hypnagogic imagery. Actual sleep may thwart this preliminary processing of accumulated experience and tends to result in grogginess upon awakening. Problems in focusing your consciousness may persist for several hours.

Before you take a nap, it is essential that you urinate so that the brain chemistry will support the soul's experiential processing. There may not be an impulse to urinate upon awakening. As a part of its processing of your experience, the soul will assess what activity might be most appropriate for you to do next and will prepare the brain chemistry to support it. You're much more likely to perceive the impulse to quench thirst after a nap, since that will help fuel the new brain chemistry.

The impulse to take a nap may sometimes be confused with the impulse to exercise. Impulses toward the Physical

Focus Menu often express themselves as an inability to concentrate, accompanied by a heaviness in the limbs, whereas the impulse to take a nap usually expresses itself as an inability to concentrate and a heaviness of the eyelids. Taking a nap when the body needs exercise instead will *not* have the beneficial effects we describe. When you awaken, you will still feel an inability to concentrate. Generally speaking, if you are unsure of which impulse you are perceiving, it is often more appropriate to exercise first and *then* take a nap —if it still feels necessary to do so. In this way, you won't be inadvertently talking yourself out of pursuing a Menu B impulse in favor of the perennial temptation to rest as much as possible.

As long as you recognize that rest is appropriate only when the body tells you so, and as long as you do not deny yourself that rest whenever the genuine impulse to sleep manifests, you will never feel exhausted or run-down. All you have to do is let those droopy eyelids close. Trust that they will open again after the briefest possible interval that will allow you to feel fully refreshed.

CHAPTER 12

The Impulse to Awaken

The impulse to awaken is the first impulse of the new day. Pursuing it by not returning to sleep will make it easier to perceive other impulses throughout the day. Ignoring it and staying in bed will have a number of negative effects. When you awaken, the body is ready for the day's physical activity. When you deny it that activity by returning to sleep, the body responds by producing dreams of a highly physical nature—chase scenes and the like. Upon awakening a second time, you will find that some of the energy meant to propel you through the day has been used up. You will feel tired and groggy for hours. The problem is not that you have gotten too little sleep, but too much.

Another negative effect of staying in bed after the impulse to awaken has manifested itself is that you have set a precedent for ignoring impulses. These ignored impulses will tend to form a logjam, competing for the time available during the day. When impulses compete for your attention, it becomes difficult for you to know what to do next. You will be forced to pursue certain impulses at the expense of others. Usually the ones you choose to acknowledge will represent the minimum requirements for ensuring the satisfaction of your needs—in other words, the Work Menu. Making a habit of oversleeping means making a habit of the Work Menu. Life will become dreary and dull because of the apparent lack of time available for other sorts of activities. Stress will begin to accumulate as a result of the impulses you ignore. You will end up expending a certain amount of energy on keeping impulses out of your awareness just so that you can stay focused on the ones you have chosen to pursue. This energy expenditure, combined with the frantic rushing-about that seems to be the only way to get everything done, will tend to shorten the day: you will exhaust yourself earlier than usual. On days when you ignore the impulse to awaken, you can lose up to *twice* the amount of time you spent in bed in the morning by also having to retire early. Never having enough time to do what needs to get done is more a result of ignoring the impulse to awaken than it is a genuine characteristic of modern life.

Your ability to perceive impulses will be so drastically affected by not pursuing the first one of the day that you will almost always pick the wrong times to do things. The line at the bank or post office will be twice as long and/or twice as slow as usual. Whenever you are trying to get from one place to another, everything will seem to conspire to slow you down. Your timing will be just enough off that you'll miss the bus and end up waiting three times the expected period for the next one, or an accident or some other unforeseen event will cause a traffic jam. To make matters worse, rushing through the projects you are involved in will almost certainly produce problems—due to inattentiveness—that will have to be corrected in days to come. The combination of exhaustion, frustration at work that has to be done over again, and the stress associated with an ever-increasing backlog of things that just aren't getting done, will greatly increase the chances of illness due to overload. To add insult to injury, the net result of living perpetually on the verge of overload will be symptoms of aging.

The only way to prevent such a hectic lifestyle from taking its toll on you is to begin your day when the body tells you to. It will be a lot easier to perceive impulses that can help you avoid annoying delays. Reducing the time spent in such delays will greatly increase your efficiency. We're not saying that by pursuing the impulse to awaken, you'll never encounter another delay in your life. But even if you do get stuck in a traffic jam now and then, your stress level will not be significantly affected.

How do you know when you have perceived the impulse to awaken that signals the beginning of the day? What of the occasions when you are awakened in the middle of the night by a nightmare or because you are cold? Or because a car door has slammed somewhere nearby? Or even because you suddenly have to go to the bathroom?

When you awaken in the middle of the night having had only a couple hours of sleep, the most likely reason is that a dream of great significance has just occurred and the soul wants to make sure that you remember it. In such a case, the soul may generate the impulse to urinate quite some time before it is actually appropriate for you to begin the day. On those occasions when you are awakened by loud noises, the soul has temporarily altered the threshold of hearing, so that sounds that wouldn't ordinarily disturb your sleep get through. It does this because something has gone awry with the dreaming process. Sometimes the attention of the part of the ego that monitors a dream begins to wander, just as the mind of a child in school can drift away from the subject at hand into a daydream. These "ego daydreams" can distort the message the soul was intending to put across. So the soul will attempt to erase memory of both the dream itself and the ego's unsolicited imagery. It allows the ego's daydream to continue and alters the threshold of hearing. The next relatively loud noise in the environment will then cause an abrupt awakening. In the suddenness of this transition back to consciousness, the dream images will be lost. If the ego's daydreamlike distortion of the soul's message is relatively minor, then the soul may lower the body temperature instead. There will be a more gradual transition back to consciousness, with the realization that you are cold. In this way, the soul can ensure that some memory of the dream's message remains intact.

Use of alcohol, drugs, tobacco, or coffee late in the evening can also cause the body to awaken you with the impulse to urinate, sometimes on several occasions. The body must purge itself entirely of these mind-altering substances in order to restore the pristine clarity of awareness necessary to begin the day. It may need to do so in several stages, depending on the amounts of these substances that you have ingested. You will then experience multiple awakenings to urinate. The body is unable to relax and refresh itself fully by morning when it has to work so hard at purifying the brain chemistry. This is one of the reasons you might feel dragged out or even hung over on mornings following such indulgences. Only after the following night's sleep will everything be restored to normal. If maximum clarity of consciousness is your goal on any particular day, then we recommend that mind-altering substances be avoided for at least six hours before bedtime. A glass of wine or beer with dinner or a cup of coffee afterward will not affect the next day's clarity to any appreciable degree.

Sometimes people may experience frequent needs to urinate in the course of the night even when they have not ingested mind-altering substances. Contrary to popular opinion, this is not the result of drinking too much water before bedtime. Such people will often be somewhat afraid of the dark or of sleep itself and may also be prone to nightmares. Their bodies are continually purifying themselves of high adrenalin levels in order to guarantee at least a modicum of rest by morning. Adrenalin, after all, is a stimulant.

Nightmares occur whenever people thwart their own growth by refusing to acknowledge or face their fears. If so many unacknowledged fears have accumulated that someone has trouble taking action on anything, the soul will force a confrontation with these fears in symbolic terms. The resulting nightmare acts as a kind of lightning rod that allows the accumulated fear to be discharged. Awakening immediately after a nightmare brings the need to release oneself from fear to full consciousness. Once again, the impulse to urinate will allow the body to purge itself of adrenalin.

In general, fear of the dark or of sleep is actually fear of dreaming. Sometimes this fear arises because people have an intuitive sense that they are somehow going against the intentions of the soul. They may behave toward the soul in the same manner that children who have done something wrong behave toward their parents—avoidance. Since direct communication with the soul takes place during the night, they will be afraid of, or will attempt to avoid, sleep as much as possible. This is often the basis of insomnia and the root of many kinds of mental illness. Furthermore, the soul often strongly encourages people to dream about emotional tangles they may prefer not to deal with in real life, such as the pain experienced in a relationship that is not going well or has ended. Fear of being emotionally "raked over the coals" of unresolved painful experiences while dreaming can also contribute to high adrenalin levels and frequent urinations during the night.

Being able to perceive the genuine impulse to awaken and begin the day requires that you also be able to recognize the states of consciousness that result from having had too much or too little sleep. If you have overslept you will feel groggy and dazed. You might have difficulty focusing your attention. There will be a great deal of stiffness in the body, as a result of your having kept it inactive too long. On the other hand, if you have had too little sleep when the impulse to urinate manifests itself for one of the reasons discussed above, your lids will still feel very heavy and your body will move to and from the bathroom in a more or less automatic fashion. There will be a sense of inward pressure to return to sleep, and you will scarcely feel any desire to resist. If you have had a particularly striking dream or a nightmare, however, you may have trouble getting back to sleep. Because the soul has awakened you specifically to recall the dream, it will not send a new impulse to sleep until after you have gone over the plot line of the dream enough times in your mind that you won't forget it by morning. But the soul would return you immediately to sleep if you just took a moment to jot down some brief notes on the dream in order to jog your memory later.

If you find yourself trying to talk yourself into staying in bed *for whatever reason,* you are arguing against the soul, which has just sent the true impulse to awaken. This includes looking at a clock and telling yourself that you have not had the amount of sleep you think you need. There is a pervasive belief that eight hours of sleep is necessary to get through a day. Unless you are seriously ill, this is almost always far too much.

When you first get up with the impulse to awaken, you may not yet be able to focus your consciousness fully. Your limbs may seem a bit heavy or draggy, but they will not be stiff, as they often are when you have overslept. You may even have a headache. Do not infer from these observations that you have not had enough sleep. Drinking some fruit juice immediately upon rising, and then moving about—perhaps doing some gentle stretching exercises for about twenty minutes—should suffice to clear up these problems. They are usually the result of the body's having run out of food with which to feed the muscles and the brain. Fruit juice will be rather quickly absorbed into the system in the form of blood sugars, which will then be distributed throughout the body by means of the stretches.

Another danger to avoid is telling yourself that you will lie in bed until you remember your dreams. This is usually just another excuse to doze off, even though it seems to be a virtuous one. Since intrusive noises tend to destroy dreams, it is generally not a good idea to awaken with an alarm. Besides the fact that all sorts of beneficial information could be lost in this way, the alarm might awaken you before both soul and body have completed their restorative processes. The entire day will be negatively affected by tiredness and irritability. Furthermore, inability to concentrate and lassitude will produce an interminably slow passage of time during much of the day. Very little will get accomplished, because a good part of your energy will be devoted to fighting off the impulse to sleep. Only through taking a nap might you be able to salvage some part of the day from being wasted in torpor.

The soul is aware of any genuine need on your part to arise at a certain time and can alter the rate of experiential processing accordingly. This is the primary reason why people often awaken just before their alarms sound. If you hate your job or dread whatever you must arise early to attend to, then you are predisposed to ignore the impulse to awaken, whether or not you use an alarm. You will tend to blame this disliked activity for the unfocused consciousness you will then experience while engaged in it. Yet the problem lies not in the activity itself but in how your attitudes toward it affect your approach to awakening. Since it is easy to ruin a whole day with oversleeping, even leisure-time activities will be negatively influenced by these attitudes. Getting rid of the obligations you resent or changing your attitudes about them are the only ways to normalize your response to the impulse to awaken.

On nights when you have stayed up quite a bit later than usual, the impulse to awaken may still manifest in the very early morning, even though you have had only a few hours of sleep. There is a danger that beliefs about needing to catch up on your sleep will not only cause you to get too much on such a day but will also cause you to assume you need more sleep the next day as well. The soul is perfectly capable of accelerating the sleep processes when you have gone to bed late. However, the brain chemistry will tend to become clogged with the adjustments that have to be made in order for this acceleration to occur. This is why there is a certain graininess to consciousness when you first awaken on mornings after you have stayed up very late. What you need to do in order to return your consciousness to a pristine state of clarity is to arise, urinate, and drink some fruit juice. Then perform some kind of fairly vigorous exercise that will stimulate the circulation for at least twenty minutes. Eventually you will feel the impulse to sleep once again. After about an hour and a half, you will wake up fully refreshed. The purpose of the exercise is to clear the body of waste brain chemicals that have accumulated in the muscles in large amounts because of the accelerated experiential processing.

If you happen to be working at a job that requires you to go to bed later than most people or that requires you to work through the night and sleep during the day, it is especially important for you not to force yourself to sleep eight hours all at once. The body functions most naturally when it is allowed to arise in the early morning, around dawn. It prefers to be most active during daylight hours. The soul will take into account your work schedule when it sends the impulse to sleep, but you will tend to awaken either around dawn or after three and a half or four hours of sleep, whichever comes first. You should then exercise vigorously for up to an hour. Wait until the impulse to sleep has manifested itself again before returning to bed. You will awaken whenever the soul and body have both completed all the processes required for you to feel fully refreshed. In this way, the body's desire to become active in the early morning or during daylight hours will be satisfied, as well as your need for rest. It will then be much easier for you to enjoy what is left of the day when you do finally get up. And if you pursue impulses to take a twenty-minute nap or two, as recommended in the last chapter, you should have little difficulty remaining brilliantly aware and awake while at your job.

If you are working at a job that gets you up much earlier than most people—at three or four in the morning, for example—don't arbitrarily go to bed at a certain time in the early evening to make sure that you get eight hours of sleep. Wait for the impulse to sleep. Make sure that you exercise at some point during the day, and be alert to impulses to take brief naps. The first of these naps will probably be quite a bit longer than the twenty minutes we recommend. The reason is that not all of the soul's deep-sleep experiential processing may have taken place during the night. Exercising before taking that nap will greatly reduce the amount of time required to refresh yourself during it. If you feel an impulse for a second nap, it should not exceed twenty minutes. The soul and the body will very likely choose for you a pattern of four and a half to five hours of sleep, with a first nap of an hour and a half after work and a second of twenty minutes at least six hours later. In this way, you will be able to function with at least as much—and probably more—clarity and focus than people with more usual schedules. And you will not lose so many hours of social time in the evening by going to bed earlier than you really need to.

Ordinarily, the impulse to awaken will be experienced as an unequivocal readiness to embrace what the new day has to offer. On some days, you may literally spring out of bed full of joyful exuberance, and on others, you may stretch luxuriantly and relish each moment of flowing back into yourself before you climb out of bed. There will never be a sense of rush or hurry. The soul takes into consideration everything that you might need to do in the course of the day when it times the impulse to awaken—the things you require of yourself, those required of you by other people, and those the soul itself requires for your growth. Only if you stay in bed too long and fall asleep again or if you get out of bed only to return to it will you have to rush and hurry to get these things done. Once again, if you find yourself telling yourself that you haven't had enough sleep, you are about to ignore this first impulse of the day. There will be disastrous side effects that will far outweigh the pleasure of staying in bed just a little longer. Because of the prevalence in this society of the belief that you need eight hours of sleep a night, most people tend to assume that if you have to subtract some sleep one day, you must somehow add it back the next. Let the soul and the body determine your sleep schedule, not an arbitrary arithmetic. Your willingness to pursue the impulses to sleep and to awaken whenever they manifest themselves is the only way to get what is truly enough sleep for you in a given twenty-four-hour period.

By far the most common cause of making mistaken assumptions about the amount of sleep needed in the course of a night is the sense of "being out of it" that results from the body's having run out of food. Tissue starvation during sleep is a primary cause of wrinkles on the face and lines on the forehead. The entire musculature actually begins to deteriorate as a result of the lack of blood sugar. This is one of the reasons your muscles can become stiff during the night. For a time, the body will shunt whatever blood sugar remains to the brain in order to keep the brain cells from suffering this same sort of starvation. If you awaken with a headache, then even this small reserve of blood sugar has been used up. If you were to live truly impulsively, then you would find yourself ingesting roughly four meals a day instead of the traditional three. The fourth meal would be a bedtime snack to ensure you against running out of the food necessary to fuel the sleep process. We shall return to this idea of four meals a day in the chapter on eating impulsively. But first, let us discuss what the impulse to eat means from the soul's perspective.

CHAPTER 13

The Impulses to Eat and to Defecate

You are already quite familiar with what eating means from the body's perspective: if you don't eat, you die. The soul, on the other hand, views food as the symbolic equivalent of experience. From the soul's perspective, everything in physical reality is symbolic. Even physical objects represent not what they look or feel like or what they are called but the energy transformations that have allowed them to come into being and sustain them. Their apparent solidity is an expression of how the process of thought becoming experience has been slowed down to create physical reality—this learning ground for purging randomness of thought. From the soul's perspective, then, the body is a symbolic expression of the soul's own nonphysical beingness. Just as your intellect collects experience to feed the soul with learning, so does your body ingest food to nourish itself.

There are several rather common phrases that hint at the symbolic nature of the digestive process. "Biting off more than one can chew," for example, refers to attempting to take in more experience than can be adequately processed. "That's hard to swallow" or "I can't stomach this" communicates that one has a certain resistance to accepting something that has just happened. You have an enormous appetite for experience. Impulses, just like hunger, will motivate you toward what will satisfy your needs. You will then begin to consume experience one bite (or dedicated time slot) at a time. As you absorb yourself in some activity, you both mull it over in your mind (chewing it) and savor it for the pleasure or other emotions it conjures up (tasting it). Ruminating on the experience will also break it down into its component parts, so that you may easily absorb it into your beingness (swallowing it). What happens to food in the stomach and intestines correlates symbolically with what happens to experience during sleep: a translation from physical-reality-based expressions into energy transformations. The energy made available through the digestion of your last meal will sustain you in absorbing further experience, just as life force is made available by the soul after it has fully processed the previous day's experience.

Mealtimes begin the process of digesting the experience accumulated since the last meal. At the same time, they provide the fuel for engaging you in further experience. The impulse to eat indicates the appropriateness of taking a time-out from experiential intake so that you may look back on what has been accomplished and project what you would like to do for the rest of the day. It is best to urinate before eating, in order to clear your consciousness for this sort of reflective thought. The state that you then enter will be rather different from the ones associated with each menu. It will be a special *blended* state that looks both forward and backward through the perspectives of each menu. By "looking backward," we mean that you will consider the various menus you have touched upon prior to the meal in terms of how they have satisfied your needs. By "looking forward," we mean that you will at the same time begin projecting which activities and which menus you may wish to engage in following the meal. *Reflection* and *planning* would be the key words applying to any mealtime.

The same thing is actually true of all the Menu A impulses: each represents a kind of time-out from experiential intake and a special blended state of consciousness that can open out into any other menu. Eating and defecating are usually the only Menu A impulses that last long enough for you to experience this. Awakening, urinating, and quenching thirst take just a few moments to accomplish. And you're rarely conscious enough during sleep to become aware of it as a special blended state of consciousness—except perhaps during brief naps. Even though the impulse to defecate lasts only a few minutes, people do sometimes use a visit to the bathroom as a kind of time-out.

Not urinating before eating tends to sustain the state of consciousness you were already in. This is fine when you intend to go right back to what you were doing prior to the meal. Chances are that you will be thinking about it as you eat, anyway. If you are in a hurry, there is also nothing wrong with tacking a quickly eaten meal onto the end of a dedicated time slot. But if you intend to do something different after you eat, you will probably experience the impulse to urinate immediately following the meal. The restful effects of the special time-out state of consciousness will not be available in these cases. If you try to occupy yourself with other things during the meal without having urinated beforehand, you may feel fatigued instead.

Besides the reflection and planning that concerns specific menus and activities, the menus themselves will make special contributions to the blended state of consciousness that prevails at mealtimes. The Physical Focus Menu will allow you to become sensitive to the body's needs in terms of which foods to eat and in what amounts. The Cycles Menu will help you become aware of how what you have accomplished thus far during the day initiates, furthers, or completes a process so that you may become clearer about what to do next. The Self-Awareness Menu will enable you to pinpoint how you feel about what you have accomplished so that you may come up with adjustments of beliefs, attitudes, or behaviors that might enhance your clarity or productivity for the rest of the day.

The Work Menu will be engaged whenever you are preparing food for yourself or for others. Once again, the Work Menu has to do with self-valuation and the satisfaction of survival needs. The more energy you put into preparing your food, the higher you will value yourself. This will have direct repercussions on your ability to draw new and interesting adventures into your life as a means of satisfying needs for self-realization—a topic we shall go into more deeply later on. Meanwhile, you may find yourself daydreaming, which can allow you to rehearse in your mind various ways of being that your life may not be currently supporting. This Play Menu aspect of the mealtime state of consciousness ensures that it will be a true time-out from actual participation in life, thus allowing the mealtime to refresh you.

The fact that this special blended state of consciousness contains within it something of each of the menus allows your mealtime thoughts or conversations to embrace everything from the day's dreams to a business deal (Self-Awareness and Work menus), from wordplay, relating anecdotes, and kidding around (Play Menu) to catching up with someone on the events that have transpired since the last time you met (Cycles Menu). There's even room for describing the workout activities (Physical Focus Menu) you will engage in if you eat too much!

Once you have finished eating, you may not experience a need to urinate. The brain chemistry necessary to support your next activity will simply be amplified from within the blended state until it has taken over the entire functioning of the self. The impulse to quench thirst may occur just before you fully engage yourself in that new activity, to help fuel the new brain chemistry.

Since the digestion of food and the soul's processing of experience during sleep are symbolic equivalents, the best activity following lunch or dinner may be taking a nap. In fact, this is one of the reasons why you so often feel drowsy after eating. Some experts say that you shouldn't lie down after eating because it's bad for the circulation. But as long as you have not overstuffed yourself and as long as you do not sleep for much more than twenty minutes, such a nap will be highly beneficial to both body and mind. If your circulation feels a bit sluggish afterward, then some form of exercise is called for.

Generally speaking, the impulse to eat will occur every six hours or so, depending on whether or not you ate too little, too much, or just enough food, given your needs at the time of the previous meal. The intensity of the experience occurring prior to mealtime may also affect the timing of this impulse. It is essential that you eat only when that impulse manifests itself. Just as you can't mistake the genuine impulse to sleep, which takes the form of droopiness of the eyelids, you can't mistake the genuine impulse to eat. Your tummy feels empty. It is not good to delay acting upon the impulse to eat, since mental clarity and productivity will diminish rapidly if you ignore it. On the other hand, it is also inappropriate to eat just because the clock tells you it's noon. The impulse to eat is just as variable in its timing as the impulses to sleep and to awaken. Furthermore, overweightness is just as often the result of eating out of habit at certain times every day as it is of eating more food than the body needs. When the genuine impulse to eat has not manifested itself, it is difficult to sense how much food the body actually needs. People will therefore tend to eat too much.

Often, but not always, the impulse to defecate will manifest itself after a meal. Because of the symbolic correlation between food and experience, the size, shape, color, and number of stools will reveal information about how you are currently processing your reality. During periods when you are beginning more processes than you are completing, there will be fewer defecations. During periods when you are actively involved in completing processes, there will be more. Constipation indicates that you are not allowing some growth process to move forward.

In general, loose stools indicate faulty or incomplete processing of experience, and firm stools indicate well-processed experience. A stool with the look of having been broken off indicates that some growth process is not yet complete. A stool that appears to be "all of a piece" indicates an experience fully processed from beginning to end. A long and continuous stool indicates that a lengthy process has just completed itself. Stools that seem to have broken themselves into many small units, each discrete and complete, indicate that a number of unrelated experiences have been completed simultaneously. A stool that appears to be comprised of a number of smaller units all packed together indicates that a number of differing experiences have been related to one another by applying the same set of principles or perspectives to each. Stools having the look of many small curlicues indicate confusion—a lack of willingness to relate a number of seemingly distinct events into a larger whole. Usually this occurs because of fear of, or resistance to, change. Diarrhea represents an extreme form of such resistance.

The color of stools indicates the degree of your participation in the processing of the experience. The usual brown indicates the usual degree of participation. Lighter shades indicate less subjective involvement. Darker shades indicate more subjective involvement. Significantly, very light stools are also often somewhat loose, indicating that more participation in the processing than you granted the experience was necessary. Very dark stools—those verging on black—often seem abnormally firm and usually appear after a period of constipation. These indicate an obsessive focus on the experience. Less participation in the processing than you granted the experience was necessary. Greenish stools are in no way abnormal but represent an intermediary stage between yellow and the usual brown.

The smell of the stool will also communicate information about the manner in which experience has been processed. A foul smell indicates that you have been too much caught up in wondering what other people might think of the self you are becoming as you undertake or complete some process. You are afraid that they might reject you. So the body produces gas. Your emotional discomfort has been translated into physical discomfort in order to encourage you to do something about releasing it. Flatulence may occur. With a perverse sense of humor, the body thus causes you to call upon yourself the very disapproval you were so worried about. The only way to free yourself of this sort of embarrassment is to remind yourself that if people reject you for who you really are—and for who the soul would have you become—they are not worthy of your friendship.

While foulness of smell indicates the extent to which fear of what other people might think is permeating your growth processes, there is also an ordinary smell. Though it might be strong, it will not seem unpleasant to you. This smell indicates that you have been relatively uninfluenced by worry about what other people are thinking.

Occasionally you will feel a sudden, intense urge to void yourself that forces you to run to the bathroom as quickly as possible. The stools will often be ill formed and tend toward looseness. Yet the color may be your usual brown. This is not the same thing as diarrhea. Even though diarrhea can also cause you to run to the bathroom with the same sense of urgency, the physical compulsion will occur several times in succession. What we are speaking about is a onetime occurrence. It indicates that an experience has occurred which requires considerable processing. For the time being, however, it must be released from your thoughts. Your mind needs to attend to other things, especially if you do not yet have the mental means required to process this new experience fully. Voiding yourself allows for a temporary discharge of the experience from your attention, so that you may begin to gather the awarenesses necessary to process it. In the meantime, the processing of this experience will continue at other levels of consciousness. It may rise to the surface of your thoughts from time to time to show you how far the processing has progressed. Successive defecations will show a tendency toward greater firmness as the digesting of the experience moves toward completeness.

When the impulse to defecate occurs after a meal, the bowels are emptied so that the next batch of as yet unprocessed experience (or food) may be digested. The soul will also time the impulse to defecate whenever you have just completed, or are just about to complete, a major growth process. You may have just completed a project or one of its stages. Or you may have just arrived at important conclusions or decisions about some aspect of your life. When the impulse to defecate occurs at any time other than immediately following a meal, it calls your attention to a specific milestone in your growth. What that milestone is can often become evident through an examination of the actions and thoughts that preceded the impulse to defecate. A good time for such considerations is while actually sitting on the john.

Unless you are suffering from constipation, the bowels will usually be working on processing the food consumed up to two meals prior to the one just taken. It is important to note that the timing of the impulse to defecate refers to the process you have been recently engaged in, whereas the symbolic messages of the stools themselves provide you with information about how you have been processing your experience *in general* since at least the last impulse to defecate. For example, the first defecation of the day may provide you with insights into how willing you have been to heed the messages of your dreams. If your dreams are bringing up issues you would prefer not to deal with, you probably won't remember them. The morning's stools will show a lighter shade and some degree of looseness.

The impulse to defecate, just like the other Menu A impulses, is fairly easy to detect. You will feel it as a stirring in the bowels. The passage of gas, often without much of an odor, may occur a little while before the urge to head for the bathroom. In this manner, the body puts you on notice that you are about to conclude an important growth process. It may wait to send the actual impulse to defecate until the moment it is most convenient for you to leave whatever you are doing.

Sometimes the soul itself will intervene. It may project the impulse to defecate because it is important for you to stop what you are doing, no matter the stage you are at. In such cases, you have gone as far as you can without frustration. Certain key awarenesses that would not only improve quality of participation and enjoyment in the process but would also considerably speed it toward completion are not yet available. You will need to shift the focus of your attention to other activities and menus until these new awarenesses emerge. (The impulse to defecate is often accompanied by urination precisely because of such shifts.)

You should try to act on the impulse to defecate the moment it arises. All too often people delay responding to this impulse because of the apparent nuisance of having to leave whatever they are doing at the time. If you don't cloister yourself in the bathroom immediately so as to meditate upon why this impulse has manifested itself, you may never become fully aware of the growth process just completed. Only when you can perceive a clear connection between your thoughts or actions and the impulse to defecate will this awareness become available. In the meantime, as you resist the impulse to defecate, you will experience a certain degree of physical discomfort that will increase as you continue to delay. The body is expressing its displeasure at your ignoring its messages. At some future point, the body will once again display its perverse sense of humor by sending you to the bathroom with the impulse to defecate, only to have you sit around waiting while nothing happens.

It should be clear from the above discussions of the impulses to eat and to defecate that your emotional state will have more of an impact on the size, shape, color, and smell of stools than the actual food ingested. But just as you can sometimes choose experiences that in retrospect seem not to have been good for you, so can you choose foods that the body may have trouble digesting. It is your emotional state, however, that draws you to these inappropriate experiences or foods. When you allow yourself to be guided by impulses toward activities that support your process of self-realization, it becomes more and more difficult to choose inappropriate experiences. Because of the symbolic correlation between food and experience, the same thing will be true of eating. But first you must learn how to eat impulsively.

CHAPTER 14

Eating Impulsively

Eating impulsively involves three things: pursuing the true impulse to eat whenever it arises, sensing what kinds of food the body needs, and responding to signals from the body to stop eating when you have had enough. We've already covered the first topic. The other two are the subject of this chapter.

People who prefer a bland diet of food also tend to prefer a bland diet of experience. Likewise, people who take risks in order to generate a certain sense of adventure in their lives will also be more adventuresome in their cooking or restaurant preferences. It may be fairly evident that one's taste for mild or adventuresome living can extend also into the realm of dining. But because of the symbolic correlation between food and experience, the reverse is also true: you can create more adventure in your life simply by eating more exotically.

In the hours following a meal the brain chemistry will be affected by the food you have eaten. Atoms and molecules that had not been previously present will be absorbed through the digestive tract into the bloodstream, stimulating new kinds of thought. The varying amounts of nutrients present in each food will also have an impact. The more exotic the food, the more unusual and interesting the thoughts. These thoughts will prompt you to make decisions about how to run your life that will be more likely to place you in unusual and interesting situations.

The word *exotic* used in reference to eating does not necessarily mean spicy ethnic foods. The range of foods you were brought up with becomes associated symbolically with the range of beliefs, attitudes, and behaviors that are ordinary and familiar to you. This diet represents your starting point when it comes to drawing experience to yourself. Since your beliefs about reality create that reality, continuing to eat these foods will tend to limit your range of available experience to that characteristic of life at home with your parents. Although returning to this diet from time to time can provide a sense of well-being and security—especially during periods of emotional turmoil or illness—chances are that when you left home you began to experiment with other kinds of food. Naturally, these foods represented your willingness to open yourself to experiences not available while you were growing up. Throughout your life, changes in diet represent intentions to change prevailing beliefs, attitudes, and behaviors. And because of the symbolic relationship between food and experience, changes in the kinds of situations you tend to draw to yourself will follow.

Some people have used radical changes in diet to heal themselves of various physical and emotional maladies. These problems were the result of maintaining inappropriate beliefs, attitudes, and behaviors that were somehow blocking the process of self-realization and therefore distorting the flow of life force through the body. The former diet tended to sustain these inappropriate beliefs, attitudes, and behaviors. Changing it created a space for healing by suspending the old ways of thinking about the self and allowing new ones to be introduced.

It is always the change in diet more than what the diet is changed to that supports the healing process. If a doctor tells you that adding certain foods to, and subtracting others from, your diet will have a certain beneficial effect and if you believe in the healing wisdom of this doctor, then the dietary changes will have the prescribed effect. The same is true of a guru who tells you that the fare provided at his or her ashram enhances spiritual growth. What neither the doctor nor the guru may realize, however, is that if a potentially helpful diet is sustained indefinitely, it can end up being just as restrictive as the one you were brought up with.

No matter the diet, eating the same thing every day means that you will always be thinking the same kind of thoughts. This keeps you locked into routine at the level of brain chemistry. Beliefs, attitudes, and behaviors will become entrenched, as will the kinds of experiences you tend to draw to yourself. For these reasons, we do not advocate any specific kind of diet as more or less likely to encourage enlightenment. The *most* spiritual diet is not a vegetarian one but that which results from following your impulses toward certain foods.

It is important to eat relatively unrefined foods as much as possible. The reason for this is that the process of refining often strips away the nutrients that would stimulate creative thought. Furthermore, the artificial colors, flavorings, and preservatives in processed food at the very least do nothing to support the brain's chemical balances and in some cases actually interfere with them.

When your body needs a particular food, it will generate an impulse to eat it. The presence of such an impulse may derive from the body's requirements for protein, carbohydrates, vitamins, minerals, trace elements, or other nutrients. But it may also derive from the soul's need to be nourished with a certain kind of learning. Impulses to eat certain foods may actually be preparing you, through changes in brain chemistry, to be receptive to the experiences that will promote such learning.

Impulses to eat certain foods manifest themselves in a number of ways. You may dream of the food, in which case you should attempt to prepare it on that very day or within a couple of days of the dream. Or you may find yourself thinking with pleasure about a food you haven't had in a while. Whether looking over the menu in a restaurant, cruising down the aisles of a grocery store, or perusing the contents of your pantry, whenever anything looks good to you, your impulses are encouraging you to eat it.

In order to eat truly impulsively you must not only be aware of impulses toward, but also impulses against, eating certain foods. The most obvious form of an impulse against is simply not being able to imagine yourself eating something. It may seem unappetizing or distasteful to you. If you were actually to take a bite of this food, it might seem bland or uninteresting or taste bad, no matter how often you have enjoyed it in the past. The amount of pleasure you experience when eating something is a sign of how much the body needs it. When displeasure is present, the body is warning you through your taste buds that it does not need such a food. Simply being tired of a food that you have often had can be an impulse against eating it.

Another way in which an impulse against may manifest itself is through the gurgling of your digestive tract as you think about a food. The body is letting you know that you will have trouble digesting it. Furthermore, if you ever experience an unpleasant burning sensation while swallowing something, the body is letting you know that you should not eat a single bite more of it. Either you never should have taken the first bite, or you have had as much as the body needs of it for now.

Sometimes people dislike a food because, as children, they were forced by their parents to eat it. The food may have tasted bad because the body didn't need it. The child makes the mistake of assuming that the food will *always* taste bad. This is not necessarily the case. If at some point the body genuinely needs the nutrients in that food, then eating it will be pleasurable.

Generally speaking, in the absence of any definite impulses

toward a particular food, such as in a dream, and as long as no impulses against the food manifest themselves while it is under consideration, you may eat anything you wish. But eating impulsively also requires that you beware of food addictions. If you are addicted to a food, you will talk yourself into including it in every meal or at least once a day. In order to avoid the inevitable paralysis of creative thought that results from such a practice, we recommend that you apply the following two principles to your diet:

1. Don't eat the same food prepared in the same way for more than three days in a row.
2. Don't eat the same food prepared in the same way for two successive meals.

Having scrambled eggs and bacon for breakfast every day violates the first principle. Having toast for breakfast and then using the same type of bread for a sandwich at lunchtime does *not* violate the second principle. Skipping just one day of scrambled eggs and bacon in favor of pancakes, for example, can break down routine enough to enable you to begin looking at the day's activities from a different perspective.

The body will support closely related brain chemistries for up to three days. During this period, the quantity of experience you have taken in and processed will have significantly changed you—enough for you to notice that a new self is emerging. That self will want to take off in new directions in order to sustain its growth. Eating the same thing every day prevents you from establishing brain chemistries that will support such growth. The result will be a generalized confusion as an increasing awareness of the opportunities life has to offer struggles against an inability to make intelligent decisions about what to do with yourself. This state of mind is exactly the opposite of enlightenment, which is knowing what to do next under any given set of circumstances.

There are so many types of grains, fruits, vegetables, meats, and seafood that you could easily vary them from one meal to the next. Yet certain other ingredients are basic to so many recipes that they are likely to appear at every single meal. Such things as milk, eggs, butter, margarine, and flour are similar to the most basic elements of your experience in that they may be recombined constantly into new patterns. If you bring creativity to your cooking, so that you don't use these ingredients to make the same dishes all of the time, then there is no problem with including them in some form at every meal.

It is important never to eat more food than the body needs. But how do you know when you've truly had enough? We have said that at the end of a meal, the blended brain chemistry will be refocused in order to accommodate the activities of a single menu—whichever one you choose. In order for this refocused brain chemistry to last for an entire dedicated time slot, it must be fueled with plenty of water. So the impulse to quench thirst will often occur at the very end of a meal. You can use this fact as a sign of when you have had enough food to eat. We recommend that you keep a glass of water handy at every meal, no matter what other beverages may also be served. Avoid drinking from it at first. Eat slowly and chew thoroughly so that you won't need to wash down your food with this water. The impulse to quench thirst will gradually grow stronger until you can no longer avoid it. You may even find your hand involuntarily reaching for the water at some point. This is a signal that your body has had enough food. Once you have drunk the water, do not eat another bite—no matter how much food may be left on your plate. In this way, you can prevent weight gain from eating too much food.

The glass-of-water technique is not infallible. It might not work if you are eating exceptionally spicy food. You may have to reach for the water glass more frequently in order to soothe your mouth or throat. Yet there is another way to tell if you have had enough food in the course of a meal. It is a bit more subtle. But if it is combined with the glass-of-water technique, it can be very reliable. When you are eating something the body genuinely needs, you will experience a great deal of pleasure. You will only be fully aware of it if you eat slowly, savoring each mouthful. This pleasure will diminish with every bite you take, as a sign of the body's decreasing need for that food. At a certain point, you may find yourself chewing away just to finish what's left on your plate. Or you may stop eating for a while to talk. Or you may notice that you have started idly pushing the remaining food around your plate. These are all signs that the pleasure is gone and you have had enough food. Be especially careful at this point not to talk yourself into taking another bite or going for another helping "because it's so good." This phrase indicates that you are trying to persuade the body it needs more food than it actually does. You'll just end up stuffing yourself, which can cause you to feel dopey and lethargic for hours. It will be difficult to achieve much of anything in such a state. And weight gain will be a distinct possibility.

Cooking creatively and eating a wider variety of foods are also ways to prevent weight gain. Overeating is often the result of insufficient variety of *experience.* Remember, diet can limit the range of experience you draw into your life. If you are bored with life, chances are you are also bored with the food you are eating and vice versa. Because the food is probably not satisfying the body's needs, you will not find it pleasurable. It will be difficult to know when to stop eating. Yet the more creativity you lavish on meal preparation, the more creatively you will manifest and process your experience. Releasing yourself from boredom in either area will automatically initiate the process of release in the other. You will then be less likely to overeat out of boredom.

When you prepare or order food, there is a third dietary principle that will help you find the meal ultimately satisfying: be sure to include at least two items of different textures.

A casserole has a different texture from a salad, or fruit juice from bread, chicken from cooked vegetables, or potato chips from a sandwich, for example. Such contrasts in food texture correspond to contrasts in experiential texture. Conscious attention to manipulating these textural contrasts in assembling a meal will help you bring more variety into the day's experience. Ideally, any single meal will provide several contrasts, with foods of different textures being either served simultaneously or successively, in the form of different courses. Including something from each of what dieticians call the four basic food groups (meat and fish, grains and breads, dairy products, and fruits and vegetables) is one way to guarantee such textural variety.

The impulse to quench thirst can be quite useful when you are eating a meal in several courses. It will manifest itself at the end of each course, at the exact moment when you have had as much as the body needs of the food being served. If you stop eating once you have quenched your thirst—even if you have had only a few bites—you will not end up stuffing yourself by the end of the meal.

As we mentioned in the previous chapter, the impulse to eat will manifest itself every six hours or so. The digestion works most efficiently when roughly equal demands are placed upon it for an entire twenty-four-hour period. Thus, to eat truly impulsively, it may be necessary to add a fourth meal to the day's agenda. This meal should be taken just before bedtime, in order to ensure that the body does not run out of fuel during the night. The size of the evening meal that precedes it should be modified accordingly. Often people eat more than their bodies genuinely need at suppertime, to tide them over until breakfast time. Thus do they dull their abilities to concentrate after dinner by overtaxing the digestive system, and then starve the muscles and the brain during the wee hours of the morning. The harmful effects of this practice include wearing out the digestive system, gaining weight, causing tissue deterioration during sleep, and accumulating symptoms of aging. In fact, one of the reasons the elderly are so often prone to falling and hurting themselves is that their muscles have been weakened through years of being starved every single night.

It is possible to add a fourth meal to the day without gaining weight—provided that you always pay close attention to the amount of food required by the body. Again, the impulse to quench thirst may be used as a means of determining how much to eat at any given meal. Usually the amount of food ingested just before bedtime will be smaller than a regular meal because the body is relatively inactive during sleep and thus does not require much fuel. The closer to bedtime that supper is taken, however, the less of a need there will be for such a meal.

You may need to experiment with the exact proportions of this bedtime meal. It may seem more like a snack when compared to lunch or dinner. The way to tell if you have had too little is by noting your mental state upon awakening. If you have a headache or feel particularly groggy and stiff upon responding to the impulse to awaken, then you ran out of fuel at some point in the night. If you should wake up feeling hungry in the wee hours of the morning, then something light, such as a glass of juice, a piece of toast, or even both, may be necessary to get you through the rest of the night.

If you are trying to lose weight, your body will modify the amount of food ingested for all four meals, using the impulse to quench thirst. Weight loss may take longer this way than it would if you were to try a crash diet, but you will be far less likely to accelerate aging. Besides, any great reduction in amount or kinds of food eaten—whether through a crash diet, fasting, or the skipping of meals—will force a drastic reduction in the amount of experience taken in. If you get bored with this reduced amount of experience, you may begin to overeat again to compensate for it. This is the main reason why willpower so often seems to fail when it comes to losing weight. The body wants to express itself in its own ideal form as much as your mind wants it to. Even so, you will be able to lose, gain, or maintain weight—depending on your intent—only if you eat impulsively. You must allow impulses not only to time your meals but also to determine types and amounts of food to be eaten.

One of the secrets of eating impulsively is to recognize that your appetite helps to coordinate the amount of food eaten during a meal with the amount of experience taken in prior to that meal. When there is an exact correspondence in symbolic terms, weight gain cannot occur. How the body gauges this correspondence will vary from person to person and from period to period in your life. So you cannot compare your appetite to someone else's—nor to your own of years past or even of yesterday. Only the impulse to quench thirst, acting in tandem with the diminishing-pleasure syndrome can be depended upon as a means of knowing you have hit upon the exact correspondence. This fact is especially important to keep in mind in situations—such as dining at a restaurant or being served by a host or hostess at a dinner party—where you are not responsible for the amount of food served on your plate.

In the case of a dinner party, there may be a temptation to eat everything put in front of you in order not to offend the cook. The body does not consider possible embarrassment to be a valid justification for overeating. Compliments to the chef, along with an apology for a small appetite, should be sufficient to excuse yourself. If a scene results, it's probably for quite another reason anyway. In the case of restaurants, the danger of succumbing to the temptation to overeat tends to increase with the degree to which you feel uncomfortable with the price of the food. The restaurant will often try to offset this discomfort by serving more than generous portions. Don't force yourself to overeat just to get your money's worth. If you can't abide the idea of simply leaving food behind when you have eaten all the body needs, ask to take the remainder home with you and reheat it for another meal.

If you have failed to eat enough food during a meal, you may experience a hunger impulse directing you to snack a few hours later. It may be hard to hit upon an exact correspondence with the experience that has not yet been compensated for—especially because you will have accumulated more experience in the intervening hours. There is nothing wrong with allowing a snack to correspond to at least some of the experience that has occurred since the last meal. But the amount of food taken in at the next meal will have to be reduced. The genuine impulse to snack will usually manifest itself as a slight daze resulting from low blood sugar. More often than not, a piece of fruit or some juice will be enough to correct this imbalance without encroaching upon the food/experience correspondence that will determine the size of the next actual meal.

Eating impulsively means eating only when the genuine hunger impulse has manifested itself and never eating more food than the body needs. It also means heeding impulses to eat certain foods when they arise and avoiding those you experience an impulse against. If you keep these things in mind, then no matter how frequently the hunger impulse may guide you to kitchen, store, or restaurant in the course of a day, you will not gain weight. Your body will use whatever you eat in order to shape itself toward its own ideal expression. And if you give preference to foods that you have never tried before or that you haven't eaten for a while, your life will become more adventuresome as well.

PART THREE

CREATING AN IMPULSIVE LIFESTYLE

CHAPTER 15

Life-Force Dynamics

THE MENUS FOR IMPULSIVE LIVING

MENU A—The Natural Schedule

MENU B—Physical Focus

MENU C—Self-Awareness

MENU D—Work

MENU E—Play

MENU F—Cycles

MENU G—Surprises

The impulses from Menus A and G—the Natural Schedule and the Surprise Menu—can be seen as signals from the soul designed to guide you in managing your life force as efficiently as possible. Knowing how to read these signals can help you become more productive. Less time will be required for you to accomplish even the most demanding tasks. You will rarely if ever exhaust yourself, and you will be less likely to accumulate stress. Wear and tear on the body will be greatly reduced, allowing you to maintain high levels of health and well-being. The secret of arresting or reversing the symptoms of aging is nothing more than preventing precious life force from leaking away. An understanding of what we call *life-force dynamics* can enable you to achieve these ends.

The first step in learning how not to waste life force is to let the Menu A impulses guide you through the day. The impulse to urinate lets you know when to shift menus. The impulse to quench thirst tells you when to shift to other activities on the same menu. The impulse to defecate points out when to leave what you are doing, either because you have finished it or because you have gone as far as you can for the moment. The impulse to eat tells you when to take a time-out from alternating between menus. The impulse to sleep indicates when you need to clear the mind of accumulated experience in order to make room for more (naps) or when it is time to replenish your stores of life force (the nightly sleep cycle). The impulse to awaken lets you know when these processes are complete.

In order to pattern a day after the Natural Schedule rather than the arbitrary subdivisions of clock time, all you need do is begin the day with the impulse to awaken. Follow the hunger impulse and prepare breakfast for yourself. Envision an impulsive framework for the day, asking yourself what you would like to get done from each of the Menus B through F and in what possible order. Note when the impulse to quench thirst indicates that you have eaten enough breakfast. Proceed into whatever menu strikes your fancy, and pursue it until the impulse to urinate manifests itself. Switch menus at that point, pursuing the impulse to quench thirst in order to fuel the next dedicated time slot. Then proceed to activities from another menu. Each time you feel the impulse to urinate, switch menus until the next impulse to eat or to defecate manifests itself. In the case of the former, take time out to think about what has been accomplished and to project the shape of the rest of the day. In the case of the latter, think about what process you may have just completed and note what your body tells you about how you have been processing your experience in general. Take a twenty-minute nap if you feel sleepy. You may continue with the process of alternating menus, and taking time-outs for meals and naps, all the way up to the point when you know that you can do no more and it is time to go to bed. After one last snack-sized meal, you are ready to let your droopy eyelids close for the night.

The life-force fuel tank is filled by the soul each night. Upon awakening, you have immediate access to this life force in order to accomplish the day's activities. The energy is equally distributed among Menus B through F. Imagine each of these menus—Physical Focus, Self-Awareness, Work, Play, and Cycles—as columns in a bar graph, all at the same level. As you use up the available energy in one column, it descends while the others remain as they were when you awoke. You can thus exhaust the energy available in one category without even tapping the energy available in others. When you shift to an activity on another menu via the impulse to urinate, two things happen. First, you get a kind of "second wind" that allows you to engage yourself productively in the new activity—even if you had begun to feel fatigued while pursuing the previous activity. Second, the energy available to all the other menus is averaged out and redistributed, thereby refueling the one you had depleted. Once again the levels of life force available to each menu will be equal—but they will be lower than they were when you first awakened. This averaging-out process explains why you can experience so much refreshment by taking a break from an intensely demanding project in order to do something else for a while. (See Figure 4.)

The soul distributes life force into one primary and one reserve tank for each menu. The primary tank contains enough life force to fuel at least one dedicated time slot. The impulse to urinate is often a warning signal that the life-force fuel tank may be nearing empty and must be refilled. One way to refill it is to shift into another menu for a while and

FIGURE 4

MENU B	MENU C	MENU D	MENU E	MENU F

a. The life-force fuel tank upon awakening

MENU B	MENU C	MENU D	MENU E	MENU F

b. After a time slot dedicated to the Self-Awareness Menu

MENU B	MENU C	MENU D	MENU E	MENU F

c. After switching to a different menu

then back to the first one. The averaging-out process we mentioned above will refill the empty tank. Perhaps you have just spent a time slot dedicated to the Work Menu. Then you shift to the Physical Focus Menu to get some exercise. Following your workout, you return to the Work Menu. You will feel fully refreshed because the Work Menu's life-force fuel tank has been replenished through the averaging out of the life force available to all the other menus. So the first principle of efficient life-force usage is this:

> *When you leave behind a time slot dedicated to a particular menu at the point of urination, dedicate the next time slot as often as possible to a different menu.*

The reserve tank contains enough life force to fuel at least two additional time slots dedicated to the same menu. So the total amount of life force available to each menu is enough to fuel at least three dedicated time slots of average length. We are speaking in purely theoretical terms here. The only way that this energy could possibly fuel three time slots dedicated to the same menu is if you went through all five menus without repeating a single one and then repeated this sequence two more times. In reality, your impulses will rarely follow such a pattern. It may take all day for you to get to a particular menu, whereas you may have touched upon several of the others two or three times by that point. In the meantime, the life force present in each menu's primary and reserve tanks will have been redistributed several times through the averaging-out process.

We do not mean to imply that on any particular day you will experience only fifteen total dedicated time slots. For the purposes of this discussion we have assumed that every time slot will be the same length and that everything you do will require the same amount of concentration. In reality, everyone will experience a different average number of dedicated time slots per day. The average lengths of these time slots will also differ from each other. Both averages depend on four interrelated factors: your flexibility of consciousness, your ability to maintain concentration, how demanding the activity is, and how much sleep you get each night. These factors can change from day to day, depending on such things as the weather and your emotional state. They can also change from one period to another in your life. Longer-than-average dedicated time slots will tend to decrease the number of time slots on a particular day. Likewise, shorter ones will tend to increase the number of time slots. Length and number of dedicated time slots depend entirely on what needs to be accomplished, from the soul's perspective, and how capable of maintaining a given focus of consciousness you might be on a given day.

The life force in each menu's reserve tank becomes available to the averaging-out process only after at least one time slot has been dedicated to that menu. So the second principle of efficient life-force usage is this:

Dedicate at least one time slot per day to each of the Menus B through F.

We call this principle the *Once-a-Day Requirement.* The soul has an investment in your pursuing activities on each of the menus every single day. This is the only way to ensure that your growth will proceed smoothly on all levels and that you will be able to fulfill all components of your life purpose. In fact, you can greatly accelerate the process of self-realization simply by pursuing an equal number of time slots dedicated to each menu every single day.

Making use of the Once-a-Day Requirement is the only way that you will be able to tap all of the life force the soul makes available to you each day. It doesn't matter whether you take all day to fulfill this requirement or run through all five menus first thing. Unstinting application of this principle will prevent you from ever wearing yourself out in the course of a day. Telling yourself that you'll get to this or that menu tomorrow instead of today, or promising yourself that you'll be sure to run through the entire cycle in the course of a week will do no good. If you ignore the Once-a-Day Requirement, you will find yourself running out of steam long before bedtime.

Once you have fulfilled the Once-a-Day Requirement for a particular menu, that menu's entire energy reserve will be redistributed among the other menus through the averaging-out process. This occurs at the point of urination. You may then choose to dedicate a second time slot in a row to the same menu or to shift to another menu.

We have said that the body has a tolerance for sustaining the same brain chemistry for the duration of two dedicated time slots. Even though the soul makes enough life force available to fuel at least three time slots dedicated to the same menu, the body will permit only two in succession. You will find your ability to concentrate petering out rather quickly if you immediately attempt a third. So the third principle of life-force dynamics is this:

> *Separate second and third time slots dedicated to a particular menu from each other by engaging in activities from at least one other menu.*

The soul respects the body's lack of tolerance for dedicating more than two successive time slots to the same menu. Thus it will never encourage you, through impulses, to dedicate three time slots in a row to the Work Menu, for example. As determined as you may be to get something done, if it remains unfinished as the second time slot comes to a close, it is best to leave it for a while and come back later. The temptation to keep on working until you're done may be great. But going right into a third time slot dedicated to the same project will not be the most efficient way to complete it. Be careful not to fall victim to the word *should* at this point—as in "I should keep working until I get this thing done." The law of diminishing returns will set in: Your ability to concentrate will diminish because the body is unable to support you in the appropriate state of consciousness. Furthermore, stress will begin to accumulate because you are ignoring other impulses. It doesn't matter whether you separate second and third time slots dedicated to the same menu with several periods devoted to other menus or only one. Once again, the averaging-out process will occur every time you shift menus.

It is entirely possible to exhaust the life force present in the primary fuel tanks for all five menus by alternating between just two menus several times. This doesn't mean that if you shift into one of the neglected menus, you will find no energy available for what you need to do. The life force in the reserve tank will fuel this new dedicated time slot.

For example, you may be engaged in a work project at home. This project requires a great deal of concentration. You need to take frequent breaks in order to maintain such an intense focus. So you alternate between the Work and Play menus every time you urinate. Each time you are in the Work Menu, you take the project to the next stage of development. Each time you are in the Play Menu, you read a couple of chapters of an absorbing novel. You can alternate between the work project and the novel for up to nine dedicated time slots in this fashion: three times each using the Work and Play menus' primary and reserve tanks, and one time each using the energy in the primary tanks for the other three menus. By then, the averaging-out process will have occurred so many times that there won't be enough energy left to sustain maximum levels of efficiency in either the Work Menu or Play Menu activities. Your concentration will flag. Errors may creep into the work project, or you may find yourself reading passages in the novel over and over in order to make sense out of them. You may even feel physically exhausted. But if you shift into any of the other menus—Physical Focus, Self-Awareness, or Cycles—the life force in their respective reserve fuel tanks will immediately become available. And if you shift to yet another menu after that, the life force remaining in the reserve tanks for both menus will be pooled together and averaged out. So the fourth principle of efficient life-force usage is this:

When you are nearing exhaustion, shift into a menu that has thus far been neglected.

The technique of alternating several times between two menus is a good one for maintaining high levels of productivity and efficiency in both areas. Generally speaking, the soul will project no more than five or six impulses to dedicate time slots to a particular menu in the course of a day. Usually it will project only three or four. The reason is that the soul has too much of an investment in your living as much as possible out of all the menus and all the components of your life purpose to favor any given one. Thus, you will never experience a day in which you have acted upon one impulse from four menus and all the rest from the remaining one. If you do, it's because the word *should* is interfering with your perception of impulses. Usually the soul will encourage you to pursue several impulses from some, if not all of the menus in the course of a day. The fact that two menus are involved in the alternation technique is what allows for the maximum number of time slots to be dedicated to each. Even though you could theoretically return in the example above to the Work Menu or the Play Menu once the reserve tanks for the remaining menus have been pooled together, the soul would probably not encourage you to do so.

The last principle of efficient life-force usage follows from the others:

For maximum life-force availability in the course of a day, pursue impulses from all five menus as early as possible.

In this way, you will have fulfilled the Once-a-Day Requirement and the reserve tanks for all five menus will have become available. As long as you continue to shift from one menu to another throughout the day, the averaging-out process will keep refilling the life-force fuel tanks for each menu.

Insomnia can sometimes be the result of inefficient life-force management. It will often occur when you have gone through the day without drawing from one or more of the menus at least once. While you may feel worn out as a result of having depleted the life-force reserves in the menus you did allow yourself to pursue, you will also feel restless. This restlessness is the result of not having tapped the fuel reserves for the menu or menus you neglected. Such untapped reserves can actually exert a pressure on you to use them—and this is what keeps you awake. Furthermore, not having access to these reserves will have diminished your productivity during the day, even if you believed that you did not have time for the menu or menus in question. The time that you apparently give up to a menu other than Work, for example, can actually redouble the amount of energy you have available for a work task. An enhanced ability to concentrate will then allow you to finish the project in much less time.

You will never wear yourself out on days when you have drawn at least once from each menu. Although the energy levels available to all menus will gradually diminish throughout the day, at the point when one more menu shift would mean utter depletion, the impulse to sleep will manifest itself. Sleep will be an easy matter. You'll feel that satisfied and happy tiredness you may recall from childhood—so different from anxious tossings and turnings or a leaden falling into bed. Even though you may have almost forgotten this ease of sleep, every night can bring the same joyous rest if you keep the principles of efficient life-force usage in mind.

Toward the end of the day, your energy may bottom out in one of the menus. You will definitely feel weary. But you must be careful not to tell yourself you're too tired to do anything else if the true impulse to sleep hasn't manifested itself yet. There may be a little unused life force still left in the other menus' fuel tanks. The last menu shift of the day will pool it to support one final dedicated time slot. Only after you have used up this energy will you feel that you can't keep your eyes open any longer. If you talk yourself out of using up this last bit of energy, you'll end up going to bed too early. Even though you may fall asleep after a relatively brief period, you will probably experience the impulse to awaken much earlier than usual. It will be rather easy to tell yourself it's too early to get up, when in fact you've had enough sleep. This is a form of arguing against the body, which knows better. If you go back to sleep, you'll have problems with stiffness, life-force availability, and sensitivity to impulses for the rest of that day.

As we have mentioned, not applying the Once-a-Day Requirement will cause you to run out of steam long before bedtime. If you misinterpret your exhaustion as the impulse to sleep, you'll have similar problems on the following day.

Up to this point, we've been speaking about life-force dynamics primarily in terms of the Menu A impulse to urinate. But Menu G performs an important function in this area as well. Because you have listed synchronicities, coincidences, unusual occurrences, unexpected happenings, and magical or miraculous events on the Surprise Menu, you have given yourself permission in advance for the soul to intervene and redirect your course of action in any of these ways. If you graciously allow whatever you are doing to be interrupted by Menu G surprises, the soul will reward you each time with an *energy surge.* This energy surge will cause the total amount of life force available to the menus to rise abruptly.

The amount of life force available each morning when you awaken varies with your degree of dedication to fulfilling your life purpose. There will be more when you are strongly focused on fulfilling your life purpose and less when you are putting up resistance. As we have said before, any Menu G experience acts as a vector force, attempting to redirect your course of action so that it aligns more closely with your life purpose. The more willing you are to be redirected in this fashion, the greater the intensity of the energy surge. Every time a surge occurs, the amount of life force available to the menus can rise to the point of equaling or exceeding its level when you awakened. Often called peak experiences, these energy surges represent a kind of built-in reward system. The soul uses the joyful sense of expansion that accompanies them to guide you toward self-realization—especially when habit is causing you to ignore your impulses.

People crave such "highs." They may seek them out through drugs, spiritual disciplines, or the excitement of living dangerously. But there is no guarantee that any of these means will be successful. The most effective manner of ensuring a plenitude of peak experiences is simply to stand in readiness for any and every Menu G surprise. Be willing to let go of whatever process you are engaged in. Resenting or grumbling about the interruption tends to diminish the energy surge—sometimes to the point that you may hardly be aware of it. In the case of unpleasant Menu G experiences, the surge will come only after you have identified the problematic beliefs, attitudes, or behaviors the soul was trying to point out to you.

It should be clear from the foregoing that Menu G and the impulse to urinate are the two primary means of shifting between menus. Your willingness to flow with the interruption caused by a Menu G surprise determines how successfully you are able to shift menus this way. In place of the impulse to urinate, you will experience the energy surge. You need not worry that you will somehow lose the ability to focus in your new state of consciousness because the old one had not been released through urination. You may notice, however, that the volume of urine discharged upon the *next* impulse to urinate will be greater than usual. The soul's energy surge will have made allowances for the processing of any waste chemicals in the bloodstream—both from the state of consciousness that prevailed before you entered the menu that has been interrupted and from the state of consciousness you are leaving behind because of Menu G.

You may occasionally find yourself in circumstances that do not support your application of the five principles of efficient life-force management. An example would be attending an all-day self-awareness seminar. Not only will you be in the Self-Awareness Menu while attending lectures and participating in group discussions, you might also make some new friends during breaks. As we have already pointed out, getting to know someone is yet another Self-Awareness activity. By the end of the day, perhaps a half dozen time slots in a row have been dedicated to the same menu. You're almost certain to feel drained. Yet taking a nap and then spending the evening pursuing activities from the other menus in accordance with these principles will tend to revive you.

It is important for you to recognize that the principles of life-force dynamics do not comprise so much a set of rules as a set of guidelines. It *is* possible to get through a day without them. But you'll get twice as much accomplished in half the amount of time—with little if any wear and tear on the body —by applying these principles. Whether or not you adopt them is simply a question of living a life of greater or lesser efficiency. The payoff for a more energy-efficient lifestyle is the increased sense of physical well-being that accompanies your emotional satisfaction at what you've been able to accomplish.

CHAPTER 16

Implementing the Menus

Considered as a system, the Menus for Impulsive Living is a set of strategies for becoming aware of, and giving yourself permission to pursue, impulses. Yet merely being able to provide yourself with lists of activities appropriate to each of the menus is not enough to guarantee an impulsive lifestyle. Several steps are required in order to create a truly impulsive approach to each day.

The first step in implementing the Menus for Impulsive Living is simply to pay attention to the Menu A impulses. When you feel the urge to urinate, see if you can figure out which state of consciousness you have left behind and which you are about to enter. Pay attention to the impulse to quench thirst. See how it tends to follow the impulse to urinate or tells you when to conclude a meal. If it occurs at some point *between* urinations, notice whether you are continuing with the same project (in which case, you are simply attempting to enhance your ability to concentrate) or changing to another one. In the second case, ask yourself if there is a resemblance between the new project and the old one. Could they both belong to the same menu?

Try to eat only when hungry. Whenever the impulse to defecate manifests itself, make an attempt to pinpoint the process that has just been completed. Did you actually finish a project or just one of the stages involved? Or was the process an internal one, expressing itself in the form of a decision or realization about yourself?

Observe the impulse to sleep. See how it manifests itself at different times each night, often having nothing to do with an arbitrarily chosen bedtime. Do you seem to lie awake for an hour or more after slipping into bed? Or do you perhaps make yourself stay up longer than you really have the energy to? Pay just as close attention to the impulse to awaken. Do you lie in bed half awake and half asleep for an hour after your alarm goes off? Or do you awaken before the alarm but stay in bed until it has sounded? When does the need to urinate awaken you naturally—before or after the alarm?

Try to sense the periods between experiencing any of these Menu A impulses as units of time—*flexible* units because they will never occur after the same amount of clock time has passed or at the same hour every day. Remind yourself that these impulses provide an alternative schedule to the clock's hours. This alternative is a more natural one, because it is based on the body's ability to maintain states of consciousness rather than on arbitrary temporal subdivisions. Keep in mind that the Menu A impulses not only represent physical needs but may also be considered the signals through which the body communicates to you how well you are using your life force. They can tell you how to ensure maximum efficiency by redirecting your use of life force in order to prevent exhaustion. The result of paying attention to such signals and of viewing them as measuring out flexible units of time is a release from the tyranny of the clock. Your life will no longer be controlled by the clock's artificially equal subdivisions, which seem to go fast or slow according to your mood. You will always have enough time to accomplish what you need to do.

Chances are that you have already begun this process of observing the Menu A impulses simply to see if the information communicated in Part II holds true for you. We are merely suggesting that you make this process as conscious as possible. In this way, you will actually begin to implement Menu A.

The second step in creating an impulsive lifestyle is to review the definitions of the other menus and to construct your own personal lists of activities for Menus B through F—if you have not already done so. (A review of the various components of the Menus system may be found in the Appendix.) Remember to list only those activities you currently practice—not things you *used* to do or *want* to do or *should* do, but never get around to. Note any apparent problem areas, or blank menus—ones with only a few activities or activities you can't seem to place anywhere. For menus deficient in choices, request that the soul help you draw new possibilities to yourself through Menu G.

The third step is to begin to apply the principles of efficient life-force usage from the previous chapter: shift between menus as often as possible; draw at least one activity from each of the Menus B through F each day; don't draw from the same menu for more than two dedicated time slots in a row; when exhausted, switch to any menu that has been thus far neglected; and try to run through a complete cycle of Menus B through F as early in the day as possible.

Living from these principles may be difficult for persons engaged in a rigorous work schedule. Later in the book we shall provide some strategies for taking an impulsive approach to the workday. For now, see if you can apply the menus at least to your free days.

Besides the five principles of efficient life-force usage, there are two additional rules you must keep in mind in order to guarantee an impulsive lifestyle. Steps must be taken to overcome the tendency to value certain activities over others, because the overvalued activities will tend to screen out impulses toward the less-valued ones. The latter may satisfy vitally important needs from time to time, however, and should be honored. In order to prevent impulse screening, especially by the Work Menu, the following rules must be applied:

1. No menu shall be perceived as of greater value than any other.
2. No activity on any given menu shall be perceived as of greater value than any other.

In this way you can prevent falling into the trap of doing what you think you *should* be doing instead of what you actually *need* to be doing, from the soul's perspective. Furthermore, you will be less likely to accumulate stress through ignored impulses.

The fourth step in implementing the menus is to begin to play with the impulsive shape of your day as consciously as possible. In this way you prevent yourself from succumbing to the mind-numbing effects of routine. Using the menus you have made up for yourself, you will have nearly inexhaustible resources for differentiating one day from the next, even if you choose only one activity per menu per day. All you have to do is make sure that you don't choose the same activities from the same menus each day.

Another means of altering the experiential coloration of each day is to draw twice from at least one menu every day, varying that menu from one day to the next as you feel the impulse to do so. You might also experiment with drawing twice from two, three, four, or all five of Menus B through F. Then you may wish to experiment with drawing three or four times from one or more of the menus.

The fifth step is to pay close attention to the seasonal variation of activities during the first year or so of applying the menus to your life. The time of year you write your first set of menus will have a great impact on what activities you record. In terms of the Play Menu, for example, summer seems to provide ample opportunity for outside recreation, whereas winter seems to restrict such possibilities. Furthermore, certain professions, such as teaching, have a seasonal rhythm. Your menus will not be complete until you have listed activities appropriate for each and every season.

In coming up with seasonal activities, you will probably find that summer is the easiest and winter the hardest. Make a special effort to find some outside winter activities toward which you incline impulsively: ice-skating, skiing, showshoeing, and the like. Thus, you will not only prevent cabin fever, you will also suffer less from the cold. Inability to warm yourself in winter is a symbolic manifestation of refusing to embrace winter as a necessary component of the life cycle, replete with its own magic, beauty, and unique activities. If you live in a climate without a winter, there may be other seasonal variations that shift the balance of your activities indoors or outdoors, such as a rainy season. If this is the case, you must make sure that you have listed things you will enjoy doing on the days when you can't go outside.

In climates with the four traditional seasons, you should also attempt to find unique seasonal activities that will help you differentiate spring and fall from winter and summer: planting and harvesting, flying kites, taking country drives to enjoy the autumn leaves, making maple syrup, picking apples, and so on. See how creative you can be in allowing your menus to align with the seasons. In this fashion, not only each day but also each season—and therefore each year—can develop its own impulsive shape. Against this backdrop of seasonal activities, you will be able to monitor your growth from year to year more clearly.

It is important not to let your life deteriorate into a dreadful sameness that supports routine. If you become blind to your *interior* seasons and cycles, you will be able to differentiate one decade from another only by how much more "over the hill" you feel physically and emotionally. On the other hand, by participating fully in the impulsive shape of the seasons, you will always find yourself not a day or year older but a day or year wiser.

This may be a bit more difficult to do in relatively changeless climates. The best way for people living in such places to monitor their growth on a yearly basis is through holiday celebrations: New Year's Day, Valentine's Day, Easter, Memorial Day, Independence Day, Labor Day, Halloween, Thanksgiving, Christmas—or any others that might seem important, whether local, national, or religious. Each holiday has its own set of customary activities that can take over the season's functions as yardsticks for growth. All you have to do is remind yourself of who you were a few weeks or months ago during the previous holiday celebration and how much you have changed since the same time last year.

Obviously, what we have said regarding the Menus for Impulsive Living can guide an entire lifetime of experience. As the years come and go, however, your interests and pursuits will naturally change. Through meeting new people and through Menu G surprises, new activities never before considered as options can become available. From time to time you may also find that certain activities have begun to bore you. In order to maintain living impulsively, it is important to be aware of such changes.

The menus exhibit those impulses which you have already given yourself permission to acknowledge and pursue. Not listing a new activity can have negative effects on the balance of daily experience. For example, you could attempt to ignore the impulse when it arises, thereby supporting the routines it was probably sent to break down. You could also allow it to become so utterly fascinating that it eclipses all other activities in importance. This often happens when you are particularly enthusiastic about a new pursuit. Other things that may be just as important will tend not to get done, which causes the accumulation of stress—even when this new activity is recreational in nature. In order to guarantee that any new activity be perceived as of no greater or lesser value than any other activity or menu, you should add it to your lists as soon as possible.

It is important that you cross off any activities that have become tiresome or dull or that you never seem motivated to pursue. Occasionally you just need a rest from doing something you have done too often. Crossing this activity off the list gives you permission to take this rest for a few months. When it seems interesting once more, you are already beginning to feel new impulses toward it. Go ahead and add it back to your lists. If you find yourself feeling guilty about having eliminated an activity, this means that the soul disapproves of the deletion.

Whenever you cross off an activity, chances are that it has already been, or will soon be, replaced by another one that you find more interesting. But if the variety of activities listed on a menu begins to diminish over time, chances are that you have been tending to favor other activities or other menus over the activity or menu in question. You should then make a conscious effort to seek out new ones.

When you make up the menus the first time, be sure to date them. You may also wish to include a date with each deletion or addition. This can help you keep track of the impulsive shape of your life as it changes gradually over time. Furthermore, it is a good idea to review the menus several times a year. Any dates will do, but we recommend that you consider the solstices and equinoxes as possible review days. There is no mystical reason for this; it is just that they divide the year equally into four parts. Looking over your menus every three months gives you the opportunity to reclaim activities that may have slipped your mind. This helps to keep you from settling into routine. Once a year—on your birthday, perhaps—you may wish to rewrite the menus, especially if they have become cluttered with additions, deletions, and dates.

Such review periods belong to the Cycles Menu. You will

not be saddled with them for the rest of your life though. After a while you may become so attuned to your impulses that you no longer need the lists. At that point, the Menus for Impulsive Living will have served their purpose.

CHAPTER 17

How to Know What Menu You Are In

If impulses originate with the body or the soul, and not the ego, then it may seem paradoxical that we say you should play with the impulsive shape of your day as consciously as possible. An impulse is like a radio broadcast: just because you haven't attuned your awareness to it doesn't mean that it has gone away. Both body and soul are constantly broadcasting impulses to you, and these impulses only go away when they have been acted upon. In a sense, then, the ego is like the hand that turns the dial of a radio. It tunes in to the different broadcasts as it pleases. Ideally, the entire spectrum of broadcasts should be covered on a regular basis. Instead, the ego often gets stuck on certain ones and ends up not undertaking important growth in other areas. The five principles of efficient life-force usage—especially the Once-a-Day Requirement—and the two rules about valuing all menus and activities equally will enable the ego to overcome stuckness and return to scanning the entire spectrum of broadcasts.

From the perspective of the soul—which exists outside of time—it doesn't matter in what order you accomplish the various tasks it poses for you. You may choose any order of menus you please and vary it from day to day. Yet the soul does have a kind of master plan for your development, which might require that particular things be accomplished during particular periods of your life. The specific day, however, may not be all that important. These broadcasts will have a certain intensity, which becomes amplified as you approach the end of the period in which the growth would best be undertaken. It is this intensity that you experience as stress and that determines a kind of impulsive priority system based upon your needs for growth. By not valuing one activity or menu over another, you allow this priority system to assert itself.

It is highly likely that you will become aware of priority broadcasts immediately upon urinating, just before you have committed yourself to producing a new brain chemistry. Such awarenesses indicate that the period you are about to enter might be suitable for doing something about one of those broadcasts. The best approach to the menus, therefore, is to choose a new menu *consciously* at the moment of urination. Then open yourself to "suggestions"—actually impulsive priorities, based on the degree of intensity—for appropriate activities from that menu. Through conscious manipulation of the experiential coloration of each day in favor of a different menu or group of menus, you can then make sure that you cover the entire spectrum of impulsive priorities. Such practices ensure not only that you will never become bored and/or stressed-out by settling into routine but also that the soul's master plan will eventually realize itself through you. Furthermore, the question of what menu you are in at a given moment will not come up: you will have decided that already at the point of urination.

One way to become aware of impulsive priorities is to do a quick mental scan of the menu you have chosen, in order to see which activity feels right or has a certain urgency about it. Anything that feels right has impulsive backing. You must be careful, however, not to try to *persuade* yourself that something feels right. At that point, you are attempting to substitute an activity you would *prefer* to do for what the soul is projecting as impulsively appropriate. Likewise, if you enter a new menu and find yourself saying "Well, I certainly don't want to do *that!*" you are resisting the pursuit of a priority impulse projected by the soul.

At all times you must beware of the word *should.* This word indicates that you are valuing one activity over another. As we have said, when you find yourself thinking "I *should* be doing X," you are unconsciously suppressing the rest of the sentence, which is "instead of Y." If you persist in doing X, you will find that you don't have the backing of the soul. It will be impossible for you to be completely present with the task. You will tend to feel distracted, restless, or bored. And the longer you persist, the more you will be overcome by feelings of grogginess.

Distraction, restlessness, boredom, and grogginess—in order of increasing intensity—are all warning signals that you are wasting life force. Each one is a kind of error message from the soul. A computer produces error messages whenever you type in something other than what it expects from you. There are times when the computer will not understand you, because the next step may require the entry of numbers and instead you punch in letters. So might the body be primed by the soul for a certain demand on its physical or mental prowess, but the ego might instruct it to do something else. The result will be an error message. In other words, distraction, restlessness, boredom, and grogginess mean that the type of activity chosen by the ego does not match the type of activity for which the soul is broadcasting an impulse—and the body has become confused.

An error message tends to intensify when you ignore it. If you make the proper adjustments right away, full ability to focus your attention will return immediately. On the other hand, if you try to keep on going with whatever you have been doing, then fatigue will certainly result. At that point, only taking a nap can return you to a pristine clarity of awareness.

It might appear through all that we have said about the soul up to this point that it is incredibly manipulative and that you don't have much choice but to do what it wants. This is to some extent true. Because you were born with a life purpose and because the soul holds the master plan for realizing that life purpose, at least some of your experience will have been predetermined. But just because the soul has chosen the *what* and *why* of your presence in physical reality doesn't mean that you have no choices at all. Free will does extend into the areas of *how, where, when,* and *with whom* you go about realizing this master plan.

For example, the service-to-the-Creator aspect of your life purpose has predetermined that you find some creative outlet for yourself. If the soul has decided that in this lifetime you are to be an artist, then the medium of creative expression may also have been predetermined. Otherwise you are free to choose any creative outlet you please—whatever seems to appeal to you. In either case, free will allows you to choose the best method of learning for you, whether from a book, from a private teacher, or from a college course (how). You can also choose between taking a class at the local art museum or an adult education center (where). You can choose to take the class in the evening or on weekends, during the school year or the summer (when). You can also choose from among a number of different instructors (with whom). The only thing you cannot choose is whether or not you will find some medium of creative expression for yourself.

As long as you content yourself with making choices in the areas of how, where, when, and with whom—without resisting the what and the why that motivate them—you will experience a harmonious relationship with the soul. The soul only steps in and manipulates you through falling levels of life force or unpleasant surprises when the ego tries to pretend that it has complete control of your destiny. In order to create this illusion of supremacy, the ego, like a rebellious teenager who refuses to do what he or she is told, will always choose whats and whys that conflict with the soul's master plan. Error messages occur whenever your choice of menu or activity is irrelevant to fulfilling your life purpose, because it stems from such resistance. The soul will often use such messages when the ideal time to accomplish certain things—because of a number of internal and external conditions of which you may be largely unaware—is *right now.* They will also be sent when you are basing your decisions about what to do on routine instead of impulse.

If you are having trouble determining what menu you happen to be in at a given moment, the problem may be that you have not declared an intent to enter a particular menu at the moment of urination. In this case, the impulses being projected to you by the soul will seem unfocused. Just saying to yourself "I'm in the Self-Awareness Menu now," for example, will bring your impulses into immediate focus. If for some reason that menu is not appropriate, given your needs of the moment, then one of the error messages will be produced. Declare another menu affiliation. If another error message is received, then you are still not properly focused. Eventually you will find the right match of menu with impulsive priority. Before you know it, you will be engaged in some activity that completely holds your interest and provides a feeling of true satisfaction.

You must be patient with yourself when you first begin to apply the Menus for Impulsive Living. You may have to resort to trial and error from time to time because of your unfamiliarity with impulses in general or with those emanating from a particular menu. How long this period of trial and error will last depends entirely on how well you develop a sensitivity to impulses. You won't have to try out all the menus every time you urinate to find the right one. But even if you do, there are only five choices to consider.

Once you have overcome any tendency to settle into routine, it becomes possible for you to know what must next be done right at the point of urination. Reduction of the amount of time spent in distraction, restlessness, boredom, and grogginess will be a measure of how enlightened you are becoming. Once again, enlightenment is nothing more than knowing what to do next under any given set of circumstances.

Another reason you may have difficulty perceiving what menu you are in is that the situation in which you find yourself has not been listed on the appropriate menu. We have already mentioned that it is easier to ignore impulses toward unlisted activities or to allow such activities to screen out impulses toward others. The problem may not be that you have delayed updating your menus but that you just aren't sure what menu some new activity genuinely belongs to. We suggest that you make up a separate list of these *misfit activities* on the pages in your notebook following your personal set of menus.

If you haven't been able to determine what menu an activity belongs on by consulting the chart in Chapter 8, the best approach to finding the right menu for it is a variation of the trial-and-error method mentioned above. At the point of urination, declare your intent to pursue activities from the menu you think the misfit might belong to. Then begin doing an activity you know for sure belongs to the menu you are now in. At some point, perhaps after fifteen minutes or so, switch over to the misfit activity. If grogginess develops, then you know the activity belongs to a different menu. If it does not, then cross the activity off the misfit list and enter it upon the menu you have been in.

Because this society tends to distrust impulses, you have not learned their language. Impulses may not always manifest themselves as a word spoken in your head or even as mental images of yourself engaged in doing something. For example, heaviness in the legs is an impulse to enter the Physical Focus Menu. Remembering a dream upon awakening constitutes an impulse to write it down and interpret it. For Kurt, hearing piano or clarinet music in his head on a particular day lets him know that it is important to practice either of those instruments. The purpose of the menus is to help familiarize you with the feel of each category of impulses. Sorting through misfit activities is an important step in this process, even if it seems to be time-consuming and awkward. The more familiar you become with the feel of each impulse category, the fewer alternatives you will have to investigate through trial and error—until finally, whenever a new activity comes up, you will know exactly how it fits into your life.

A large number of your misfit activities will probably belong on the Cycles Menu. This affiliation may not be immediately apparent, because the impulses to do these things come up rather infrequently. The cycles they conclude may be so long that you have not been aware of them as such.

Once again, it is your intent in engaging in some activity that determines its proper menu affiliation. There is always one particular brain chemistry that will best and most efficiently support *you* in that activity. Grogginess results when the prevailing brain chemistry and the one demanded by the activity conflict. If an activity tends to drain you rather than provide a feeling of satisfied accomplishment, then you may have listed it on the wrong menu or you may be approaching it with an inappropriate intent. The area in which this is most likely to happen is play. Because play can provide a break from fulfilling one's life purpose, many people in this responsibility-obsessed society feel guilty about providing themselves with playtime, so they tend to define play as work, in order to feel better about it. An example would be an executive who has bought a sailboat. Whereas he could derive enormous pleasure and relaxation from sailing, in order to feel better about such an idle pastime he might become obsessed with winning races. Approaching play as if it were work will take all the fun out of it, precisely because two different brain chemistries will be in conflict. We're not saying that our executive-sailor shouldn't enter competitions but that he should do so for the fun of sailing, not just to win.

Yet another reason why you may have difficulty perceiving what menu you are in is that you may not have been specific enough in constructing one or more of the menus. For example, if you have written "being at the office" as the only item on your Work Menu, then you have not perceived the enormous variety of activities that can take place at the office—not all of which are necessarily work activities. The best way to approach sorting these activities into the appropriate menus is to declare at the moment of urination that you will dedicate the next time slot to work. Begin with an activity you know to be work of some sort, and trust that all other impulses originating during that period will also emanate from the work menu. Make note of each specific task on Menu D. Nonwork impulses that may arise during this period will result in grogginess. These should be added to the misfit list and dealt with as mentioned above. Generally speaking, the more refined your perception of the multitude of smaller jobs that constitute your work, the easier it will be for you to perceive impulses toward any of these activities in any time slot dedicated to work. This will greatly increase your efficiency. For if you have genuine impulsive backing for the task you are engaged in, you also have access to peak levels of concentration and clarity about how to proceed.

There may always be periods you can't identify. Don't worry about them. As long as you fulfill the Once-a-Day Requirement each day with activities that you are sure of, you won't inadvertently neglect one or more of the menus.

CHAPTER 18

How to Avoid Error Messages

One of the secrets of achieving efficiency with the Menus system is to make sure that as few activities as possible from menus other than the one to which you have dedicated a particular time slot creep in. Even though your thoughts may occasionally stray to topics more appropriate to other menus, or you may need to drop what you are doing for a moment to get something from another menu out of the way, in order to keep the brain chemistry as clear as possible, you should try to sort out activities and thoughts that don't belong to the menu you are in. Conflicting brain chemistries—which are often experienced as "having too much on one's mind"—are the cause of inefficiency. Generally speaking, the soul will honor the fact that you have dedicated a time slot to a certain menu by broadcasting only impulses from that menu. Anything else will probably be a distraction—especially if the word *should* appears in connection with it.

There may be times when to shift into, and out of, another menu momentarily and without urinating may be unavoidable. For example, perhaps you are out shopping for clothes (Cycles Menu). A novel in the window of a bookstore (Play Menu) catches your eye as you pass from one clothing store to another. In all likelihood, the bookstore has no public rest room. Furthermore, you may not even feel the impulse to urinate. Will the soul send an error message if you go into the bookstore? Will you begin to feel so groggy that only taking a nap as soon as possible will get you through the rest of the day? And yet you do feel an impulsive draw to examine the novel. What should you do?

The soul will never send an error message when you are following a true impulse. Only when the activity you have begun to pursue is distracting you from another activity that is more necessary will you receive an error message. If you had been impulsively guided to go shopping for clothes but proceeded to check out all the bookstores in the area one after another, then you probably would receive an error message—unless, of course, it was more necessary for you to find something you might enjoy reading than to shop for clothes in the first place. In any event, the important thing is always to follow your impulses. Don't get caught up in worrying about whether the soul might send an error message. Just do what you feel an internal prompting to do. And if you begin to feel distracted, restless, bored, or groggy, stop doing what you think you *should* be doing and try to uncover the impulse you have been suppressing.

One way to ensure that you will not receive an error message when you have shifted into another menu momentarily is to shift right back into the original menu immediately afterward. We call this technique *nestling,* because you have nestled one menu in between two periods of pursuing another. In our example above, you would just return to clothes shopping after your visit to the bookstore. That way you have nestled the Play Menu within the Cycles Menu. If you intend to make a full-fledged switch from one menu into another though, it would be best to urinate first. The longer you spend in the nestled menu, the more likely you are to receive an error message. Switching immediately back into the original menu will cancel out this error message before you have become so groggy that only a nap will enable you to recover. Remember, if a Menu G surprise has been the cause of switching to another menu, the soul will take care of all adjustments to the brain chemistry. There will be no error message, even if you do not return to the original menu later on.

The Menus system works best when you pursue activities from a particular menu all the way up to the point of urination. Let us say that you have shifted into the Cycles Menu. The first thing you do is make your bed. That takes only a couple of minutes. It is unlikely that you will then feel the impulse to urinate. So you should allow yourself to become aware of another Cycles Menu impulse: some clothes scattered around the room need to be put in the hamper. Still the impulse to urinate has not manifested itself. There are a couple of bills to pay, and your checkbook needs balancing. Maybe after you have finished these activities, the impulse to urinate will signal the importance of shifting to another menu. If not, then keep trying to come up with further Cycles Menu activities to pursue. You will be surprised at how much can be accomplished in this fashion.

There may be times when you feel the need to shift menus and no impulse to urinate has manifested itself. Perhaps you are working an eight-hour day. You have just spent two time slots dedicated to work, and you would like to shift to another menu for a while to guarantee maximum productivity in the Work Menu for the rest of the day. You act upon the impulse to urinate and decide to enter the Cycles Menu. First, you spend a few minutes straightening up your desk. Then, you take a break and catch up on the goings-on in the life of one of your coworkers. Finally, you make a brief telephone call to your mate to check on how his or her day has been going so far. Twenty minutes or so have elapsed. You feel sufficiently refreshed to return to work, but the impulse to urinate has not manifested itself. You also don't want to spend any more time in the Cycles Menu for fear of a reprimand from your boss. What do you do?

Go to the rest room and prepare to urinate. Think for a moment about the activity or activities you have just completed. Then imagine the activity you wish to perform next. Think: "Shift from Cycles Menu [or whatever menu you are in] to Work Menu [or whatever menu you would like to shift to]." Once you have declared your intent, you will find yourself able to urinate. We call this the *quick-shift technique.* You may use this technique whenever you feel it necessary to shift quickly from one menu to another after a short period in the first. There will be a decreased volume of urine, one, of course. But even five minutes of full focus within a menu will produce a small trickle. Making frequent trips to the rest room in this way may seem like nothing more than a ritual. But such a practice will allow you to maintain a maximally focused and clear consciousness far better than prolonged periods between urinations.

There is one thing to keep in mind whenever you use the quick-shift technique. Only a few minutes in a certain menu may not be enough to fulfill the Once-a-Day Requirement. The only way to guarantee that you have fulfilled this requirement is to spend one full dedicated time slot per day on the pursuit of activities from that menu. So the quick-shift technique should be considered nothing more than a stopgap measure. It is most useful when you are trying to avoid dedicating three successive time slots to the same menu, as in the example above.

What makes the quick-shift technique work is the fact that at the moment of urination you are declaring your intention to become available to another set of impulses. The soul will hold you to such an intention, which is why it sends error messages if you get sidetracked. Yet it will also support you in any *change* of intention, as long as you honor the Once-a-Day Requirement.

Perhaps there are a couple of things from one menu that

you would like to get out of the way before you settle into a more-demanding activity from another. As long as you have clearly declared your intention to pursue this other activity, you will not receive an error message. We call this technique *attaching* one menu to another. It is especially helpful when there are not enough of these small tasks to fill an entire dedicated time slot. An example would be making your bed and getting dressed to begin the day (Cycles Menu) just before settling down to read the morning paper (Play Menu). It is also possible to attach one menu to another at the end of a dedicated time slot, such as when you shower and dress (Cycles) after a workout (Physical Focus). You should not consider the brief period spent in an attached or a nestled menu as sufficient to fulfill the Once-a-Day Requirement.

Under certain conditions you may pursue activities from two different menus concurrently without receiving an error message. All you need do is *subordinate* one to the other. Perhaps listening to music is one of your Play Menu activities. And perhaps you have found that putting music on in the background while you are working helps you concentrate. You have subordinated the Play Menu activity to the Work Menu activity. Or perhaps you have taken a novel with you to the Laundromat. While waiting for your clothes to go through the wash cycle, you read. After you have shifted them to the dryer, you continue to read. Then perhaps you end this dedicated time slot by folding the clothes, returning home, and putting them away. At the beginning of this period, you had subordinated the Cycles Menu to the Play Menu. Both focuses of consciousness were present from the beginning as a result of your intention to subordinate one to the other. For this reason, there was no conflict in brain chemistries when you allowed the subordinated activity to come to the fore toward the end.

Whenever you use the technique of menu subordination, you have fulfilled the Once-a-Day Requirement for *both* of the menus involved—but in a single dedicated time slot. If you are working long hours at a job and feel that you may not have time to dedicate yourself to pursuing one activity from each menu daily, you could use this technique to your advantage. For example, you could subordinate the Play Menu to the Physical Focus Menu by exercising while listening to music. That way you release yourself from the obligation of pursuing activities from these menus in two separate time slots. For any of the activities on your Play Menu that are also listed on the Physical Focus Menu, such as a softball game, the same thing will be true. You can subordinate the intent to have fun to the intent for exercise or vice versa. In either case, you will have fulfilled the Once-a-Day Requirement for both menus in a single time slot.

Not every activity on your menus can be subordinated to something else in the manner we have described. Many will require undivided attention. It is often possible to engage your hands in one activity while at the same time thinking about something else. This is another form of subordination. As long as what you are thinking about doesn't interfere with this activity, there's nothing wrong with using the subordination technique in this way.

In some cases, it will be clear that one menu must be in the forefront of your consciousness, while the other is in the background. In others, you may find that your awareness alternates between the two menus. It might be difficult sometimes to say which menu has been subordinated to the other. Yet you are still using the same technique: only one menu is in the forefront of your consciousness at a time.

If you are not sure whether the subordination technique will work for you, we suggest the following experiment: in the course of a dedicated time slot, try alternating between two activities from different menus every five minutes or so; if you are able to maintain concentration in both activities and can get something accomplished without distraction, then you have successfully subordinated each to the other. While simply being able to maintain concentration in this fashion can be one means of developing flexibility of consciousness, the technique is only truly useful when you have perceived a significant enhancement of your ability to concentrate on either activity. Don't link more than two menus at a time in this way. It is highly unlikely that you will be able to divide your attention among three or more menus and achieve much of anything.

In a conversation, the topic may drift from one thing to another, but there will usually be an overall theme. That theme should be traceable to one of the menus. The topics that belong to other menus will be nestled, attached, or subordinated to that main theme. Perhaps you have gotten together over lunch with your closest friend. The main theme of the conversation is what has happened in your respective lives since the last time you saw each other (Cycles Menu). In the midst of this conversation, you describe a movie you have seen (Play Menu). Then you return to the main theme. At another point, your friend places you momentarily in the Work Menu by asking for your advice on a certain matter. Once again, you return to the main theme afterward. It would be useless to try to decide whether these other two menus had been nestled within, or subordinated to, the Cycles Menu. Yet you *can* use this conversation to fulfill the Once-a-Day Requirement for Cycles. This approach will work just as well with periods of solitary thought. In either case, you may have to nudge the flow of topics back to the original theme or menu from time to time. The more focused within a single menu such a period of thinking or talking happens to be, the less likely you are to become fatigued by it.

The last tip on how to avoid error messages has to do with public rest rooms. The entire Menus system depends on your responding to the impulse to urinate. When you are away from home, a little investigation might be necessary in order to find out where the nearest rest rooms are. This can prevent a great deal of both physical and mental discomfort. The feeling of fatigue that can build up while one is shopping is usually the result of inadvertent menu switches when passing from store to store. You can help prevent this fatigue by pursuing the impulse to urinate whenever it manifests itself and either dividing up your errands into as many different time slots as there are menus or nestling one kind of shopping within a menu dedicated to another.

None of the techniques listed in this chapter are absolutely essential to the understanding and application of the Menus system. Yet the learning of any skill can pass through ever-increasing degrees of refinement. This is certainly true of learning how to manage your life force efficiently. There may come a time when you have mastered the basics, and the soul will begin to guide you toward an ever greater efficiency. It will probably use error messages in order to accomplish this end. You may then find these more advanced applications of the system tremendously helpful.

CHAPTER 19

Exercises in Impulsive Living

We shall now provide you with a number of exercises that will enable you to become more proficient in living impulsively. You may add them to the Self-Awareness Menu if you wish. Since each of them requires a bit of writing, we suggest that you use the stenographer's notebook in which you initially recorded your menus.

EXERCISE ONE
Flexible Time Units

The purpose of this exercise is to help you become aware of the approximate number of flexible time units available per day. Only one page of the notebook will be required. If you work, then write "Workdays" in the left column and "Nonworkdays" in the right. You will need six days to complete the exercise—three for each column. They need not be consecutive. In both columns, write "Day One," "Day Two," and "Day Three," skipping a couple of lines after each. If you do not work or if you make your own hours, then only four days are required, and you need not concern yourself with the columns. Keep the notebook with you on each day you do the exercise, and mark a slash next to the number of the day every time you act upon the impulse to urinate. Do not proceed to the next exercise until you have completed this one.

It may seem silly at first to pay such attention to what your society considers little more than a minor annoyance. But the impulse to urinate is the very backbone of the Menus for Impulsive Living. In order to release yourself from the feeling that there aren't enough hours in the day to accomplish what needs to be done, you must first become aware of just how many flexible time units are available to replace those hours.

EXERCISE TWO
Dedicated Time Slots

Keep your notebook with you from four to six days. Each time you act on the impulse to urinate, decide upon a menu and then engage yourself in whatever activities suggest themselves impulsively. Keep track in the notebook of both the menus and the activities. Whenever you change activities in the midst of this dedicated time slot, notice whether there is a smooth transition or whether you become groggy. If you become groggy, make note of the activity on the misfit list and try to find the appropriate menu for it later. Once again, be sure to include both workdays and nonworkdays in your sample.

The purpose of this exercise is to begin the process of purging each flexible time unit of activities not supported by the prevailing brain chemistry. In this fashion, they become truly dedicated to the pursuit of activities from a particular menu. The result will be increased ability to concentrate, enhanced enjoyment and satisfaction, and reduced likelihood of fatigue.

EXERCISE THREE
The Once-a-Day Requirement

For two or three days after you have completed the previous exercise, continue keeping track of the menus and activities to which you have dedicated each flexible time unit. Make sure that you have pursued at least one impulse from each of the Menus B through F each day. Make note of your mental state at the end of the day: are you exhausted, or do you feel a sense of happy tiredness? For the next two or three days, try to *leave out* one or more of the menus by not following any impulses from them. Once again, make note of your mental state at the end of each day.

The purpose of this exercise is to familiarize you with the difference between what we call *energy-debit* and *energy-neutral* states of consciousness. The energy-debit state occurs whenever you have not applied the Once-a-Day Requirement. Its symptom is a feeling of being utterly depleted by the end of a day. The energy-neutral state occurs when you have pursued at least one impulse from each menu by the end of a day. Its symptom is drowsiness, accompanied by a satisfied feeling of accomplishment.

EXERCISE FOUR
Experiential Coloration

Each day has its own particular feel to it, depending on which of the menus has predominated. The day's experience will have been colored by these feelings. It is possible to distinguish between the experiential coloration of a day in which the Work Menu has predominated and one in which the Self-Awareness Menu has predominated. In order to release yourself from routine, you must first become aware of these distinctions, which we call *feeling tones.*

The first step of the exercise is to identify each of the

Menus B through F with one of the colors of the rainbow. One approach you could take is to write the names of the menus on successive lines in the left column of your notebook. Use both their letter names and the labels we have assigned them (for example, "Menu B—Physical Focus"). Then, in the right column, write down the following colors: red, orange, yellow, green, blue, purple. Clearly there will be one more color than there are menus. The next step is to draw a line between each of the menus and the one color that best seems to express your feelings about it. Red could stand for the Work Menu—perhaps because your job demands an aggressive stance. Or it could represent the Physical Focus Menu, to symbolize strenuous physical activity. Green might signify the refreshing aspects of the Play Menu. Or perhaps blue could express the fact that play allows you to cool down from the Work Menu's aggressive focus. Purple, since it is often associated with mysticism, could easily be linked with the Self-Awareness Menu. And if you use furniture polish with a lemon scent, yellow would of course be the natural choice for the Cycles Menu!

Be spontaneous in your choices; don't deliberate for long. The reason that we recommend that you use six colors instead of five is so that there will still be *some* element of choice left when you have come to the last menu that needs a color match. It is important that there be at least a tenuous connection between menu and color, even if it is nothing more than liking one of the two remaining colors better than the other. Once all of the color associations have been made, you should rewrite the list of menus in the left column of the next page in your notebook, with its identifying color in the right column. You may then tear out the page on which you worked out these matches and throw it away. Here is Kurt's list of menus and color associations, by way of example.

FIGURE 5

MENU B—Physical Focus	RED
MENU C—Self-Awareness	BLUE
MENU D—Work	YELLOW
MENU E—Play	GREEN
MENU F—Cycles	ORANGE

The remainder of the exercise is best undertaken at the end of each day. Just before you retire, take your notebook in hand and write the date on the top line of a fresh page. Then write the letter names of Menus B through F in the left column with several lines between letters. Think back over what you accomplished in the course of the day. On the same line as the letter name, mark a slash just to the left of the center line for each time slot dedicated to the menu in question. Then list as briefly as possible which activities you chose each time you drew from that menu in the right column. If you find it difficult to recall exactly what you did, then carry your notebook with you during the day and make the slashes as you enter each dedicated time slot.

You should not count menus that you have nestled within, or attached to, others. On the other hand, you may make note of anytime you have used either the quick-shift or subordination technique. In the case of the latter, mark a slash for both of the menus involved. If a Menu G surprise has shifted you from one menu into another, count both.

After you have finished marking slashes for each menu, add them up to see which menu has received the most attention. At the top of the page, across from the date, write the color associated with the predominant menu. (For an example of this procedure, see Figure 6.) As you conclude the exercise, tell yourself "This is what a ——— Menu day feels like," depending on the predominant menu. Then close your eyes and run through your memories of the day's activities while pretending to be looking through glasses tinted with the predominant menu's color. This will help you become aware of the feeling tone of a day colored by that menu.

Ten days are required for this exercise—two for each menu. They don't have to be consecutive. It will be fairly easy to identify the Work Menu's feeling tone, because of the large number of days in which that coloration predominates. In order to become aware of the feeling tones of days on which the other menus predominate, you may have to use nonworkdays. Decide in advance that you will allow a particular menu to predominate on a particular day, and then dedicate as many time slots to activities from that menu as you can. Make sure that you are consistently meeting the Once-a-Day Requirement, or the only feeling tone you will come up with is exhaustion. Also, try to avoid pursuing activities from the same menu during more than two consecutive dedicated time slots. Even if you have collected only one slash more for the menu you want to predominate than for one or more of the others, the day will still be colored by that menu enough for you to become aware of its feeling tone. It is entirely possible that you may get to the end of a day and discover that two or more menus have exactly the same number of slashes next to them. For now, do not count such days as a part of your exercise. These *blended feeling tones* will become important later.

The last part of the exercise requires that you write a phrase or two that describes how the feeling tones of each of the nonwork menus differs from the Work Menu. You might find that you feel powerful or strong on days colored by the Physical Focus Menu, quiet and inward on days colored by the Self-Awareness Menu, focused and productive on Work Menu days, spontaneous and carefree on Play Menu days, and methodical and pragmatic on Cycles Menu days. These are just a few hints to get you started with identifying your own personal feeling tones. If you come up with negative

FIGURE 6

September 13	YELLOW
MENU B /	massage
	steam room
MENU C /	dream interpretation
MENU D ⵌ /	work on poetry
	chat with agent
	book work (4)
MENU E ////	listening to music (3)
	sketching at the
	art museum
MENU F /	chat with Mom /
	pay bills

NOTE:

[a] On this day I used the subordination technique to combine the Work and Self-Awareness menus in a single dedicated time slot: I had my word processor print up several chapters of this book while in another room I devoted the main part of my attention to interpreting the previous night's dreams.

words to describe how you feel, then something has gone wrong. Chances are that you are operating out of energy debit because of having neglected the Once-a-Day Requirement. After you have written these descriptive phrases you may move on to the next exercise.

EXERCISE FIVE
Release from Routine

If every day seems more or less the same to you, then the problem may be that you are allowing one menu to screen out impulses from the other menus. The purpose of this exercise is to help you play with experiential coloring so that you can make your days as much *unlike* each other as possible. As you release yourself from routine in this fashion, you will no longer dread the succession of days as endlessly dreary. Rather, you will awaken with feelings of eager anticipation, ready to throw yourself into realizing the day's endless possibilities.

This exercise concentrates on bringing greater variety into the workday. It will require about five workdays to complete. This time we recommend that as many of them be consecutive as possible. On the first day, all you need do is allow the Work Menu to predominate, while making sure to act on at least one impulse from the other menus. You will also want to dedicate more than one time slot to another menu in order to ensure maximum life-force availability. But be sure that you do not allow any other menu to equal or exceed the number of time slots dedicated to work. At the end of this day, write the color associated with the Work Menu at the top of the page.

For the next four days, choose a different menu each day, and dedicate the same number of time slots to it as to work—while continuing to apply the Once-a-Day Requirement. This creates a blended feeling tone for the day. If, for example, work has been assigned the color red and cycles the color orange, at the end of a day during which you have spent an equal number of time slots dedicated to the Work and Cycles menus, you will write "red/orange" at the top of the page.

The point of this exercise is not so much to be able to differentiate between blended feeling tones as to demonstrate how you can vary the experiential coloration of every single workday. Whenever workdays begin to seem endlessly the same, you may want to do the exercise again in order to break up your routine.

EXERCISE SIX
Blended Feeling Tones

There is no set number of days required for this exercise. You may do it anytime after you have completed the previous exercise and for as long as you wish. It is an excellent way to maintain an impulsive lifestyle indefinitely. Also, if you ever find yourself lapsing back into routine after having lived impulsively for a while, this exercise is a good way to return you to an impulsive lifestyle.

Continue to outline the impulsive shape of each day in your notebook. On nonworkdays you may wish to experiment with allowing two menus other than the Work Menu to predominate equally. Once again, write the two colors associated with those menus at the top of the page. There are ten possible feeling tones to experiment with when you allow two menus to predominate. If you wish, you may use Figure 7 to select menu pairings in advance.

FIGURE 7

B + C B + D B + E B + F	C + D C + E C + F	D + E D + F	E + F

You may also blend feeling tones by dedicating equal numbers of time slots to each of three different menus. Once again, there are ten possibilities, as shown in Figure 8.

FIGURE 8

B + C + D	C + D + E	D + E + F
B + C + E	C + D + F	
B + C + F	C + E + F	
B + D + E		
B + D + F		
B + E + F		

And of course, you could also dedicate equal numbers of time slots to four different menus. In this case there are five possibilities, as shown in Figure 9.

FIGURE 9

B + C + D + E	C + D + E + F
B + C + D + F	
B + C + E + F	
B + D + E + F	

If you consider that there are five possible feeling tones when only one menu predominates and only one possible feeling tone when time slots have been dedicated to all five menus equally, then there is a total of thirty-one different feeling tones. That's enough that if you were to try a different one every day, it would be a whole month before you repeated yourself. Once you have completed this exercise it may be hard for you to believe you could ever have perceived the progression of days as endlessly the same!

You might want to copy these charts into your notebook and check off each feeling tone as you have experienced it. That way you can be sure to cover them all if you wish. It is not necessary that you be able to describe the differences between these blended feeling tones in words.

EXERCISE SEVEN
Over- and Undervalued Activities

By now, you have collected quite a bit of material about the impulsive structure of your days. We recommend that you compare these records with the menus themselves in order to discover which activities or menus you tend to over- or undervalue. You cannot live a truly impulsive lifestyle without reminding yourself from time to time that all menus and activities must be valued equally.

So that you don't have to keep flipping back and forth between the pages of your notebook, you may want to photocopy the menus. Then mark a slash next to every activity listed on the menus that also appears in the right-hand column of your daily record. By the time you have finished, it will be abundantly clear which activities you tend to favor and which you neglect. Chances are that the neglected possibilities have not been valued as much as the overabundant ones—unless they are simply out of season or are Cycles Menu activities that need only be done infrequently, such as getting the piano tuned. Finally, tally the number of slashes you have collected on each menu. Add these figures together and divide the total by five. Compare the number of impulses per menu with this average. If you are living a truly impulsive lifestyle, no single menu will be too far above or below the mean. Furthermore, if one is very high compared to the mean, then this menu is screening out impulses from the others.

All you have to do in order to combat this kind of impulse screening is to keep in mind which activities you tend to overvalue. Whenever you find yourself thinking about undertaking one of these activities, check to see if a genuine impulse toward it exists. If you are trying to persuade yourself that this is something you *should* be doing, then there is no impulsive backing from the soul.

Also keep the undervalued or neglected activities in mind. Whenever you find yourself thinking about one of them *for any reason,* the soul is probably broadcasting an impulse for you to pursue it. This is especially true if your thoughts express themselves in either of the following manners: "Gee, it's been a long time since I did thus and so," or "It's a shame that I never have time to do such and such."

EXERCISE EIGHT
Menu G Vehicles

The current exercise may be performed by itself, or in tandem with Exercise Four, Five, or Six. Its purpose is to aid you in becoming aware of the energy surge that results from pursuing a Menu G impulse. It will also help you release the vehicles whereby surprises come into your life from the effects of emotional blacklisting. Whenever you refuse to pursue a Menu G impulse because of annoyance at the interruption it causes, the vehicle can no longer convey further Menu G experiences to you. If your life seems to be devoid of adventure, the problem may be that the usual vehicles have become unavailable in this fashion.

As you conduct your experience surveys at the end of each day, write a plus sign next to the color whenever a Menu G surprise has occurred. This symbolizes the state we call *energy credit.* Whenever you allow yourself to pursue a Menu G impulse, you will feel highly energized—even elated—because of the energy surge from the soul. This energy surge raises the levels of life force available to all menus to equal or exceed their levels upon awakening. You are likely to have a highly creative and productive day as a result. If no Menu G experience has occurred and if you feel a satisfied tiredness, then, next to the color, place a zero for the energy-neutral state. If you feel deeply dissatisfied with what you have accomplished during the day and if you also feel exhausted or stressed out, then, next to the color, write a minus sign for energy debit. The slashes you have been recording for the number of time slots dedicated to each menu will tell you if the problem has been a failure to apply the Once-a-Day Requirement. If, however, you have indeed pursued one impulse from each of the Menus B through F on that day, then some other type of life-force mismanagement has been responsible. You may want to think back over the day to see if you violated any of the other principles of efficient life-force usage. If not, chances are that the problem originated in your not having arisen with the impulse to awaken. It is possible to experience a Menu G energy surge and still feel exhausted at the end of the day—especially if you neglected to pursue any impulses at all from one or more of the menus. In this case, write a plus-or-minus sign (±) at the top of the page. (In the case of the example given in Figure 6, there were no Menu G experiences and no instances of mismanaged life force. The rating would therefore be "energy neutral." Kurt would then have written "Yellow 0" at the top of the page.)

A Menu G impulse is *always* accompanied by an energy surge. Yet resistance to releasing yourself from whatever you have been doing can desensitize you to it. This will be equally true when you refuse the opportunity for adventure outright as when you go along with it reluctantly. *Always* award a rating of "energy credit" to a day in which anything unusual has occurred, even when you may not have felt the energy surge. Wondering why you didn't notice anything will automatically make you more sensitive to the next surge, or at least to the grumblings that have been causing you not to perceive such surges all along. Eventually you will come to recognize these life-force infusions even when the soul's redirective measures are minor in degree and gentle in persuasion.

For the next part of the exercise you will need a second notebook. This will serve as a "Menu G journal." It need not be a stenographer's pad. The first entry will be a list of the several varieties of Menu G experiences: synchronicities, coincidences, unusual occurrences, unexpected happenings, magical and miraculous events. Head the next page "Menu G Vehicles," but leave it blank for now. Skip over the next several pages to make ample room for this list. Then begin your journal with a dated entry that describes the latest Menu G surprise. The description need not be an elaborate one—just enough that in looking over the journal later you will be able to recognize and remember it. After you have written this description, determine the nature of the Menu G vehicle involved and write it on the "Vehicles" page. If the surprise was a phone call from an old friend you haven't seen in years who just happens to be passing through town and wants to have lunch, then the vehicle is the telephone call. (The two Menu G experiences that Kurt describes at the end of Chapter 9 can serve as examples of Menu G journal entries. In the first case, the vehicle was a near accident; in the second, it was an encounter with a stranger.)

At first you may find that you make entries in your Menu G journal rather sporadically. But as you become used to the idea of following impulses in every area of life, you will also become more comfortable with allowing yourself to be interrupted by adventures emanating from the Surprise Menu. The average length of time between entries will diminish until you have at least one adventure every single day. By this time, your list of vehicles should encompass nearly every situation in which you characteristically find yourself. These situations may be quite ordinary in themselves. Yet the more you become aware of the extraordinary possibilities inherent within even the most mundane aspects of your daily life, the more magical and adventuresome your life will seem.

PART FOUR

SPECIAL APPLICATIONS

CHAPTER 20

Strategies for the Office

This chapter explains how to get through an eight-hour workday using the menus to ensure maximum productivity and minimum wear and tear on the body. The first step is to analyze the day in terms of uncommitted time. Obviously, the eight hours of the workday will be primarily committed to the Work Menu. Usually that period will be broken up by a lunch hour and possibly a couple of other breaks of perhaps twenty minutes each. There will be an uncommitted period before you arrive at work. It may consist of several dedicated time slots following the impulse to awaken. After work there will be another uncommitted period, lasting until the impulse to sleep has manifested itself and you retire for the night. The second step is to see how you can use these two uncommitted periods to satisfy the Once-a-Day Requirement with activities from menus other than Work.

Several important things need to be accomplished in the early morning. You'll probably want to eat breakfast and may need to shower, shampoo, dry your hair, shave or apply makeup, brush your teeth, and get dressed. Furthermore, some kind of commute may be involved in getting you to your place of employment. The more time slots you are able to dedicate to menus other than Work before you arrive there, the greater the amount of energy available for work.

When you fulfill the Once-a-Day Requirement for a particular menu early in the morning, that menu's reserve tank has been tapped. The averaging-out process that takes place every time you shift menus can replenish the Work Menu again and again.

The number of time slots that you could dedicate to prework activities from other menus depends on how much time you have available between arising with the impulse to awaken and arriving at work. If you don't force yourself to sleep until the last moment possible, there will probably be time for several menus.

A good way of looking at the time available before work is to assume that there will be the equivalent of three dedicated time slots. One will be dedicated to the Cycles Menu, as you prepare your self-image for work. Another comprises the commute to work, within which certain kinds of Play or Self-Awareness activities could be pursued. The third time slot will be a sort of free period, within which you could choose to pursue activities from any menu *except* Work. You should vary what you do during this free period each day. Remember that mealtimes have their own special state of consciousness that flows easily into any one of the menus afterward. So breakfast will not really comprise a time slot of its own.

If you would like to get some exercise during the free period, a good way to go about it is to drink a glass of juice immediately upon arising and then do some gentle stretches. Yoga is ideal. Following this period of stretching, you could go running, lift weights, or do any of the other activities on the Physical Focus Menu. The purpose of the stretching is to begin to oxygenate the muscles and to feed them with the juice. In this way, you will be unlikely to hurt yourself during the more-strenuous exercise that comes later. Exercising immediately after having eaten a large breakfast is usually not a good idea, since solid food takes a longer time than juice to become available to the muscles. If you plan to exercise more extensively later in the day, then the period of stretching alone will be sufficient. If you are able to leave at least an hour after breakfast before undertaking more-strenuous exercise—and still get to work on time—then stretching immediately upon rising will not be necessary. Always warm up slowly, so as not to damage the body.

It is essential that you eat breakfast at some point after you have arisen—enough food to digest the dream experiences of the night and to fuel the morning's activities. Eating the same foods every day will guarantee the monotony of the upcoming workday. To apply creativity to the satisfaction of this need demonstrates your willingness to apply creativity to the impulsive shaping of your day. The soul will certainly respond.

Skipping breakfast is not a good idea. The emotional work accomplished during the sleep period needs to be digested in order to feed you. Skipping breakfast not only delays this process but causes it to become tangled up with the various concerns of the morning's first work periods. The result is a diffusion or dispersion of that emotional work, requiring that it be run through again the next night. Fatigue and weariness during the morning hours, plus sleep that doesn't refresh, will result. Skipping breakfast causes you to enter an endless loop of repetition: each day brings up the same set of lessons that are completed in the sleep state, ignored upon awakening, and then confronted yet again the next night. Furthermore, not eating when there is need creates rifts between you and your body and soul. Confusion, frustration, and the tendencies to hurry, rush, worry, and express abrasiveness, irritability, and moodiness will follow. Making yourself sleep longer to compensate for fatigue will complicate matters further with impulsive logjams. For these reasons, not eating breakfast and getting more sleep than you need are the primary causes of friction between coworkers.

If you have recalled any dreams upon awakening, this should be considered an impulse to record and interpret them. Try to capture these often fleeting images immediately upon awakening. That glass of juice can also be helpful here. As the brain is fed with the blood sugars derived from it, an increasing clarity of thought will help you remember your dreams better. It is not essential that you write them out in detail right away; just make some notes for later. Be sure to write down enough that your memory will be jogged.

You could dedicate a prework time slot to the Self-Awareness Menu by spending time with your dream journal. Or you could think about what the night's dreams mean while doing other things—exercising, preparing breakfast, or taking a shower. In this way, you can use the subordination technique on the Self-Awareness Menu. The commute to work could also provide an opportunity to think about your dreams.

If you are eating breakfast with a partner or a friend, dreams could become the topic of conversation. If you are able to arrive at some sense of what they mean, then you have fulfilled the self-awareness requirement for the day. It doesn't matter whether you accomplish this by writing, thinking, or talking. Just try to avoid answering the question "What does it mean?" with the summary dismissal "I have no idea." Even if you have very little knowledge of the mechanics of dream interpretation, the dream will have elicited some feeling upon your awakening. Write, think, or speak about how it makes you feel. Free-associate with the recent events of your waking life to come up with an emotional match. These approaches may not yield the totality of the dream's message, but they will at least acknowledge the relevance of the dream. This will encourage the soul, during the next night's dreams, to come up with another set of images that will possibly be more accessible to interpretation. If you are wrong, these dreams will offer a correction.

The impulse to awaken will generally ensure that you have sufficient time for this activity before you leave for work, while the dreams are still fresh. The soul will make sure that you are not overburdened with more dreams than you have time for. Of course, you could always address them later in the day if there are other things that must be done before leaving for work.

Reading the morning paper at the breakfast table can provide you with a prework Play Menu activity. But just because the paper arrives each morning on your doorstep doesn't mean you have to read it right away. The news will be just as interesting during your lunch break or after work.

These recommendations on how to structure your prework hours impulsively must not become a routine. Several time slots will be available, and these are merely suggestions for how you could fill them beneficially. Since neither exercising nor writing down your dreams—nor reading the newspaper, for that matter—are "required" by the soul before you go to work, you could do a different one during each morning's free period, shifting the others to the postwork hours. Of course, you could pursue a genuine impulse from *any* menu during this time. Just stay away from the Work Menu until you actually arrive at your place of employment.

At some point before you leave home for work, you will probably dedicate a time slot to the Cycles Menu activities of showering, shampooing, drying your hair, shaving or applying makeup, brushing your teeth, and getting dressed. Try not to think about work at all during this period. Meditate instead on the growth that has been accomplished since you did these same things a day earlier. There is nothing wrong with thinking about things that happened at work the day before, especially interactions with coworkers. But do try to avoid furthering work projects in your mind during this period. Your life consists of much more than what you do at work. And the Cycles Menu is your opportunity to integrate your awarenesses of how both work and nonwork activities have contributed to your growth.

While showering, cleanse your mind of any of yesterday's experiences that may have been unpleasant or difficult, thereby creating a tabula rasa upon which the new day can record its uniqueness. While brushing your teeth, tune up your smile for the world, releasing any vestiges of a bad mood possibly left over from the day before. While shaving, speculate on the positive growth that the previous day brought: how is it that you are not a day older but a day wiser? While applying makeup or getting dressed, consider how to match colors with moods: perhaps to enhance the good feeling with which you have awakened, perhaps to incite you to action, perhaps to attract adventure.

How you dress can actually shape the impulsive content of your day. The choice to wear the same clothes—either in ensemble or in part—will indicate an intention to carry over some aspect of the previous day into the current one. To wear the same cut and type of clothes every day will ensure that your moods and attitudes, as well as the kind of experiences you draw to yourself, will vary hardly at all. Continually wearing the standard business suit supports continually living from the same set of moods and attitudes. The business suit originated from the intention to maximize productivity through minimizing the possible distraction of adventure—of Menu G. Because this intention promotes routine, it actually causes productivity to break down.

If you dress with the intention of expressing who you are—even if there are certain limitations placed upon you by your employer—then you will draw to yourself experiences that support who you are. You will be much more satisfied with time spent at work than if you dress like everyone else and are treated like everyone else. The creative mixing and matching of the items in your wardrobe declares to the soul that you are willing to apply the same kind of creativity to the impulsive shaping of your day. The soul will respond by supplying you with the appropriate raw material—impulses—and you will rarely be bored.

If you do not feel the impulse to urinate after you have prepared yourself for work, then see if there are any other

Cycles Menu activities that you could do before leaving. When that impulse finally manifests itself, you will have completed the Cycles Menu requirement for the day. The energy reserve available to the Cycles Menu can now support you at work. Just keep in mind that there may be other impulses toward the Cycles Menu later in the day.

Now we come to the commute. If you are able to walk or ride a bicycle to work, then clearly this period allows you to participate in the Physical Focus Menu, both before and after work. More exercise may be required, however, if the walk or ride is brief; your body will let you know with that feeling of heaviness in the limbs we have mentioned.

If you drive, then you might want to listen to the radio or to cassette tapes of music (Play Menu). Don't listen to the same old things over and over again though. This sort of routine will end up encouraging you to think about work, because it doesn't engage enough of your attention.

You might also consider employing the Self-Awareness Menu during this period. There are any number of taped programs in self-improvement for business persons who spend a lot of time on the road. Listening to tapes of channeled entities or of psychic readings you have received are other possibilities. Many books—of both the self-awareness and play types—have been put on tape. These, too, could provide you with an interesting backdrop for your drive.

If you use a form of public transit to get to work, then you will be able to read as you commute. Again, you could choose works that engage the Self-Awareness or the Play Menus. Try not to read anything that has to do with work. Newspapers, self-help books, novels, poetry, and short stories are all possibilities. If it seems likely that you might not be able to sit down while commuting, then carry a portable cassette player or radio with you and listen to tapes or to radio programs. You could alternate between reading and listening to tapes on different days for variety.

If you travel to work with a buddy, as in a car pool, then the conversation could become a means of satisfying the Once-a-Day Requirement for a particular menu. Make a deal with the person(s) you are with that you will not talk about work at all. Talk instead about special interests, hobbies, or sports (Play Menu); your families or the things you did over the weekend (Cycles Menu); or problems that may have come up in your life (Self-Awareness Menu).

Clearly, all of this will apply equally well to the commute after work. Choose to do things that allow you to look forward to both commutes, no matter how long or how fraught with delays they might be. A tremendous amount of energy that could otherwise be available for both work and after-work activities can be used up in frustration with rush-hour traffic. Ostensibly, you could fulfill both the Play Menu and the Self-Awareness Menu requirements for the day during either of these two commuting periods. Time that had been previously fallow suddenly becomes productive. No longer a necessary evil but a functioning portion of the impulsive structure, these commutes can contribute to, rather than detract from, your overall well-being. Your stress level will fall. There may be other Play or Self-Awareness impulses later in the day, however. You shouldn't ignore them just because you've already drawn from either of these menus once. This will be especially true if the commute is relatively brief. It may not be quite enough to fulfill the Once-a-Day Requirement in this area.

Now we come to the workday itself. Clearly you will want to change your focus of consciousness immediately upon arriving at work, through urination. The eight or so hours of the workday may be broken down into several time slots dedicated to work. If you have a number of different projects going on at once or if your job specifications require several different kinds of work, try to dedicate each Work Menu time slot to something different. This will add variety to your day. Following your impulses about what to do in each of these time slots will also increase your efficiency. Procrastination is a form of arguing against the soul about what truly needs to be done next. If you can avoid it, you should have no trouble making all of your deadlines on time. Because your impulses can tell you when your state of consciousness is best suited to a particular activity, you will never waste time with mental blocks. Furthermore, you'll get done more quickly and thoroughly what needs to be done. You'll be less likely to fall behind.

Remember that it is not a good idea to dedicate more than two successive time slots to the Work Menu. If you experience the impulse to urinate only once between your arrival at work and your lunch hour, then as long as you do something other than work during lunch, you need not worry about becoming fatigued by having strung too many work periods together. If you do tend to urinate more than once, you will want to insert a break of twenty minutes or so between the first and second or second and third periods, using the quick-shift technique. This break could be dedicated to the Cycles Menu activities of catching up on the happenings in your coworker's lives, straightening up your office or desk, checking in with your mate about how his or her day is going, or writing a personal letter to a friend. You might even be able to spend some self-awareness time with your dream-journal. Hanging out and joking around with coworkers would be Play Menu. Through using the menus, your efficiency and productivity will have increased considerably. This is reason enough for your boss to overlook these break periods, whether or not he or she knows or understands why they might be important. But don't sneak around or look guilty while you are engaging in them. This will only draw inappropriate attention to yourself.

Your lunch hour is one of the most important parts of the workday. Aside from the fact that it allows you to satisfy the impulse to eat, it also offers a free period that you can dedicate to a menu other than Work. Guard it jealously against any incursion by the Work Menu. If you must use it for business purposes, try to direct the conversation into other areas as much as you can and still accomplish what the meeting was intended to do. This will allow you to subordinate the Work Menu to some other menu. The Self-Awareness Menu will be involved if you and your client(s) are first getting to know each other. The Play Menu will come up whenever the conversation turns to hobbies, recent movies, or sports happenings. If you are already moderately familiar with aspects of your client's personal life, questions about the well-being of his or her family or recent vacations will bring up the Cycles Menu. Far from obstructing the business that must be accomplished, these diversions will enhance your relationships with clients by putting them on a personal level. Demonstrating that you care about your clients is one of the surest ways to win them over. At the same time, you will be fulfilling the Once-a-Day Requirement for a menu other than Work, because you have subordinated the Work Menu to that other menu. When you use the subordination technique in this way, it is possible to circumvent the principle of life-force dynamics that recommends against dedicating more than two time slots in a row to the same menu. The fact that a menu different from the original one is predominant changes the brain chemistry just enough that the body will not resist. This approach should be used as a stopgap measure only: the body can be very sensitive to moments when the original menu gains the upper hand, and you could suddenly find yourself deeply fatigued.

Lunch with coworkers should be conducted along similar lines. If the conversation turns to certain problematical aspects of the work situation, do some brainstorming about a possible solution rather than just complaining. This would be a self-awareness activity rather than a work activity.

If you eat out alone, have some nonwork reading matter with you. Or prepare a lunch in the morning before you leave home so that you won't have to wait for service at restaurants. In the time remaining after you eat, take a walk in the local park (Physical Focus Menu). Go shopping for clothes (Cycles Menu). Visit a nearby gallery or museum (Play Menu). Browse for interesting novels to read or recordings to buy (Play Menu). If the weather is nice, you might even be able to find a place outdoors to take a twenty-minute nap, in order to clear your mind of the experience you have accumulated up to that point in the day. If you belong to a nearby health club, you could first work out (Physical Focus) and then eat your lunch later. You could also use this time to catch up on your dream journal or to read a book by your favorite channeled entity (Self-Awareness). Follow your impulses. But don't even think about work.

Once you have returned from lunch, the afternoon work periods will be conducted along lines similar to the morning ones. Again it will be important not to allow more than two successive work periods without a break between the second and the third, using the quick-shift technique. If you must work overtime, take another free period similar to the lunch break before you start—with or without dinner, as you prefer. Overtime will become less and less necessary with the increase in efficiency and productivity that comes from following the menus. In fact, because of the nature of the Once-a-Day Requirement, you should dedicate at least one time slot to work every time you have a day off. If not overdone, this will increase both enjoyment and energy availability on days off. But you must also pursue the impulse to awaken, even though you don't have to get up and go to work. Overtime could be greatly reduced with such a practice. There are even offices that run on the plan that as long as you put in your forty hours a week, you can arrange your daily schedule as you please. Clearly this situation would be ideal for following the menus. You could take longer breaks during the workday, dedicating a full flexible time unit to some activity other than work rather than using the quick-shift technique. You might have to stay a little longer at work, but this could put you on the road home at a less-crowded hour. Or perhaps you could come in later. Then you would have the opportunity to pursue a greater number of menus before work. You could also shift some of your work hours to the weekend in order to fulfill the Once-a-Day Requirement.

When you get home at the end of the day, it might be a good idea before you do anything else to take a twenty-minute nap. This will clear out the experience of the day so that you will be able to focus more fully on what the evening has to offer. You won't wind down or wear yourself out too early this way. Your first priority—depending on whether or not the impulse to eat has directed you toward taking supper—will be to engage in activities from any menus that have not yet been touched upon in the course of the day. In this way, you can avoid experiencing energy debit due to not having met the Once-a-Day Requirement. Once you have fulfilled this requirement, anything goes until the impulse to sleep indicates that it is time to go to bed.

In order to guarantee efficiency of life-force usage during the evening, keep the other principles of life-force dynamics in mind. Shift menus as often as possible. And be careful not to dedicate more than two periods in a row to the Play Menu. Endless hours of watching television, for example, is just as stressful as endless hours in the Work Menu. While taking a break from the intensity of work through the Play Menu is certainly important, there are many other impulses that could greatly enrich your life just waiting to be noticed and acted upon during the evening hours. Don't allow an overvaluation of the Play Menu to block them.

We have said that cooking and grocery shopping belong to the Work Menu. If you cook for yourself, you may feel disinclined to prepare an elaborate meal after a long workday. This is understandable: you've already spent quite a bit of time in the Work Menu. You'll feel a lot better if you switch to other menus once you have left work. But you still have to eat.

Several options are available. You can eat out, in which case the Work Menu won't be involved at all. Reading, thinking, or conversing with a friend will determine which menu you have dedicated this time slot to. Or you can prepare a simple supper—anything from a recipe that takes little time at all, to microwaving leftovers or frozen foods. Because of the special blended state of consciousness that prevails during mealtimes, cooking can be attached, nestled, or subordinated to another menu rather easily—as long as the preparations don't take up a full dedicated time slot on their own. You could listen to music while you cook, thus subordinating the Work Menu to the Play Menu. The subject of your thoughts or of conversations with anyone you may share meal preparations with can allow you to subordinate the Work Menu to another one. If you decide to read as you eat, then meal preparation has been attached to the beginning of a Play Menu time slot. Furthermore, if you shop for groceries in the midst of doing other errands, you have nestled the Work Menu within the Cycles Menu.

Any of these techniques will work just as well at breakfast or lunch time—as will eating out. If you prepare a lunch for yourself before you leave home, you could nestle that activity within any of the prework menus.

Cooking elaborately for every one of the three or four meals you eat regularly could easily cause the Work Menu to predominate every single day. To avoid this, you should avail yourself of attaching, nestling, or subordinating one menu to another. You will then be able to vary the experiential coloration of workdays more freely. On weekends or days off, if you want to put the office entirely out of your mind, you can meet the Once-a-Day Requirement through grocery shopping and/or through preparing more elaborate meals. It is essential that such meals take at least one full dedicated time slot to assemble.

If you live with someone who doesn't mind cooking for you, then obviously none of this applies. Still, a new dimension could be added to the relationship if you were to take over the cooking from time to time, perhaps on weekends. Preparing a special meal for a partner is one of the best ways to express gratitude for his or her presence in your life.

C H A P T E R 2 1

Strategies for the Traveler

Vacations are times of leaving behind habit and routine. They often allow people to reestablish a sense of spontaneity in their lives. While living out of impulses may become habitual, when the Menus system has been diligently applied, its very nature prevents habits themselves from forming. It is not a good idea to leave the system behind with all the other concerns of daily living when you go traveling. You will get more enjoyment out of your vacation if you work within the dynamics of life-force flow, because you won't wear yourself out. This means that pursuing the impulse to awaken is essential. It also means that you should continue to meet the Once-a-Day Requirement. It is of the utmost importance, therefore, that you dedicate at least one time slot per day to the Work Menu, even though you are on vacation. Just shift the experiential coloration of the day from one in which the Work Menu predominates to one that emphasizes the Play Menu.

We recommend that as you plan a vacation, you also keep in mind the kinds of activities you can take along from each of the menus. In fact, it might be a good idea to make up a special set of *travel menus.* On the Physical Focus Menu, you should include activities that can be accomplished anywhere, such as yoga or running. Some hotels have health clubs, and many towns have a local YMCA or health club whose facilities you could use. Hiking in the mountains or swimming in the ocean are two possibilities that might be available, depending on the vacation spot you have chosen. If you have children along, strenuous outdoor play might fit the bill. Make up a special Menu B in which you have already thought out the possibilities of exercise that will be available to you. That way it will be easier to perceive impulses toward the Physical Focus Menu while you are away.

You will also want to make up a special Self-Awareness Menu. This might include meditating, writing down and interpreting dreams, and reading a spiritual or self-help book. Again, you should try to come up with activities that are portable.

When it comes to the Work Menu, all you need to do is find a couple of work projects that don't take up much space and that you could devote yourself to once each day. You could also read a book on some topic related to your field.

The Play Menu will always be easiest when you are on vacation. The place you choose will often be full of opportunities for play. It would be a good idea, though, for you to list them on a travel menu. That way it will be easier to perceive genuine impulses toward them. You won't be so likely to overvalue them just because you are on vacation. Do some research to find out what tourist attractions, historical sights, tours, museums, concert series, or shopping opportunities can be found in the area you will be going to. Also keep in mind the kinds of activities that allow you to subordinate the Physical Focus and Play menus to each other, such as sailing, canoeing, or waterskiing. If you are not traveling alone, be flexible with your plans so that you can also accommodate the interests of your partner or your children.

When you travel, the Cycles Menu can involve not only the usual care of self-image but also packing and unpacking, keeping the space you are staying in neat, writing letters or postcards about what you are doing, and keeping a diary of what you have done or thought each day.

The best part of being on vacation is the prevalence of the Surprise Menu. The soul is aware of your greater flexibility in responding to impulses on vacation. It will make every attempt to renew and refresh your ability to perceive and act upon them with all sorts of adventures. This can be true even before you actually arrive at the vacation spot. You might meet someone on the plane or train who would give you hot tips about places to go you hadn't heard of. Or while driving, you could stop at a roadside attraction of some sort.

The higher level of energy and sense of well-being felt upon return from a vacation is directly proportional to how much you abandoned yourself to such surprises. And the key to successful reentry into the world you had left behind when your vacation began is to carry forward this willingness to be guided by your impulses, especially those arising from Menu G. Keeping a log of these surprises as they occur would be an excellent self-awareness exercise. After your return, you could read over what you had written whenever you might need to remind yourself of the soul's magically supportive presence in your life. Yearning for the adventures of a recent vacation can be a powerful means of drawing new ones into your life, even while you are at home.

When you are camping out or backpacking, it may be difficult to carry much more than tent, sleeping bag, clothing, food, and cooking utensils. Yet it is still possible to live out of the menus. Hiking will easily fulfill the Physical Focus Menu requirement. Thinking (if you are alone) or talking (if you are with others) can help you touch upon the other menus. It would also be a good idea to include a dream journal and a novel to read, in order to guarantee time in the Self-Awareness and Play menus. The dream journal could double as a diary—as a Cycles Menu activity. Setting up and breaking camp also belong to the Cycles Menu. And cooking for yourself or others will provide you with opportunities to fulfill the

Work Menu requirement. If you don't mind carrying the extra weight, you may be able to think of other portable activities to bring along for greater variety, such as a field guide to birds, trees, wildflowers, mushrooms, or stars (Play Menu).

Travel menus can also be useful for the business traveler. Since the purpose of the trip will have been defined by the Work Menu, it is important that you find ways of including the other menus in your daily diet of experience. This will be especially true of the business seminar or convention, which often runs unbroken for many hours. Try to get everything you can do from other menus accomplished before things get started. The more menus you are able to put in before the business part of the day begins, the more energy you will have available for the seminar or convention. Arising early with the impulse to awaken will be essential. Also, try to shift into other menus during meal times. Remember that getting to know someone—during a meal, perhaps—is a self-awareness activity. After the seminar or convention is over for the day, you would do better to stay up awhile longer through switching menus than to go to bed right away, no matter how fatigued you may be from the often unavoidable long hours in the Work Menu. Watching television in your hotel room would be one not-too-demanding way of doing this. If you go to bed too early, the impulse to awaken may come so long before breakfast is offered by the local coffee shop that you will be sorely tempted to go back to sleep. That means you will have a rather stressful day.

Business seminars and conventions are set up on the principle that a lot must be accomplished in a very short time. This kind of scheduling may not support the menus system. Time for naps and opportunities to switch to other menus may not be available. Your ability to take in information or effectively engage in wheeling and dealing will suffer accordingly. You will have to ask yourself one question: Is my doing what I have been sent here to do more important than maintaining the integrity of my relationship with the soul? If not, you should take an occasional break to take a nap or switch to another menu. Trust that while you are at the convention, the soul will guide you toward any and all essential business connections, which will take place effortlessly because of Menu G. As you are sitting in a seminar, remember that boredom is an error message from the soul: what you are doing does not match up to what the soul requires of you at that moment. You might want to consider doing something else instead.

We are not advocating shirking responsibilities or goofing off with these suggestions. Impulse-motivated behavior can actually be more "responsible" than so-called responsible behavior, inasmuch as it allows you to be vastly more efficient in all work situations. If anyone questions your choices of action during a seminar or business convention, simply remind them gently that it is hardly possible to learn new sales strategies or pave the way to an important deal when you feel like a zombie and that an hour break here or there ensures maximum concentration and productivity.

A few words about mode of transportation. If you are flying or taking a train or bus, be sure to carry with you a number of things that will allow you to switch back and forth between several menus during the trip. When you are packing and making up your travel menus, keep these activities in mind. With a certain amount of creative thinking, you should be able not only to find enough to keep yourself occupied for the duration of the trip but also fit it all into a single piece of carry-on luggage. Simply having one Self-Awareness, one Work, and one Play menu book, magazine, or tabloid with you, and perhaps some writing utensils for a dream-journal entry, a crossword puzzle, or a Cycles Menu letter might be enough. You could even carry a portable cassette player or radio with you as further Play Menu activities. You may wish to consider positioning yourself in such a way that you will not inconvenience others by making several trips to the rest room. If you are traveling with a partner, your conversation could be a means of touching upon several menus. Or you could play cards or some other game you have brought along. Either before your trip or after it, you should pursue impulses from any of the menus that will not be touched upon by the trip, especially the Physical Focus Menu.

If you are taking a very long flight or train trip and it doesn't seem possible to touch upon the Physical Focus Menu, the following stopgap measure may be used. Buy a magazine or a book about exercise, the workings of the body, or how to improve your participation in such a sport as skiing or tennis. Dedicating a time slot to reading it will allow you to touch upon the Physical Focus Menu. We call this a stopgap measure because it does not address the body's need for stimulating the circulation. Under other circumstances, there is nothing wrong with engaging in such reading as a Physical Focus Menu activity, but you should also dedicate at least one time slot to actual exercise.

The same principles apply to traveling on an ocean liner as to taking a plane or a train—except there may be opportunities for Physical Focus activities such as dancing, swimming in a pool, walking briskly on the deck, or doing stretching exercises, yoga, calisthenics, or sit-ups in your cabin. There may even be exercise facilities available.

If you are driving a long distance by yourself, you will be able to get more miles in without exhaustion if you do a couple of menus before you leave and a couple after you arrive at your motel or final destination and if you make a good number of stops along the way. For example, you could arise with the impulse to awaken, eat breakfast while thinking about your dreams, and then interpret them in your dream journal. After this period in the Self-Awareness Menu, you could do some stretching exercises, yoga, calisthenics or sit-ups in your motel room in order to touch upon the Physical Focus Menu. Then you could shower, shampoo, shave, pack your luggage, and arrange everything in the car (Cycles

Menu). You could even write a postcard or two. If you have arisen with the impulse to awaken, it is possible to get all this accomplished and still be on the road by as early as nine o'clock. Because you now have access to the life-force reserves available to three of the menus, you will have quite a bit of energy available for driving.

While on the road, be sure to stop every time you feel the impulse to urinate, no matter how often. Otherwise you will find yourself growing fatigued and sleepy at the wheel. You could listen to tapes of music or of the spoken word (novels, for example) or to the radio while driving (Play Menu). You could listen to self-awareness tapes. Furthermore, you could dedicate any number of time slots to thinking. Try to come up with solutions to a personal problem by running through a number of possibilities in your mind (Self-Awareness Menu). Or devote some attention to a work project and come up with ways to further it (Work Menu). Plan the fun things you expect to be doing at your destination (Play Menu). Think about the cycle you are just ending, such as what sorts of things have happened since the last business trip or vacation and who you have become as a result. You could even imagine yourself to be writing letters to people close to you about what you are seeing or thinking about along the way (Cycles Menu).

For a time slot dedicated to thinking to count as a means of fulfilling the Once-a-Day Requirement, you must consciously direct your thoughts. Keep them focused as much as possible on the menu you have chosen. Otherwise your mind may just run through old tapes of things you've thought about yourself before—usually negative. If you turn your attention to these tapes and start dismantling them, then you can dedicate a time slot or two specifically to the Self-Awareness Menu. Because of this tendency of the mind to play old tapes—and because they have often become so much a part of the "background chatter" of one's consciousness—it is often difficult to notice them. All too often, thinking consists of long periods of such background chatter interrupted momentarily by a very brief actual thought. Use of thinking to fulfill the Once-a-Day Requirement only works when a sustained effort has been made to ignore or dismantle the background chatter and increase the amount of time spent in real thought.

You will probably find yourself much more capable of driving long distances without fatigue if you dedicate as many time slots as possible to a different menu. So, for example, you could listen to music for two time slots in a row (Play Menu) and then switch to a self-awareness tape. Perhaps by this time you have gotten hungry. Stop at a restaurant along the way, and while you eat, spend some time reading the Work Menu book you have brought along. This will help refresh you so that when you get back on the road, you can return to listening to music for another two dedicated time slots.

Be sure to take a twenty-minute nap at some point. Whenever droopy eyelids signal the presence of the impulse to sleep, it is far better to pull off the road into a rest area, state park, or parking lot and get some shut-eye than to force yourself to stay awake with coffee. If you have stopped at a rest area or state park, you may want to combine your nap with a period of Physical Focus activity. You could take a hike, run through the park, do some calisthenics, or spread a blanket out on the grass and do some yoga or stretching exercises. Getting the circulation going and unkinking parts of the body that have become stiff from being in the same position a long time will greatly relax you and increase your ability to concentrate. You will be able to drive longer distances and to arrive at your destination without being completely worn out.

Kurt often takes a jump rope with him when he drives long distances. It is easy to carry and can be used even when there is not much space for running around. It also provides an excellent way of stimulating the circulation in a short amount of time, allowing him to get back on the road more quickly. Be sensitive to the needs of your body for exercise. You may need more than one such period when you travel—once before you begin, one or more times en route, and once after your arrival.

All these stops we are recommending may seem to interrupt the journey too many times. Whenever you travel alone, you will have to ask yourself which is more important—getting to your destination as fast as possible or arriving without having worn yourself out. In spite of the many stops, if you follow the menus while on the road, you will not only be free of fatigue when you arrive, but you will also be able to drive *at least* as many miles as you would otherwise—and probably more. However, driving between five and six hundred miles a day is about all the body can take and still run efficiently. It is possible to go further if you have a partner to share the driving.

When you have arrived at your destination for the night, the first temptation may be to go to bed right away. We recommend that you switch menus instead. Pick a menu that hasn't been addressed in the course of the day. After all, to avoid complete exhaustion it is essential to meet the Once-a-Day Requirement. But even if you have already touched upon each menu once, it is still a good idea to shift into one that has hasn't been engaged as frequently—the Work Menu, perhaps. Keep switching back and forth between menus until the genuine impulse to sleep has manifested itself. If you go to bed too early, the impulse to awaken will get you up too early. You'll probably go right back to bed. By the time you get up, a good part of the energy that would have been available for the next day's driving or for enjoying your vacation or attending your seminar will have been used up.

Everything that we have said about driving alone applies equally well to driving with a partner—except that you may add conversation to the list of available acitivities. Such conversations should be shaped so as to allow a single menu to predominate. In the meantime, the two of you can take turns driving. The person not driving can take a nap or read while the driver thinks about something or listens to music. So you need not always be interacting with each other in the same menu. Once again, it is important to honor the impulse to urinate whenever it arises for either of you. You should stop even if only one of you feels it. The same is true of the impulse to eat. You could also carry a Frisbee or ball of some sort with you to toss back and forth at a rest area to get the circulation stimulated (Physical Focus Menu).

If you are traveling with a family, you should resign yourself to making frequent stops. When small children have to urinate, they will only make everyone in the car miserable if you try to keep going. Anger doesn't do any good, because their bodies or souls have been responsible; it's not at all a matter of failure of willpower. Trying to keep children busy while on the road also requires making up special travel menus. These will primarily involve play: small bags of toys and games, comic books and other reading matter; games that involve everyone in the car (looking for license plates from every state, for example); singing songs together; reading stories aloud; and the like. Be sure to provide children with plenty of opportunities to stretch their legs at rest areas, parks, or playgrounds (Physical Focus Menu). It will greatly benefit your own cramped-up body if you participate as well. It is a good idea to have a special bag of surprises that you can dole out whenever the children become restive.

When there are several children in a family, the biggest problem will often be that the older children may not have to urinate when the youngest ones do. This is because older children have a greater concentration span. If they pass up an opportunity to go to the bathroom when the youngest children do, they may have to go themselves before the next time the youngest child has to. You must ask yourself if getting to your destination as fast as possible is more important than allowing everyone to enjoy the ride. It is best not to make your children suffer by not stopping again right away. Demonstrating such care and concern for their needs will considerably lighten the atmosphere in the car. They will be less likely to make your life miserable in return by being grumpy and fighting among themselves.

There *is* one way that you can address this problem without making the children suffer: each time you include the entire family in some activity by playing a game or singing or reading aloud, everyone will be in the same state of consciousness. When the child with the shortest attention span can no longer maintain concentration and you stop, everyone will experience the impulse to urinate at more or less the same time. The reason is that you will all be leaving the activity to which the time slot has been dedicated together.

CHAPTER 22

Strategies for the Home

The first step in applying the menus to homemaking is to break down a typical day and analyze it in terms of activities and menus. Such a day may include preparing meals for yourself and your partner, cleaning house, doing laundry, running errands, buying groceries, shopping for clothes, paying bills, balancing the checkbook, and the like. All of these things are either Cycles Menu or Work Menu activities.

Care and feeding of pets will also belong to the Work Menu, as an aspect of service to all life. Houseplants or yards, on the other hand, are a part of your environment. Anything you do that concerns them, such as watering or cutting the lawn, belongs to the Cycles Menu. These activities, too, allow you to fulfill service to all life.

Anything you do exclusively for the benefit of your partner belongs to the Work Menu, such as buying clothes for him or her. If you are buying clothes for yourself at the same time, then you have subordinated the Work Menu to the Cycles Menu.

It should be clear that just about everything involved in running a household comes from either the Work Menu or the Cycles Menu. Because of the Once-a-Day Requirement, you'll need to make time for pursuing activities from the other three menus: Physical Focus, Self-Awareness, and Play.

This will be even more true if you have a full- or part-time job, since you will then be dedicating a certain number of time slots to the Work Menu, in addition to the other Work or Cycles slots. All you need do is apply the five principles of life-force dynamics, and you'll have no trouble getting through the day in the most productive and efficient manner possible.

If you have chosen to have a family, things become a bit more complex. Again, the Work and Cycles menus will tend to predominate. Doing things exclusively for the benefit of your children, such as bathing them or driving them to and from doctor's appointments or extracurricular activities, belongs to the Work Menu.

There will always be a number of needs on the part of your partner or your children that may seem to interfere with the satisfaction of your own. It does no good to resent having surrounded yourself with a family, since this may be part of your life purpose. You will drag yourself down with such resentment—which wastes a tremendous amount of life force—unless you find, or make time for, yourself alone. So what you should be looking for as you analyze the structure of your day are the periods of time alone in which you can do the things that you enjoy or that will further your own growth. This will be just as true of the single parent or the divorced one who has the children only on weekends as of the mother and father of the traditional nuclear family.

The presence of children in your life requires that you be more or less constantly on hand to satisfy their needs. You must design your menus not only so that this will be possible but also so that you can accomplish the things you need to do for yourself. There is no reason for you to make yourself a martyr to your children. Some careful planning will allow you to balance your time between them and yourself. The key to avoiding such martyrdom is to be aware of which of your menu activities *require* aloneness to be accomplished and which could admit the presence of children. Also, you will need to be aware of the conditions under which you are most likely to be alone. If the child is very young and has not yet gone off to school, then the frequent and sometimes extended nap periods become opportunities for solitary activities. If the child has gone to school, then those hours, as well as any that the child devotes to extracurricular activities, become available for the satisfaction of your personal needs. Although having children with you while running errands can sometimes be an annoyance, it is more possible to accomplish those errands in their company than to meditate. We recommend that you analyze your menus from this standpoint and mark all of the activities that require solitude.

Another way to create time alone for yourself is to find activities within which children can absorb themselves completely for extended periods. Television or video movies can be useful for this purpose. So can toys, games, building blocks, crafts-type projects, coloring books, and the like. Developing a large store of such activities—and keeping some surprises on hand for rainy days, when children tend to get bored easily—can keep them out of your hair. If children insist on "helping" you, give them something to do that seems important but will not distract you from what you are doing—even if it doesn't really need to be done. Freely giving a child the opportunity to feel that his or her presence somehow contributes to the well-being of an adult will cause him or her to stop pestering.

Persons with a very young child at home may feel that their Physical Focus Menus have been restricted. They may not be able to leave the house to go running, for example. Some health clubs have a space set aside for child care. There is also the possibility of having an exercise bicycle at home to use during a child's nap periods. Furthermore, exercise programs are shown on some television stations and can be bought on audio or video cassette. You may find that a child's needs may not always leave you free at the same time every day for a television show, so the cassettes could be especially useful. You could vary these prerecorded programs so as to enrich your Physical Focus Menu. Other possibilities include yoga or having a set of weights or other home exercise equipment available. There are all sorts of books with fully illustrated exercise programs. The important thing about any type of exercise practiced alone is not to overdo it. If at all possible, you should periodically place yourself in a position to be corrected by an instructor so that you will not do subtle damage to yourself through incorrect form. During some hours of each day your partner may be home, and this could give you the freedom to go outside for a bicycle ride, a run, a brisk walk, or a visit to your health club.

Pushing a stroller or baby carriage or carrying a child in a sling while taking a walk can be considered Menu B activities. The same thing will be true of walking a dog. Make sure to focus strongly on your presence within the body so that proper posture and use of the musculature never leaves your mind. In this way, you become much less likely to cause damage to the body, especially the lower back. If there is any degree of discomfort, then make some adjustments. Slow down. Realign yourself within the body. Try several different approaches to the posture or use of the muscles. If the discomfort continues, cease practicing this activity. The body is trying to let you know that it is damaging.

The Play Menu will require some careful handling. You should divide the activities listed there into two categories: adult play and child play. Adult play will consist of things such as reading novels, attending concerts, going out to movies, or watching television shows or video movies inappropriate for children. Child play will include activities you can enjoy sharing with your children. Remember that the structure of play indicates that a life situation has been isolated and taken out of context so as to pose a challenge that must be overcome through strategy development. Playing games increases flexibility of consciousness in dealing with real-life situations. If you play a variety of games to which you are impulsively drawn, you will be exercising a variety of mental faculties against the possibility of their becoming necessary in real life. If a game bores you, then you have no need of exercising the mental faculties it develops. If your children can't grasp the rules of a game, it is too early for them to grapple with the faculties involved. In terms of flexibility of consciousness, some games are better suited to children than to adults and vice versa. But many of the perennial favorites will be equally playable and absorbing to both.

Be patient with your children as they learn to play games that pose intellectual challenges, such as chess. Since they are just beginning to develop certain of their mental faculties, some awkwardness is to be expected. You, however, will be trying to keep these same mental faculties from atrophying. If a child isn't given an opportunity to win sometimes, he or she will become frustrated and give up. But seeing that you win somewhat more often will challenge him or her to develop better strategies. Teaching a game is much more than simply going over the rules. At subtle levels you will also be teaching a child how to become a more fully realized human being as well. Eventually he or she will have grown to the point of challenging you. At this point, it is just as important that *you* not give up out of frustration if the child begins to win more often. This means that you are stuck in old mental strategies that may no longer be effectual in real life as well. Keep playing in order to develop new ones.

Children may seem relentless in their demands for attention and affection. This is because they are following their impulses, which are equally relentless. At one time or another, many parents view their children as constantly impending threats of interruption of "more important" tasks. Moments of offering undivided attention to the child are rare. Children sense this abstractedness. And because they do not understand the adult concerns that have caused it, they fear that there might be something wrong with them, that they are somehow unworthy of attention and affection, and that their parents don't love them. They therefore redouble their efforts at winning back the attention and affection they feel has been denied them. In short, they become nuisances.

There are two ways to remedy this situation. The first is simply to maintain a more or less constant awareness of the presence of your children in your life—no matter what you are doing. Never put them completely out of mind for any reason. Your loving thoughts are like a lifeline to them, which they sense telepathically. One sure way to call them to your side is to cut off such thoughts. In fact, you may wish to try the following experiment to prove to yourself the telepathic nature of this bond. (It will work best for children between the ages of three and nine.) Go into a room some distance from where one of your children happens to be. Take up a project that demands quite a bit of concentration. Tell yourself that you don't want to be interrupted and imagine pushing the child out of your mind. It won't take long for him or her to appear. Try the same thing on another occasion, but instead of thinking about not wanting to be interrupted, see if you can maintain a warm and loving connection to your child by thinking of him or her occasionally as you work. Keep an image of the child playing happily in your mind and mentally say that you love him or her from time to time. You'll be much more likely to be uninterrupted this way.

The second way to prevent children from becoming nuisances is for each parent—or both together—to dedicate at least one time slot per day to giving the child undivided attention and uncompromised affection. If there is more than one child, spending time with all of them at once is certainly acceptable. Be sensitive to the children's needs, however. Older children will often benefit more from a one-on-one involvement with adults—and will also require such attention less often than younger ones. There is no need for you to give up all your free time for the sake of your children.

However, it is just as much a part of your life purpose to serve them as to serve your own needs for self-fulfillment.

In order to keep from being bored with this period spent with your children, because it may seem to have little to do with your usual matters of concern, you will have to enter the child's world. Try to participate with the child in the wonder of a world full of so much freshness of possibility. In so doing, you will reconnect with your own playful, impulsive spontaneity. There will be an increased ability to sense your children's needs and how to satisfy them. The children themselves will become less constantly demanding—more like happy puppies that are content to play by themselves all day long than like bawling brats that never seem to shut up. Furthermore, they will no longer resort to doing bad things simply because this is the only way to get an adult's undivided attention.

All negligent, self-destructive, or ill-meaning behavior in a child has its origins in feeling unloved. The degree of intensity of problematic behavior is directly proportional to how unloved the child feels. You may "know" that you love a child, but if you are unable to keep this love from being alloyed with worry about unrelated things during time spent together, he or she will feel unloved to the extent that you are abstracted.

Keep in mind that children need to develop relationships with each parent individually. Both parents should try to find time to be with them alone. Children also need to sense the supportive network of the family surrounding and nurturing them. So some activities that involve everyone at once are also important. Without doing things as a whole family from time to time, a child can feel unprotected from the unknowns of the outside world, which he or she may not be ready to face. It is the terror of these unknowns, which comes up whenever parents seem too absorbed in them to provide attention and affection, that actually causes disruptive behavior.

Children of broken marriages will often be high-strung and insecure as a result of feeling that they are personally responsible for the absence of their father or mother. This may cause them to cling to the parent they live with. They will be extremely sensitive to parental abstraction. The more capable a single or divorced parent is of projecting love mentally to a child, even while engaged in the most-demanding activities, the less likely the child will be to create disturbances.

To play with a child properly during your time together may mean giving up all pretense of being an adult. After all, that's what most of adulthood is—a pretense of "being responsible" made for the benefit of parents, bosses, and society in general. In this sense, being responsible means not following impulses—which means not becoming who you truly are for the sake of gaining the approval of others. This is the root of the conspiracy against discovering your life purpose that we mentioned toward the beginning of this book. Learn to play again as a child plays, with irrepressible imagination and wild abandon, and you will have done much to overcome hesitation about becoming yourself in other areas.

If you devote one full dedicated time slot to play with your children each and every day, without fail and with undivided attention, they will stop nagging you. When they pester you to play, it is usually because you are ignoring your own impulses toward the Play Menu. You may be afraid fully to engage in such play, which can often become quite rambunctious, because of what other adults might think of you. It is never appropriate to live your life out of what you think other people are thinking about you—unless you are a highly skilled telepath. Besides, they're probably too busy worrying about what you think about them to have passed judgment on you. Such thoughts only bring up your own fears about social acceptance. Other adults are much more likely to watch you playing with your children and feel guilty that they are not so free with their own time and energy. They might be envious of what a good parent you are for doing what they tell themselves they're too busy to do. And they will certainly yearn for the joy and exuberance that shines forth from your face in the midst of such activities. Don't play to humor your kids, however. They will resent this just as much as you. Select activities that you can both enjoy.

As children grow older, they will eventually prefer to play with other children of their own age. But there will often be times when their playmates are not available, such as vacations, rainy days, and sick days. So keep the possibility of playing with them yourself for such times. A sick child will heal faster when you provide him or her with such attention. As a matter of fact, susceptibility to illness in children is often the result of the child's doubting his or her parents' love.

If a child knows that you have reserved some time for play every day, he or she will look forward to that time all day long. As long as you are absolutely dependable with it, you have a certain advantage. You can determine when it will be, and you can let your child know that he or she must not disturb you for a certain period of time while you get some things from another menu accomplished first. The child will so look forward to the play period that he or she will do everything in his or her power to be good—for fear that you might renege on your promise. However, this technique will only work if you *never* renege.

Racing or tumbling about with a child is often called play. In the context of the menus, however, it could just as well be on the Physical Focus Menu. Keep in mind that the more strenuously you involve yourself in such activities, the better the exercise you are getting. Also keep in mind that this kind of strenuousness will tend to use up some of the excess energy of the child, so that naps or bedtime will be more willingly accepted as necessary. Naps may also last longer, which would then give you more leeway for solitary activities. All of this will also be true of playing with a dog.

Putting younger children to bed to get them out of the way

will often lead to resistance on their part. You're afraid that they'll distract you from whatever it is you would rather be doing, such as attending to guests. But their protestations about being put to bed will probably distract you just as much as their presence. The problem is that they are telepathically picking up that they are not wanted, and once again they feel unloved. Furthermore, the impulse to sleep may not yet have manifested itself for them. Forcing them to deny their own impulsive schedules will cause much frustration and confusion. The kind of inability to recognize needs or respond to impulses that most adults feel will be the inevitable result. It would be much better to let them see what it is you wish to exclude them from so that they will eventually become bored and then can easily be put to bed.

It is certainly possible to carry on an intelligent conversation with other adults while petting a dog. In certain situations it can be useful to think of the child in this manner. Holding and stroking the child can often keep him or her relatively quiet. As far as going to bed is concerned, it is always best to wait until the genuine impulse to sleep is clearly apparent than to enforce an arbitrary bedtime.

Another parental decision that can lead to problems in later life has to do with the child's impulse to awaken. If you have had difficulty breaking down the belief that you require eight hours of continuous sleep to function normally, the reason is that your parents ingrained that belief in you when you were very young. In all probability there was a period in your life when you were punished for waking up your parents before they had had what they felt was sufficient sleep. You may not have actually been struck. But a grumpy parent's harsh words telling you to go back to bed when you were full of exuberant eagerness to begin a new day—and the interpretation of parental annoyance as lack of love—were far worse than any corporal punishment could have been. In a way, you were told that you were lovable only if you denied yourself this early-morning exuberance and waited until your parents had arisen first. Sleeping late became a kind of symbol of loving and taking care of yourself, even as it robbed you of essential energy to get through the day. Furthermore, when you first began to deny the impulsive imperative to awaken, you probably went through a period of bed-wetting. The conscious mind, terrified of punishment, was simply suppressing the impulse to urinate that naturally accompanies awakening. The body, however, responded to its genuine need anyway.

When you were an infant, you were likely to awaken your parents at any hour of the night with your needs. They had no power to stop you from doing so, no matter how miserable they might have felt in the morning. Once they could begin to control your behavior with words or punishment, however, one of the first things they probably did was to compensate for your earlier interruption of their sleep patterns by enforcing their own unnatural schedule on you—the same one forced upon them by their parents, for the same reason. The relationship with the soul begins to deteriorate when the impulse to awaken is ignored. It becomes less easy to sense other impulses when the first one of the day has been denied. And so, year after year, life would become less and less wonderful and ever more stressful and confusing. Meanwhile, the body's natural process of maturing would become greatly distorted as aging. Why pass on this "gift" of your parents to your children? Why not find a way to break the power of the eight-hour belief in your own life and never allow it to influence the lives of your children?

If children (or restless pets, for that matter) awaken you in the early morning, you must trust that satisfying their needs is more important than your own for sleep in that moment. In fact, it is quite likely that your own soul has simply used these stirrings as a natural alarm clock to make it easier for you to perceive the impulse to awaken. Telling yourself that you haven't had enough sleep—whether because of the eight-hour belief or because your sleep has apparently been interrupted—only leads to oversleeping and resentment. Yet the souls of all people present in a family that lives together will always seek to time impulses for the benefit of every family member. The lack of energy experienced at the start of a new day is usually more the result of oversleeping than of interruptions. The soul is quite capable of making sure that you have as much rest as you need, regardless of how many times you have to get up. It will not punish you with a lack of energy for getting through the day because you have responded once or several times in the course of the night to the service-to-family aspect of your life purpose.

To battle the deeply entrenched eight-hour belief, all you need do is suggest to yourself each night as you retire that you will be completely refreshed and energized when you awaken, no matter what unexpected demands your family may make in the course of the night. And if you are awakened by such needs, remind yourself of this suggestion when you go back to bed. If you cannot sleep, find something to do until the impulse to sleep manifests itself once more. If you feel tired when you awaken in the morning, it may be that you just need to get your blood circulating again.

If you live with a partner, then both of you should engage in Play and Physical Focus activities with your children on a daily basis. When the working member of the family has returned home, he or she could give you the opportunity to pursue solitary activities while involving him or herself with the children. Or you could all play together. If the working partner is weary from a long day at the office, give him or her a chance to take a nap first.

In addition to making room in your day for solitary activities and for being with your children, you will also need to devote time to the relationship with your spouse or partner. Certainly, after the children have gone to bed you can have your special time together. You can also keep track of what is going on in each other's lives through phone conversations between your respective places of employment or between home and office (Cycles Menu). You should also engage yourselves as a couple in various activities from the menus. You could exercise together or share your dreams. You could help each other with work and creative projects or engage in Play Menu activities with or without the children. You could also cook or clean house together. Or you could alternate with one another in performing these activities. Such alternation is essential in providing both you and your partner with time alone.

What breaks up many marriages is resentment. The working partner often feels that his or her obligations to the family stop at breadwinning. Thus, when the working partner returns home from the office, he or she will focus on solitary activities, leaving the children in the care of the homemaking partner—where they may have been all day. This apparently selfish devotion to solitary activities on the part of the working partner compensates for his or her idea that the homemaking partner does anything he or she wants to all day long. Furthermore, the working partner will tell himself or herself that he or she is too exhausted from time spent at the office to do anything so strenuous as playing with children or helping to clean house. This exhaustion would dissipate if the working partner would simply apply our strategies for the office to time spent at work. Helping to clean house or playing with children afterward would then become important as a means of redistributing the energy levels in the life-force fuel tank. In this way, there would be enough energy available for all sorts of evening pursuits.

While it may be true that homemaking can lend itself somewhat more easily to an impulsive lifestyle than a forty-hour-a-week job, this doesn't mean that the homemaking partner has been engaged only in selfish solitary pursuits while his or her counterpart is away at the office. Raising a family can be just as much work as what goes on at the office, so it is patently unfair for the working partner to take the attitude mentioned above.

The homemaking partner must also beware of resentful attitudes. It can sometimes be easy for him or her to be jealous of the fact that the working partner has an almost daily opportunity to get away from the hubbub at home. Thus, he or she should not expect simply to turn the kids over to the working partner at the end of the workday. There must be a perfect balance of responsibilities. Each partner must share in the work of keeping the household running and caring for the children while also supporting the other in finding time alone.

Our final words to parents concern day care and baby-sitting. Do not hesitate to take advantage of such services—for the sake of your own processes of self-realization as individuals and as a couple. Children will benefit more from parents who have fully realized themselves through a modicum of selfishness than from ones full of resentment due to martyrdom. Remember that as long as you follow your impulses, the soul provides you with an inexhaustible supply of life force. This life force will allow you both—as individuals and as parents—to accomplish everything that must be done in the course of a day. But only if you unflaggingly pursue the impulse to awaken will you be fully capable of pursuing your career, spending quality time with your partner and your children, *and* finding time alone for personal development.

CHAPTER 23

Children and the Menus

Children do not have the same configuration of menus as adults. When a child is born, its impulses emanate solely from Menu A: sleeping, awakening, urinating, quenching thirst, eating, and defecating. As a child begins to crawl and eventually to walk, the Physical Focus Menu comes into being. At this point, the child will begin to require periods of exercise. These can be timed to coincide with the adult's Physical Focus Menu, as we have said. Very young children may not yet be capable of strenuous exercise. So the adult must pay particular attention to the requirements of his or her own body, which may need a separate Physical Focus period when he or she can be alone for a while. As the child gets older, you could enjoy taking walks, chasing or running about, or kicking or tossing a ball with each other. Again, the more strenuous these activities, the more refreshed you will feel afterward. Wearing out the child in this fashion so that he or she requires a nap will then allow you to get a number of solitary things accomplished.

Although the child dreams from earliest infancy, these dreams have more to do with the formation of the physical body and the development of coordinated movement and speech than manipulation of beliefs, as with adults. Hence, the Self-Awareness Menu does not become functional until adolescence. At this time the child attempts to create a sense of personality independent of the parents, through acceptance, rejection, or modification of the parental belief systems. It is no accident that by the time a child has entered high school, literature classes have begun to focus on the symbolic nature of the works read. Only when an individual is capable of understanding the meaning of a symbol is he or she ready to begin the interpretation of dreams. This activity is the very basis of the Self-Awareness Menu, since it represents the most readily available technique of belief manipulation.

To younger children, both dreams and fairy tales are more real than symbolic. Although the child may recognize the fantastic element in both and may come to realize that the events described do not take place in exactly that fashion in waking reality, he or she will sense that dreams and fairy tales are genuine experiences. They are simply of a different order than the ones prevalent in waking reality, but they nevertheless possess their own set of laws and logic of interrelations. At the point where the concept of symbols has been grasped, the process of translation between the symbolic nature of physical reality and the energy transformations embodied in it can begin. It is then that the Self-Awareness Menu comes into existence.

A child may relate a dream to an adult, and the adult might be able to interpret it. But the child will not see the connection between the dream experience and its hypothetical meaning. Nor can a child interpret omens, though he or she may act upon them unquestioningly. For most people, the attempt to interpret literature symbolically can lead naturally to the possibility of interpreting dreams in much the same way—if they choose to pay attention to their dreams. Once dream interpretation has been mastered, then it becomes easier to perceive all of reality as in some sense symbolic. Learning to interpret omens, by which we mean the redirective measures of Menu G, naturally follows. The ultimate goal of the Self-Awareness Menu is to enable the individual to recognize how the appropriateness of his or her beliefs, attitudes, and behaviors is constantly being commented upon through the symbolic content of both dreaming and waking experience.

With the exception of comforting a child who has had a nightmare, it is best not to broach the subject of dreams until adolescence. Encouraging the child to share his or her dreams at the breakfast table and then discussing them can provide a first experience of the Self-Awareness Menu. Children are often fascinated by their dreams. If it were not for the fact that most adults are antagonistic toward dreams, calling them irrelevant, children would openly share them. They have an intuitive sense that their dreams are special, unique to themselves, and very precious. In fact, their dreams at this time are beginning to shape an individuality different in many respects from the atmosphere of acceptable beliefs, attitudes, and behaviors prevailing in the household. Asking a child to speak of his or her dreams at this point, therefore, is a demonstration of genuine care and concern for who the child truly is. A skilled dream interpreter will be able to pick up from the child just where the storms and stresses of adolescence lie and will thus be better prepared to guide the child through this period. The child may also come to realize that his or her inmost secrets have effortlessly come out into the open in this way. And the adult has demonstrated nothing but care and concern, if not also wisdom and insight. So the child's worst fears—that he or she would be rejected by the parents if they only knew what was going on inside—will be allayed. Open lines of communication will be established.

The breakdown in relations between parents and children during adolescence is the result of the child's process of rejecting and modifying parental beliefs, attitudes, and behaviors in order to create an independent personality. There is a tendency to identify parents with the beliefs, attitudes, and behaviors they exhibit. Rejection of these things becomes confused with a rejection of the parents themselves as human beings. The child is desparately afraid that if this rejection were ever to come fully to the attention of his or her parents, he or she would be rejected by them in exactly the same way. It is a question of survival.

Adolescents usually know that they are not ready to make it alone in the outside world, so they conceal their feelings and bottle up the inward changes. Meanwhile, various actions will be perceived by their parents as rebellious. Considerable strain occurs in their families. All of this could be circumvented through the sharing of dreams.

In the course of the breakfast table conversation we have recommended, the adult should also share a dream or two, with interpretation. This will reveal to the child that even adults are struggling and growing. A sense of camaraderie can then develop. The child will be able to demonstrate his or her care and concern to the parents by offering personal insights into these dreams—even if these insights seem awkward or silly at first. Regardless of their usefulness, the parent should recognize what is actually occurring here: the child has by now become aware that his or her previously godlike parents have problems. He or she would like to offer help and encouragement. But there is a question of how to do so tactfully. The child doesn't want to be told to mind his or her own business, because the well-being of one's parents *is* his or her business. The sharing of dreams between both parties can become a bit like exchanging secret information about the self in a code that allows parent and child to become comfortable with each other, in preparation for more-direct communications.

The Work Menu does not become operational until the child enters school. The educational system is based on progression through levels of understanding, with grades as the means through which progress is evaluated. This setup allows the child to perceive rising levels of self-valuation, so learning how to read, write, and manipulate numbers is associated with the Work Menu. Even though at the most elementary levels, this sort of learning begins to prepare the child for fulfillment of a life purpose.

The Play Menu comes into being whenever the child starts to play games that involve some form of imagination. Simple rough-and-tumble play belongs to the Physical Focus Menu. But any kind of role-playing belongs to the Play Menu. All of the games the child plays at this point—from let's-pretend to puzzles, coloring books, and building with blocks—generally involve identifying and putting into place various components of the world. The child is developing its capacity for observation, whether of modes of behavior (duplicated in role-playing games), how parts fit together to make a whole (puzzles), or how things are really shaped or colored (coloring books). Card games and board games will become possible a few years later, as reasoning faculties begin to develop. In fact, they aid in refining such abilities.

Reading aloud to younger children is an important Play Menu activity for them—especially as the plot lines of the stories have an archetypal cast, as in fairy tales, myths, legends, and fantasies modeled on heroic quests. The subject of such tales (or the life situation taken out of context) is usually the process of discovering and fulfilling one's life purpose. The stories actually provide the child with maps or recipes for how to accomplish these ends. Such stories affect the development of a child's consciousness in much the same way that dreams do, even though the child may not have developed sufficient consciousness of self to have a bona fide Menu C. Such tales invoke the mental faculties involved in the self-realization process, so that they do not remain dormant or atrophy before the soul has need of activating them.

In the early years, children are exploring and learning not only how to manipulate the environment and their own responses to it but also how to master their presence within the body. Their days will consist in an alternation between many, often brief periods of Physical Focus and Play activities punctuated by the Menu A impulses. A more or less equal balance between these two types of activities is essential: strenuous physical exercise actually speeds the process of learning about the environment.

Remember that experience and food are symbolically equivalent. What nurtures the muscles of the body comes from the digesting of food. Likewise, what feeds the mind is the digesting of experience. Strenuous physical exercise increases the flow of nutrients to the muscles. What actually occurs is that learning acquired mentally becomes stored as cellular knowledge throughout the entire body. The short attention span of small children is indeed the result of a limited capacity to take in information. But all the physical restlessness that accompanies or follows a period of taking in information is essential to the process of assimilating that information. This is one of the reasons that recess is so important in elementary school. Insisting that a very young child sit still and forcing him or her to do so for extended periods can be detrimental to the development of information storage and retrieval skills.

The Cycles Menu comes into being as a child begins to become aware of his or her own growth. Interest in changes in weight or height or in casting aside clothing that no longer fits, along with the association of certain privileges with an age or height (what it means to be a "big" boy or girl), can indicate the development of the Cycles Menu. However, it would be somewhat more precise to say that as children begin to be capable of dressing themselves, brushing their own teeth, tying their own shoes, and bathing and picking up after themselves, the Cycles Menu slowly begins to take shape. At this point, a period of such activities can be added to the beginning and ending of each day, including getting dressed or undressed, getting ready for bed, brushing teeth, bathing, and picking up one's belongings or clothes. Although a child will have had occasional haircuts and fingernail and toenail trimmings and will certainly have been bathed and shampooed regularly before this time, he or she will have little or no awareness of what these activities mean. Only when such activities are voluntarily requested or undertaken on his or her own can they become part of the Cycles Menu. Up until that point, they represent Work Menu activities for the parents. Once the child begins to spend a number of hours each day away from home at school, then another kind of Cycles Menu activity becomes possible: conversations about what happened there.

As you can see, the Cycles Menu creates a certain independence from the parents. Care of self-image, which is the hallmark of this menu, only becomes possible when the child can in fact perceive himself or herself as an entity distinct from the parents. This doesn't happen at once. New activities will be added year by year as a sign of maturation, until finally the child is capable of living completely independently of the parents.

Magic and miracles are a regular part of a child's understanding of how the world is put together. At Christmas the presents appear underneath the tree magically, as far as the child is concerned. Even though the child may not yet understand what a symbol is, he or she will know intuitively that the magic read about in fantasies and fairy tales is a symbolic representation of how the universe takes care of each and every person, allowing everyone to become who he or she truly is through miracle after miracle of need satisfaction. But the belief in magic is usually dead by early adolescence. When anything out of the ordinary happens after that point, it is indeed a surprise. The category of miraculous phenomena to which it used to belong no longer exists, except as a "childish" notion.

The Surprise Menu only becomes necessary as the child's relationship with the soul becomes strained. Ironically, religious indoctrination and parental guidance about right and wrong are usually responsible for this strain—and hence also for the loss of belief in magic and miracles. They substitute an indirect and highly filtered perception of the soul's reality for the child's direct knowledge. We say "highly filtered" because the soul has no need for religious law or moral principles. What is right is any action that will further the child's becoming who he or she truly is. What is wrong is the violation of anyone else's process of self-realization. Children have an instinctive understanding of these two rules of conduct. After all, what will help them become who they truly are brings happiness and satisfaction into their lives. In this sense, there is nothing more basic than the pleasure principle, which is one of the soul's primary means of inspiring growth.

When parents ignore, or are for some reason incapable of figuring out, a child's needs, the bond between the child's ego and soul begins to disintegrate. Forcing the child to eat a food that he or she is actually experiencing an impulse against (which is why it tastes bad), or putting the child to bed long before the impulse to sleep has manifested itself in order to get him or her out from underfoot, are two ways in which this disintegration is actually encouraged. Punishment according to an adult code of ethics, which will always be incomprehensible to the child, is yet another. Adult moodiness often transmits frustrations felt into other areas into annoyance at a child's behavior. This makes punishments seem arbitrary. The child can't understand the source of these frustrations, which originate in the adult world. And the child's relationship to the soul and his or her inner sense of right and wrong will collapse as a result of not being able to figure out why the punishment occurred. One goal of child rearing should be to keep the child's relationship with the soul intact. Punishment, if it is ever truly necessary, must be completely unaffected by mood. It must be consistent in application and, as much as possible, derived from the two rules of conduct we mentioned above. Most bad behavior in children is simply the result of not getting enough attention at critical points, when important needs are going unsatisfied. For example, when a child becomes upset that parents haven't bought a toy he or she desires, what is really going on is that in the absence of any clear sign of love from parents distracted by adult cares and concerns, the toy has become a symbol of restored affection. The real need is playtime with the adult, not the toy itself.

Even though not all of the menus are as yet fully developed, the Once-a-Day Requirement is still important. The school day provides a guarantee that whatever menus are active in the child's life will be touched upon at least once.

As rigid and inflexible as the school environment may seem to the child, it actually provides a good model for how to structure one's day. The scheduling of a school day involves alternating between time slots dedicated to work, play, and physical focus. The opportunity to urinate is often available in between classes. The only problem is that the choice of activities and menus is not spontaneously determined. The Work Menu is represented by the academic subjects: English, mathematics, science, social studies, and foreign languages. The Physical Focus Menu is represented by recess, gym class, and intra- or extramural sports. The Play Menu is represented by art, music, band, orchestra, chorus, acting, shop, home economics, creative writing, and certain extracurricular activities, such as cheerleading or clubs of various kinds. While there may be certain students who will become artists, writers, actors, or musicians and who will therefore take these classes much more seriously than other students, the emphasis is not so much on producing quality work for a grade as on having a good time using artistic or musical materials in one way or another. In a way, these classes offer structured recess periods. The same is to some extent true of shop or home economics. In each of these cases, skills possibly useful for the Work or Cycles menus are being rehearsed out of context—that is, for their own sake, and not because there is a genuine or immediate need to match them to some real-life situation.

On weekends and during vacation periods the child may need some guidance in order to ensure that a Work Menu activity is undertaken. This will not be a problem if the child has homework to accomplish, a test to study for, or a paper to write—and does so willingly. During the summer months, encouraging the child to pursue a course of study in some field of passionate interest connected with "what I want to be when I grow up" can offer possibilities for the Work Menu. Trips to the library to find reading matter on the subject or classes at a local museum or other children's resource center would be valuable in this regard.

There will also be a tendency for the child to delight in sharing what has been learned from such pursuits with an adult. The adult's attentive listening and asking of questions—even if he or she knows the answers—will encourage the child to demonstrate how much has been learned. This allows the child to be worthy of the adult's attention, and therefore brings about a rise in the child's level of self-valuation—the hallmark of the Work Menu. In a sense, the adult is the self that the child will become. And to children, who practically worship the adults in their lives, an adult's interest symbolizes how much he or she has been able to realize that goal.

C H A P T E R 2 4

Relationships and Life Purpose

What is a relationship? From the soul's perspective, a friend is someone with whom you share a passionate interest. This passionate interest could be in exercise or athleticism, in which case your friend may be a workout buddy who supports you in fulfilling the service-to-the-body aspect of your life purpose. Much of what you do with such a friend will emanate from the Physical Focus Menu. Or the passionate interest could be in your own and each other's inner workings and personal problems. Such a friendship could allow you to get in touch with your own greater expressive range as a human being (service to personality). Or it could support you in accomplishing the learning your soul requires of you (service to the soul). Furthermore, in caring enough to provide each other with advice and to consider following it, you would be touching upon the service-to-family aspect of each other's life purpose. This sort of friendship would be strongly focused in the Self-Awareness Menu.

A third type of friendship would be with a fellow artist, a coworker, or colleague. The passionate interest would be your careers—not so much in terms of "getting ahead" as in terms of service to the Creator, humanity, or all life, depending on the type of work involved. Such a friendship would be strongly biased toward the Work Menu. A fourth type of friend would be the one you choose to go out and have fun with—a playmate, as it were. The passionate interest in play shared with such a person would give you opportunities to take a break from the rigors of fulfilling your life purpose. But remember that play can also help you develop or refresh ways of being not supported by the Work Menu. Such a friendship may permit getting in touch with a wider range of mental, emotional, and physical expressiveness—through games, role-playing, or even just plain kidding around. In this way, it can allow you to fulfill the service-to-personality aspect of your life purpose. Obviously, this sort of friendship will be focused primarily in the Play Menu.

Finally, there is the type of friend with whom you share a passionate interest in your own and each other's growth—in any particular area of fulfilling your life purpose or in all of them together. This is the person to whom you will relate the events of your life, thereby providing you with an opportunity to become aware of what kind of growth has been accomplished since the last such communication. Such a friendship will emanate from the Cycles Menu.

While passionate interests and their associated activities may bias a friendship toward a particular menu, this doesn't mean it should be confined to that menu. Every friendship will develop its own unique blend of passionate interests, impulsive menus, and aspects of life purpose. The more these things are shared, the deeper will be the friendship.

It should be clear from the above that we believe friendships and fulfillment of your life purpose go hand in hand. Passionate interest indicates that the soul is providing you with high amounts of life force to fuel your pursuit of the activities involved. This means that any passionate interest is linked in some way with discovery or fulfillment of your life purpose. Yet the interest and its associated activities may not always represent aspects of your life purpose themselves. As we have said in the case of the Play Menu, their function may sometimes be to let you take a break from fulfilling your life purpose. It is these passionate interests—often called "having things in common"—that draws people together as friends.

Both passionate interests and friends will come and go in the course of your life. Sometimes they can appear as clues directing you toward an aspect of your life purpose that you may not have previously been aware of. Once you have absorbed the messages of such clues, you are ready for others—and the passion may disappear from particular activities you no longer feel motivated to pursue. If some of your friendships were solely based on pursuit of these activities, they may tend to evaporate as well.

Some passionate interests, however, will be lifelong. These represent essential aspects of who you are. Friendships that support these interests will tend to last longer—and could themselves become lifelong. Occasionally some of these essential interests may be neglected for a period, usually because of lack of time or energy. A lot of life force had once been available to fuel your passionate pursuit of such interests. When you began to neglect them, however, that life force began to diminish. To neglect pursuing passionate interests means to lose a good deal of enthusiasm for living. Obviously it is of great importance to both your general well-being and your fulfillment of your life purpose to maintain connections to these essential interests. It is your friendships that help keep them (and you) alive.

You will note that we have not described a passionate interest in sex as one of the conditions of friendship. While the most rewarding sexual relationships must have a strong basis in friendship—which means there will certainly be passionate interests and support in fulfilling each other's life purpose—the sexually intimate relationship serves a somewhat different and highly important function in life.

In olden times, when mankind was dependent on relationships within the tribe for survival, an individual might be ostracized if he or she was found to be different from the others. Such ostracism was often a kind of death sentence, since the individual probably would not be able to care for himself or herself out in the wilds without tribal support. Even though this sort of dependence on the tribe is no longer the order of the day, many people behave emotionally as if it were. They dare not do anything to distinguish themselves from other people for fear of rejection—even though rejection is no longer a death sentence. This fear survives in such statements as "I would just die if so-and-so found out." The process of becoming who you truly are, however, is a process of differentiation or individuation from others. A strong pressure is exerted by the soul in this area, and it is often met with resistance deriving from the fear of rejection for being different. People's actions will usually be split evenly between doing things in order to gain acceptance and doing them in order to maintain individuality.

We have already said that fulfilling your life purpose allows you to become who you truly are. Your life purpose can also be described as your function within the whole of mankind. As such, it represents both the ultimate individuality *and* the ultimate sense of belonging. Yet the process of discovering your life purpose cannot even begin if you fear rejection for being different. The pressure from the soul to differentiate yourself from the rest of humanity ends up being redirected into developing harmless and inoffensive eccentricities that you then mistake for your true personality. In many people, these idiosyncrasies will be blended with a desperate craving for approval. Such people will be almost entirely controlled by what they think other people are thinking about them. They will either become obsequious, or they will attempt to manipulate and control other people's thoughts as much as possible to get this approval. The conspiracy against fulfilling one's life purpose begins here.

Everything in the universe is poised on the fine balance

between union and identity. Union holds the atom together, and identity makes sure that the various parts maintain their integrity. The same is true of humanity. Without union you cannot be a part of humanity; without identity you cannot fulfill your function, which is different from that of everyone else on the planet.

The most intimate relationships—with a boyfriend or girlfriend, a lover, or a marriage partner—provide you with the opportunity of learning how to balance union and identity. And sex is the mechanism whereby this learning comes about.

When both members of a couple have experienced an orgasm, the electrical charges in every atom of their bodies will line up in such a way that the barrier of skin separating them will seem to dissolve. At that point, they are experiencing a special kind of union—a momentary recognition that at the soul level they are each part of a larger whole, a couple. And yet neither of them has lost individuality in coming to this recognition. It is a small step from experiencing this sort of love to feeling a oneness with all mankind. Yet there are defenses against intimacy that prevent people from achieving a lasting sense of union at either level. These defenses are really just fears of rejection or ostracization for becoming who one truly is. They originate in trying to protect the idiosyncrasies that have been mistaken for one's true personality against union. Union tends to dissolve such false personality in order to allow one's actual identity and place within humanity to emerge. It follows, then, that the less a person knows who he or she really is, the more frightened of genuine intimacy he or she will be.

Every human relationship—be it with a friend or with a partner in love—must confront these defenses against intimacy and overcome them. This is what relationships are all about. Each one will help you work in certain areas of your life to overcome the fear of rejection for becoming who you truly are. And the sum total of all of your relationships will support you in your quest to discover and fulfill your life purpose.

Every relationship has the potential for passing through five stages of intimacy: attraction, togetherness, involvement, union, and permeation. Attraction indicates that there is the possibility of love. Note that we are not saying "a possibility of *making* love"! The possibility of love is what has drawn you to every friend in your life, no matter how that love expresses itself. You could think of such love in terms of the other person's understanding and acceptance of who you really are. Thus, attraction also means the possibility of finding such understanding and acceptance. If you feel comfortable allowing such possibilities to realize themselves, you begin to move into the next stage of intimacy. Through simple enjoyment of being with each other and doing the things associated with your mutually shared passionate interests, attraction has become togetherness.

The involvement stage begins at the point when the lessons that will be learned in a new relationship start to emerge. Because these lessons have to do with letting go of defenses against intimacy, this stage can often be difficult. Not every relationship gets to this point. Togetherness may provide enough understanding and acceptance. But if a relationship goes beyond togetherness, a lot of work will be done by both people in determining which needs can be satisfied by each other and which ones cannot. All sorts of expectations will come up, some fulfilled, some denied. Since emotional pain is often the result of denied expectations, there may be periods of feeling hurt. You may also feel at times as if your identity is being threatened in some way by the other individual. What is actually being threatened, however, is the false personality you have erected to ensure acceptance by society. Fights, arguments, periods of not speaking to each other, intense frustration, competition, and hurtful lashing out can all occur at this stage. But the more you know who you truly are, the less false personality will there be to give up. This can make your passage through involvement considerably less difficult.

The intimacy level of any relationship will deepen with the sharing of your secrets, from the mildest to the most protected. Everybody has things about themselves they are afraid for anyone else to know—for fear of rejection. These secrets are often connected with who one truly is in some way. And because peers, family, or authority figures seem to disapprove of the beliefs, attitudes, and behaviors behind such secrets, the secrets are guarded almost desperately. Trusting at least one other person enough to share these secrets gives you the opportunity to see that you may not be rejected for this or that aspect of who you truly are after all. Your friend or partner can then begin to support you in moving toward fulfillment of your life purpose in this area.

At the point when you have no secrets from your friend or partner, you have moved into the union stage of intimacy. As a result of many shared experiences, there will be a strong sense of bondedness. A unique brand of humor will have developed, full of in-jokes and code words no one else understands. In fact, when the two of you are together, you will have a sense of being in a special, often magical world, somehow removed from the everyday. The rules of conduct that apply in this magical world have been created by your years of being together, fully accepting of each other, and supporting each other in releasing all concerns about whether the rest of society thinks you are strange or different for being who you really are. You will feel safe to express yourself in whatever way you might feel moved to.

In the union stage, it will be easy to talk about anything going on in your lives. You will tend to provide each other with detailed reports of everything that has occurred since the last time you communicated or were together. Both of you will be completely wrapped up in, and supportive of, each other's every major decision. There may still be a few vestiges of the involvement stage, however. From time to time, tensions may arise as either of you pull in temporarily because of fear of losing your identity. But for the most part this stage of intimacy will be experienced as smooth sailing, when compared with the previous one.

All happy and satisfying relationships—whether with best friends or with partners in love—have achieved union. Many relationships never quite make it to this point. They can often get stuck in the bickering and arguing of the involvement stage. Only a very, very few ever progress through union to permeation.

Imagine a glass bubble in which two gasses are contained. Each gas has its own separate chemical identity, and yet every atom of one exists between atoms of the other. Such is permeation. Every portion of your beingness and that of your partner will have penetrated each other. Yet there will be no fear of loss of identity. By this time, you will have so successfully supported each other in discovering your mutual life purposes that your personalities will have been entirely purged of defenses against intimacy. All those harmless and idiosyncratic behaviors that had once been mistaken for your true individuality will be gone. You will have *become* your respective functions within mankind. And since no two people can have exactly the same function, you will never lose your individuality with the other person. This is the ultimate expression of union, and the ultimate awareness of identity. Regardless of how the external situation of the relationship might change, you will be bonded with such a person for life. That bond will survive every vicissitude—even years of separation.

Permeation can only be achieved in a sexual relationship. In fact, the lineup of electrical charges in the cells that occurs during orgasm can provide momentary glimpses of permeation right from the start, urging you onward in your attempts to overcome defenses against intimacy. Once permeation has been achieved through a sexual relationship, however, it becomes possible with anyone, regardless of whether the relationship is sexual or not.

The soul sets the goal of achieving permeation with at least one person as one of the requirements of each lifetime in physical reality. That one person will come to know exactly who you are in every detail and will accept it fully. If there is one such person in your life, it doesn't matter any longer how much your life purpose may seem to separate you from the masses of humanity. You will have all the love you need to achieve it—and more.

From the foregoing it should be clear that love and your life purpose are not mutually exclusive. Yet many people hold beliefs to the contrary. Some choose to work in isolation, believing that love would only interfere with their true work in life. Others choose relationships that will not support them in fulfilling their life purpose: friends or partners who are antagonistic toward it or who are so needy and demanding of attention that there seems to be no time for personal growth. As difficult as such situations may seem to the individual caught up in them, the soul is unswerving in its insistence that you achieve both union and identity through permeation and that you fulfill your life purpose. The soul may require that you give up your associations with people who obstruct these goals. But it will never require you to become a hermit. If you are not involved in an intimate relationship that is moving toward permeation, the next chapter will show you how you may draw one into your life.

If you find yourself in an intimate relationship that doesn't seem to be supporting you in the fulfillment of your life purpose, see how that involvement might change as a result of your applying the information in this book. If the other person becomes threatened or withdraws from you because of the positive changes that have come from following your impulses, be patient. Don't try to force your new beliefs, attitudes, and behaviors on him or her. The greater sense of fulfillment and happiness that derives from an impulsive lifestyle will be obvious. Only someone desperately frightened of being rejected by society for becoming who he or she truly is will ignore these things and seek to pull you down. If no amount of support or tenderness seems capable of melting this fear, you need to ask yourself if this person is actually thwarting fulfillment of your life purpose. Don't be too quick to answer yes. You may just be passing through the involvement stage. Eventually your partner may come around. After all, he or she wants to be happy just as much as you do. In the meantime, it is possible to be relatively unaffected by his or her fearful moodiness. But you must first become clear about the true nature of responsibility.

What exactly is responsibility? From the soul's perspective, the word does not mean "response-ability," as some would say. Rather, it means "answerability." Ultimately, you are answerable only to the soul itself for every decision that you make. The soul bases its judgment of how well you have lived your life on what you yourself have learned from it. Thus, you are *always* going to be the most important person in your universe, no matter how much you may care about someone else. Giving up becoming who you truly are for the sake of supporting someone else's process of self-realization is more an act of personal self-destruction than of love. Even so, supporting other people in becoming who they truly are can be just as much a part of your life purpose as taking time alone for your own fulfillment. Clearly, some sort of balance between privately pursuing self-realization and enabling that of others must be found. Impulses can provide that balance.

Ironically, impulsive behavior is often considered irresponsible. Whereas it is not at all irresponsible to the soul, it *is* perhaps irresponsible from society's perspective. In this case, being irresponsible means "not conforming" and could bring about ostracization. Someone who desperately fears becoming a social outcast will do everything he or she can to avoid following impulses. If you are intimately involved with such a person, the more you become who you truly are, the more pressure this individual will feel to drop the false personality that has been erected in order to gain the approval of others. An inner battle between soul and society will ensue, as each lays claim to defining who he or she is. You must be patient and very loving. If the soul wins, the two of you will begin to move toward permeation. If society wins, the relationship will dissolve. Your partner will be incapable of helping you fulfill your life purpose.

Even though you must consider yourself to be the most important person in your universe in order to achieve the soul's plans for your growth, this doesn't mean that the soul sends you impulses that completely disregard your relationships with others. All souls have an equal investment in guiding you in your process of self-realization and in making sure that their plans and your actions do not thwart the growth of others. While you may be the most important person in *your* universe, you are not the most important in *the* universe.

At any given moment, the soul could broadcast to you a wide variety of impulses, each of which would allow you to fulfill yourself in some way. It selects impulses on the basis of how easily they may be pursued, given the current circumstances of your life. At any moment that involves interaction with others, the soul will select the impulses that not only will best move you toward becoming who you truly are but also enable at least one other person to do the same. Therefore, involvement with other people—no matter the degree of intimacy—need not be a matter of alternating between selfishness and martyrdom.

In terms of the menus, relationships will go smoothly as long as you are clear about which impulses require that you be alone and which can admit the participation of someone else. The other person doesn't even have to know what the menus are. Just ignore any remarks that you are going to the bathroom too much!

If you are living with someone with whom you are very

close, you will be surprised at how often both of you feel the impulse to urinate more or less simultaneously. This will be especially true if both of you are following the menus. As you both enter the new flexible time unit together, take a moment to consult with each other about your needs: Is there a need for togetherness or is there a need for solitary pursuits? Attune yourselves to your impulses, and trust that your souls are broadcasting to you what will best fulfill each of you in both areas.

Intimate relationships often grow stale because lovemaking gets stuck in one particular menu. Yet impulsive lovemaking can sustain an intimate relationship for years. And by "impulsive" we don't mean just "doing it" whenever you feel like it! Rather, we mean allowing your impulses to guide you into a different menu each time you make love.

There is nothing wrong with sex as long as it is an expression of love. The soul views any sexual act that is not motivated by love as a kind of perversion. This is why we prefer the term "making love" to "having sex." It is just as appropriate to make love to oneself through masturbation as to make love to a partner. And from the soul's perspective, the gender or sexuality of one's partner is irrelevant—as long as there is love and as long as the relationship provides an appropriate space within which to learn the meaning of true intimacy.

Because lovemaking is one of the categories of experience we mentioned in Part I, it can arise from any of the Menus B through F. Not only will the approach to lovemaking change, depending on the menu, but also the orgasm itself will have a completely different feel. Here's a brief rundown of how lovemaking expresses itself through each of the menus.

Menu B

When making love manifests itself through the Physical Focus Menu, it will tend to be vigorous, possibly physically exhausting. The orgasm may be experienced as a release from tension held in the body. While this experience may not be unpleasant, it will rarely be as pleasurable as the other types of lovemaking. At most, it will be relaxing. If you or your partner grant yourselves no other opportunities in the course of a day to fulfill the physical-focus requirement, then making love will automatically manifest itself through this menu. After a while, you or your partner will become dissatisfied with the quality of the orgasm. One of you may react negatively by withdrawing from lovemaking or even going so far as to consider ending the relationship because it has gotten boring. Yet the simple act of shifting lovemaking into a different menu by changing your approach may be all that is necessary to revive it. The first step in doing so is to find another sort of exercise!

Menu C

When making love manifests itself through the Self-Awareness Menu, it will tend to be gentle and exploratory. There will be a tendency to try out new things with one's partner. One might also experiment with finding ways to focus one's consciousness in order to heighten his or her own sensitivity. The buildup to orgasm will often be prolonged and highly sensual. The orgasm itself may become a kind of ecstatic peak experience. Often the Self-Awareness Menu will be rather prominent at the beginning of a relationship. But this doesn't mean it will disappear as a relationship matures. There will always be new frontiers of intimacy and sensuality to explore—if you are daring enough to give up boredom!

Menu D

Making love may also manifest itself through the Work Menu. This doesn't mean that helping your partner to achieve orgasm must be a lot of work! The Work Menu and your ability to value yourself are closely linked, as we have said. To make love to someone through the Work Menu is to do special kinds of things that demonstrate how much you value that person—or to allow that person to value you in the same way by being receptive to his or her devotions. The traditional formula for a romantic evening—candlelight dinner, a gift of flowers, soft music, and champagne in front of a glowing fire —encapsulates what is involved when making love through the Work Menu. Attending to all the little details of creating an ideal setting for love—as long as this is a genuine expression of love, and not merely an attempt at seduction—is a kind of work. Every act, from preparing dinner or giving a gift, to the first embrace, the flaring of passion, and the final languid lying in each other's arms, should be imbued with appreciation for the presence and devotion of one's partner. The kind of ecstasy that results from a mutual appreciation in this fashion will be quite different from the one associated with the Self-Awareness Menu. There will be a high degree of passion in it. Passion is actually a form of appreciation for the inward or outward beauty of your partner. It always disappears from a relationship in which either party takes the other for granted. Making love as a show of appreciation (Work Menu) can often rekindle it. All you have to do is remind yourself of all the things you value about your partner and how much you would like him or her to know it.

Menu E

Making love through the Play Menu will be playful and spontaneous, of course. Often there will be a lot of verbal banter, perhaps some playacting or a chase scene. The whole experience will be light and full of mischief, fun, and laughter—and so will the orgasm.

Menu F

Making love through the Cycles Menu usually occurs after lengthy periods of separation or on dates significant to the development of the relationship, such as anniversaries, Christmas, and birthdays. At such times, you are likely to become aware of how your feelings for your partner have changed when compared to the last time you were together or the last celebration of the anniversary. In this way, you may chart the growth of the relationship, in terms of both your personal evolution and the evolution of yourselves as a couple. There will be a tendency to measure the feeling of depth or meaningfulness that occurs while making love against the previous occasions. Hopefully, you will become aware of a growing intimacy and a deepening bond. This awareness, too, will color an orgasm, making it different from those experienced through the other menus. It will feel especially deep and significant, even awesome. There will be a sense of having surpassed all previous levels of intimacy. Afterward both partners will often feel an urge to talk about how the relationship is growing and developing, trying to put these feelings into words. What they are really trying to do is articulate the nature of the cycle that has just ended and of the selves each of them has left behind.

Conclusion

There are a couple of things to keep in mind about impulsive lovemaking. If a genuine impulse exists, *both* you and your partner will feel it. The question of who should initiate lovemaking will be absolutely irrelevant. Don't talk yourself into it if your partner seems interested and you are not. This means that other needs are more important to you in that moment. For similar reasons, it is inappropriate to talk your partner into making love. On the other hand, don't talk yourself *out* of it by telling yourself you should be doing something else. That's a sure sign that the genuine impulse is present and that you're frightened of becoming more deeply intimate with your partner.

A relationship won't end just because other needs of yours or of your partner are more important than making love at a given moment. Relationships should help you, not prevent you, from fulfilling your life purpose. A relationship in which this is not understood is utterly inappropriate from the soul's perspective.

Once again, your life purpose makes you uniquely different from everyone else: only you can fulfill that specific function in mankind as a whole. This can be a pretty lonely proposition without the love and support of an intimate relationship continually affirming your essential beingness, value, and lovability. If the soul requires that you draw such a person into your life in order to achieve intimacy, it will also do everything it can to help you sustain that relationship once you have discovered it. All you have to do is follow your impulses, and both fulfillment of your life purpose and the development of true intimacy will ensue. There is no other recipe for bliss.

CHAPTER 25

The Treasure Hunt

By constructing your own set of menus, you have created a framework within which it is easier to perceive impulses. Before, it was not so much that impulses were few and far between but rather that you had no way of perceiving them clearly. The same is true of Menu G impulses. If you had a framework that made it easier to perceive them, they would seem to manifest themselves much more frequently. The subject of this chapter—the treasure hunt—provides such a framework. It is a means of bringing magic and adventure into your life on a daily basis.

The treasure hunt is a method of drawing to yourself what you need. There are certain needs without the satisfaction of which it might be difficult for you to fulfill your life purpose. The treasure hunt works best when linked with such needs. One of them might be for a new place to live—a house, apartment, or condominium. An environment that surrounds you with well-being and comfort can actually make it easier for you to move toward fulfillment of your life purpose, especially in the service-to-family area. Another one might be for new friends who share passionate interests, perhaps in the areas of service to the Creator or service to personality. Or for a new relationship in which the possibility of permeation enables you to overcome all defenses against becoming who you truly are. The treasure hunt can also help you find a career that is more closely aligned with the service-to-humanity aspect of your life purpose. But whatever you are seeking, this technique should be undertaken only when there is a genuine need for its object. In order for it to work, you must first adopt the following belief: *The universe satisfies all needs.*

There are two ways in which you can inadvertently prevent the universe from satisfying your needs: not believing that what will satisfy your needs exists and not feeling worthy of having your needs satisfied. Your ideal mate could live only a block away from you. But you're certain that it would be impossible for you to find all the qualities you think will make you happy in one person. Because your beliefs create your perceptions of reality, you may never see this individual for who he or she really is. Even if you *were* to see all the qualities you think will make you happy in one person, you will probably tell yourself you're not good enough for him or her. The same would be true of the ideal job: either you will see no evidence that it exists or you will tell yourself you're not good enough if you do. The treasure hunt allows you to address these two problematic beliefs in a systematic fashion so that they will no longer prevent you from drawing what will satisfy any genuine need into your life.

When we say, "The universe satisfies all needs," what we mean is that for every need of yours, the universe contains a corresponding satisfaction. It is actually the soul that determines the nature of your needs.

What exactly is a need, from the soul's perspective? In our view, a genuine need is a lack of something essential without which you will be less able to become who you truly are. Your well-being is diminished in some way whenever your needs go unsatisfied. Needs can be physical (food, water, air, shelter, protective clothing), emotional (love, nurturance, support, healing), intellectual (information, understanding, passionate interests, new ways of thinking), or spiritual (realizing the soul's master plan).

The soul will not cause you to need something that doesn't exist or cannot be made to exist. On the other hand, the ego is capable of inventing needs that can never be satisfied, thereby distracting you from the real ones. The way to tell the difference between genuine and invented needs is to pay attention to your thoughts. Whenever you find that you are telling yourself over and over that if only you had a certain thing you would be happy, you are dealing with an invented need. The key lies in the words *telling yourself.* This is an instance of trying to persuade or convince the soul, which knows better. It won't do any good. The only way you will ever be truly happy is if you work toward satisfying genuine needs.

Perhaps you are telling yourself over and over that if only you had a child you would be happy. But you're not involved in a relationship at this time. Clearly there are certain needs that must be fulfilled before you can bring a child into the world. You must first establish the deep bond of true intimacy with another person. This is the only way a relationship will be stable enough to rear a child properly. Yet your obsession with having a child could actually prevent such a bond from forming. You may not care so much who you are with as long as the child eventually comes along. Potential mates will avoid you because they know instinctively that you view them more in terms of their reproductive capacities than as people.

It should be clear from this example that some needs can be satisfied only after others have been satisfied. Only the immediate need is the true need in such cases.

Invented needs often block genuine needs. That's why the ego creates them. It tries to make itself feel miserable by denying the satisfaction of a true need. All the while, it pretends that the universe and the soul are actually responsible, because neither of them are working to satisfy the invented need. In this way, the ego is able to generate the following argument: "I know that I'm here to fulfill my life purpose and that the universe satisfies every need that might be contingent upon my doing so. But look—my needs are going unsatisfied. The universe is not keeping its part of the bargain. So I am not required to keep mine."

This sort of thinking is rather common. It underlies all instances of feeling sorry for oneself. It is especially dangerous because it invariably leads to a diminishment of life force available from the soul. Stress, illness, and symptoms of aging will be the result.

The soul not only determines the nature of your needs but also knows exactly what will satisfy them. In fact, the timing of your impulses, especially those from Menu G, will be designed to lead you toward what will satisfy your needs. Thus, it is not so much the universe, or even the soul, that satisfies your needs. Ultimately it is yourself alone who ensures this satisfaction—with your willingness to follow impulses. Without the belief that what you need truly exists and without the level of self-valuation that will allow you to feel worthy of it, these impulses simply can't get through.

Self-valuation is determined entirely by how close you are to fulfilling your life purpose. It stands to reason that the more actively you pursue becoming who you truly are, the more worthy you will feel of having your needs satisfied—and the more apparent it will be that the universe satisfies all of your needs. You will have to give up being attached to all invented needs. The best way to do this is to remind yourself that anything you *tell* yourself will make you happy will *not.* True happiness is the result of larger amounts of life force flowing through the body. Since life-force availability increases only as you move toward fulfillment of your life purpose, it is impossible for satisfaction of any invented need to make you happy. So stop wasting mental energy on it. That mental energy could be put to much better uses—such as creating genuine happiness.

The treasure hunt works best when you link it with your life purpose. That guarantees you will be dealing with genuine—as opposed to invented—needs. For example, if you use the treasure hunt to draw a new relationship into your life, it is better to seek someone who offers the possibility of permeation rather than someone who's good in bed. There are ways in which lovemaking can aid in the fulfillment of your life purpose, as we indicated in the previous chapter. But the universe may not honor a request to fulfill a "need" for sex. Sex won't make you happy. But the possibility of permeation will.

To begin the treasure hunt, you must make up a treasure map. You could use the Menu G journal we recommended in Chapter 19, or you could make up a special treasure-hunt journal. A regular notebook will do; it doesn't have to be a stenographer's pad. The treasure map will consist of two lists of characteristics pertaining to the new living space, job, friend, or lover you are seeking. The first list comprises everything you feel you must have in order to be fully satisfied with the object of the treasure hunt. The second list comprises everything you feel you must *not* have in order to be fully satisfied with the treasure. While it is fine for you to deliberate in your head about what to include on such lists, the treasure hunt will not begin until you have actually written them down.

Use what you liked or didn't like about past living spaces, jobs, friends, or lovers as you make up your lists. Any unpleasantness connected with these things usually represents ways in which you have not valued yourself. You put up with this unpleasantness because you thought that this was the best you could do or that you didn't really deserve better. If you don't make up a list of "must not haves," you will not be able to rise in level of self-valuation. You could continue to draw the same kinds of unpleasantness to yourself again and again. It is of the greatest importance, therefore, that you really look at how badly you may have been treated or how much you hated a certain situation—no matter how painful this might be. Yet even the most difficult situations usually involve some degree of pleasure at some point; otherwise you would not put up with them. Be fair in your scrutinization of the past so that you do not neglect including such things on your must-have list.

It is best to list abstract or general qualities rather than specific ones. When you are looking for a new living space, it is vastly more effective to list a general idea of location, price range, number and kinds of rooms, their approximate size, and how you would like to feel there than it is to specify a particular neighborhood, square footage, layout, or design.

The same approach is necessary when looking for a new relationship. Writing down "interested in physical fitness" is better than "has a great body." The universe may not honor a request that your new boyfriend or girlfriend look a certain way, because looks have nothing to do with what you may need to learn from an intimate relationship. Remember that attraction means the possibility of love. If there is a genuine possibility of love with someone, you will certainly be attracted to them, whether they look like your preconceived notions of handsome or beautiful or not.

Similarly, how you would like to feel in a new job will be more powerful than an actual job description. You will find greater satisfaction when the new job allows you to take the talents and skills you have developed over the years and put them to use to further your life purpose. The best way to do this may not look anything like your previous job descriptions. Once again, it is important not to be too specific. It is better to target a field you are interested in going into—one for which you have, or can develop, some qualifications—than a particular company. If you are not only dissatisfied with your career but also have no idea how you could best serve humanity, we recommend that you read a book entitled *Do What You Love and the Money Will Follow*[10] before you undertake a treasure hunt in this area.

Once you have made up your must-have and must-not-have lists, the treasure hunt begins. The universe will begin to offer you clues that what you are looking for actually exists. Clues depend on the type of treasure hunt you are engaged in. Thus, a clue might be a For Sale sign on an attractive house or a realtor's ad in the newspaper. It could be a job possibility you have heard about through a colleague or a classified ad. It could be an interesting or attractive person you have just met. Every one of these clues will appear as a surprise and may redirect your course of action in some way. Be open to such adventures; they emanate from Menu G. You will experience an extra infusion of life force from the soul every time you allow yourself to flow with them.

At first, only a few items on the must-have list may appear in each clue: you may see only one or two things that appeal to you. These things may also be combined with qualities from your must-not-have list. In each successive clue, more items from the must-have list will appear and fewer from the must-not-have list. We strongly recommend that you keep a record of every clue in your treasure-hunt journal, at least for the first treasure hunt. It is important that you be able to look back over these clues to see how they have increased in resemblance to your treasure map, if for no other reason than to prove the efficacy of the technique. Such a record often provides startling evidence for how well your soul is guiding and taking care of you.

As you gather clues, some will show you things you didn't know you needed in a treasure. Add them to the must-have list. Likewise, you may see things you didn't know you *didn't* need. Add these to the must-not-have list. You might also discover that things you once thought you needed are no longer important to you. Cross them off the must-have list. The treasure map will evolve while you are engaged in the treasure hunt. Most people are not sufficiently aware of their true needs to make up a treasure map that will never change. In fact, the soul will often guide you toward people or situations that grotesquely exaggerate some of the things on your list that aren't really necessary, precisely so that you can develop greater clarity about your true needs.

The series of clues thrown in your path by the universe demonstrates that the qualities you want in a treasure actually exist. First, the universe proves to you that they can exist separately, in different jobs, people, or living spaces. Eventually it will prove that they can come together into a single whole. Keeping a record of the clues helps you overcome doubts that this is possible. Your journal can also help you accept each clue *as* a clue.

The closer you get to the treasure, the more appealing each clue will become. But a clue, by definition, is lacking in at least one item from the must-have list and/or is spoiled by the presence of at least one item from the must-not-have list. It follows that the treasure by definition exhibits *every* characteristic on the must-have list and *none* on the must-not-have list. If this seems too good to be true, then you have some work to do on your ability to value yourself. If you settle for the clue, you are giving in to a belief that you don't deserve better. While there is nothing inherently wrong with accepting a clue as if it were the treasure, whatever is missing from the must-have list or present from the must-not-have list will become so annoying to you that your association with this job, person, or living space will be rather short-lived. You'll become fed up and leave it. Why bother investing yourself in a clue when you'll just have to go through the often complicated and emotionally wrenching process of extricating yourself almost right away? It is far better to hold out for the treasure than to act out of desperation because you're afraid that a clue is the best you can do.

Every time you see a clue and accept it as such, declining to involve yourself with it in any way, you rise in level of self-valuation. With each such rise comes a greater sense of being worthy of having your needs satisfied by the universe. This is what makes it possible for the universe to keep providing you with clues that resemble the treasure ever more closely.

One sure test of whether you are dealing with a clue or the treasure—if comparison of the must-have and must-not-have lists has not already convinced you—is to pay attention to your thoughts. Are you trying to *persuade* yourself that the clue is the treasure. If so, you are simply arguing against the soul, which knows better. On the other hand, you may try to talk yourself *out* of committing yourself to the treasure when it appears. Once again, you are arguing against the soul. The treasure will often represent a level of self-valuation you haven't quite attained yet. Overcoming the tendency to tell yourself you're "not good enough" is all that is required to become worthy of it.

When the treasure finally appears, both the soul and the universe itself have an investment in your recognizing it as such. A veritable fireworks of Menu G surprises will accompany the appearance of the right house, job, friend, or lover, leaving no doubt in your mind. Everything will happen easily and smoothly to bring about your association with the treasure. In fact, this ease and smoothness and the spectacular nature of the events surrounding the treasure's appearance are further tests of whether you are dealing with the treasure itself or just a clue.

It is entirely possible that once you have settled into an involvement with the treasure, you may see a few things from the must-not-have list. Don't abandon this treasure under the assumption that it must only be a clue. There are times when some of the things on the must-not-have list actually represent unfinished lessons from previous living spaces, jobs, friends, or lovers. The universe will make sure you don't see them until you are enough settled into the association that you will be willing at last to work them out. In fact, the universe will make sure that one of the special qualities of the treasure will be its capacity to help you confront these difficulties in as gentle and supportive a manner as possible.

We must also warn you that your association with a particular treasure may not last forever. Each treasure will be ideal for the self you are at the time it comes into your life. You could grow out of it at some point, either because you experience a rise in level of self-valuation or because you form a clearer idea about the nature of your life purpose. Things you didn't know you needed or didn't need will accumulate until you can no longer stay with the treasure. At that point, you may wish to create another treasure map based on these new awarenesses. Don't leave the old association until you have at least seen the first clue—if not the treasure itself. You could be inventing a need for a new treasure just because you're not willing to work out the difficulties that have come up with the old one. The universe will not support you in avoiding such growth.

The ultimate treasure hunt is the discovery of who you truly are. A new living space, job, friend, or lover, important as each one may seem to you at a given moment, is itself just a clue on that treasure hunt. You must not allow such things to become more important than your own process of self-realization. Simply move from clue to clue and from treasure to treasure, never becoming attached to them. If they no longer support your growth, release them and move on. Adventuring in this way, with the soul as your guide, you will surely find your daily life full of magic, and you will be happy.

EPILOGUE

You must not conceive of the Menus for Impulsive Living as a burdensome system to be rigidly executed for the rest of your days. After all, its very purpose is to help you break down routine so that you may free yourself from stress and arrest or reverse symptoms of aging. Although we have presented you with a structure that you may use to shape your daily experience, this structure is entirely dependent on your needs for growth and self-realization. It will change from moment to moment, even as your awareness of yourself and of what you need to accomplish in order to fulfill your life purpose changes.

The Menus system does not so much provide rules for conducting your life, but strategies or teaching aids designed to wean you from the clock's hours and release you from the tendency to overwork. Once you have developed the ability to perceive and act upon your impulses on a moment-by-moment basis, you may refer to the system only when something has gone wrong—such as when stress, exhaustion, or world-weariness set in. But if you find yourself spending more time wondering what menu an activity belongs to than in establishing the clearest focus within it, you have missed the point.

The menus will help you improve relations between body, soul, and ego, so that each aspect of yourself works in harmony with the others in enabling you to become who you truly are. The information on life-force dynamics, including the Once-a-Day Requirement, provides ways of "auditing" your use of life force to achieve your goals. Just as your home may be audited to check for heat loss, thereby allowing for savings of natural resources and money, so may you audit the flow of life force through you. Using the concepts of energy credit, debit, and neutral you may heighten both efficiency and productivity in all areas of your life.

Auditing is a form of self-observation, not of self-judgment. Don't get down on yourself if you're not able to attain maximum efficiency in managing your life force right away. The Exercises in Impulsive Living will show you how certain ways of structuring your day contribute to your well-being and satisfaction, while others throw you off center and drain you.

In a sense, this book provides you with a set of reeducative measures that will put you back in touch with the spontaneous and virtually timeless flow of experience characteristic of childhood. In order to do this, you must rid yourself of dependence on the clock's hours, which are not unlike training wheels: an artificial support system that makes sure you will not collapse into lassitude and slothfulness. Applying the Menus for Impulsive Living can actually remove these supports. You may find that you are a bit unsure of yourself at first, like a child trying a bicycle without training wheels for the first time. If you become frustrated that you can't seem to sustain the highest levels of energy availability and productivity all the time, gently remind yourself that a child doesn't throw away the bicycle just because he or she is experiencing some difficulty riding it.

While you are engaged in converting your lifestyle from one dependent on the hours to one fully guided by impulses, you may wish to consider the following experiment. Stop wearing a watch. Reduce the number of clocks in your living space. If you are ever curious about the time, just keep in mind that there is probably a timepiece nearby—in the next room, down the hall from your office, on a building along a road you use frequently, or on the wrist of a friend or passerby. Literally getting rid of the hours in this fashion will help you wean yourself from dependence on them.

Your life may be filled with important appointments that have been set for a certain hour. Try to schedule such appointments impulsively—those on both your business and social calendars. It will not matter how far in advance an appointment has been made; the soul will time the impulses of that day in order to accommodate it. To guarantee being on time for them, you may certainly return to using a watch. But after having made the experiment of living without one for a while, the meaning of time will have changed for you. It will no longer be the controlling factor of your life but merely a means of ensuring that your impulsive schedule and someone else's are aligned when an important exchange needs to take place.

In order to achieve enlightenment—the state of knowing what to do next under any given set of circumstances—all you have to do is follow the guidance of Menus A and G as they shift you all day long between the other menus. Enlightenment results not from how dutifully you accomplish the activities listed on Menus B through F, but from shifting always to the most appropriate menu at the most appropriate time, using the bodily impulses of Menu A and the spiritual impulses of Menu G.

Every impulse—no matter how seemingly insignificant—is a clue on the treasure hunt of becoming who you truly are. Ignore them and your relations to both the body and the soul deteriorate. You will experience malaise, world-weariness, existential boredom, and a sense of purposelessness—not to mention stress and symptoms of aging. If you acknowledge your impulses and yield to their gentle but insistent guidance, however, you will find your life far richer, far more exciting and adventuresome than you had ever hoped or dreamed.

The treasure you seek is genuine happiness, which can

only manifest itself when you are fulfilling your life purpose. The menus will help you juggle the various components of your life purpose—including those having to do with career and family, which can often seem to obstruct your own process of self-realization—without dropping and losing track of any of them. The soul provides explicit instructions on how to accomplish this. All you need to do is learn how to perceive and act upon its quiet, impulsive messages.

What could be more satisfying than living a life in which each moment contributes to an ever-increasing sense of joy? We hope that you will be able to use the assumptions, beliefs, concepts, techniques, and exercises contained in this book to create such a life for yourself.

NOTES

1. In *Seth Speaks: The Eternal Validity of the Soul,* by Jane Roberts (Englewood Cliffs, New Jersey: Prentice-Hall, 1972), the trance-channeled entity Seth outlines a sleep schedule quite similar to the one Charles advocates. This sleep schedule breaks down the usual division of a twenty-four-hour period into two large blocks, one of waking activity and the other of sleep. Citing numerous physical and psychic benefits for altering this pattern, Seth recommends a six-to-eight-hour maximum per night, with a nap or two during the day as a supplement. This material may be found on pp. 115–125.

2. Dr. Ida Rolf, a biochemist, developed a method of working on the body to release deep-held tensions causing postural misalignments. The rolfing practitioner uses pressures of various kinds (fingers, knuckles, elbows) to soften the connective tissue, or "fascia," that surrounds the muscles. When this tissue hardens because of stress or artificial restriction of the body's movement potential (induced by sitting long hours at a desk, for example), the body becomes inflexible, and the posture sags. Rolfing seeks to correct these problems in a carefully sequenced set of ten sessions.

The Alexander technique originated in the late 1800s with an Australian actor, F. Matthias Alexander, who was trying to correct a persistent voice-loss problem. It involves gentle manipulation of the head and neck to release tension and distorted posture in that area of the body. However, people often find that postural problems in other parts of the body tend to correct themselves as a result of this work. Actors and musicians—especially singers—find the Alexander technique useful in freeing up tensions that hinder their performance abilities.

3. Moshe Feldenkrais, an Israeli physicist, invented the Feldenkrais Method. This method is characterized by two different approaches. One is called "Functional Integration," in which a trained practitioner moves portions of the client's body through a series of simple but unusual movement patterns designed to reprogram the parts of the brain responsible for motion. The other is called "Awareness Through Movement." It involves a series of classes that use movements similar to those encountered in the private sessions but initiated by the participants themselves under the guidance of a teacher. Because these movements tend to increase flexibility and range of motion, such classes have been especially beneficial to the elderly.

There are many types of bodywork besides the ones that Charles mentions. Different regions of the country even have their own schools of thought, generated by individuals who have developed unique methods and have drawn to themselves circles of convinced disciples and clients. It would be impossible to review them all in a note such as this. Furthermore, the fact that Charles mentions three of the best-known contemporary bodywork methods does not necessarily mean that he endorses them or, conversely, that he disapproves of the ones not mentioned. The book *Bodywise: Regaining Your Natural Flexibility and Vitality for Maximum Well-Being,* by Joseph Heller and William A. Henkin (Los Angeles: Tarcher, 1986), provides a brief discussion of some of the major approaches to bodywork that have evolved over the centuries, as well as more recent ones (see pp. 63–86 therein). There is also a useful bibliography citing works by Alexander, Rolf, Feldenkrais, and others.

4. A useful guide for persons interested in beginning to work with their dreams is *The Dream Game,* by Ann Faraday (New York: Harper and Row, Perennial Library, 1976). The book covers topics such as how to keep a dream journal, how to encourage the remembering of dreams, how to interpret them, and how to become aware of ESP and other altered states of consciousness in dreams.

5. *Create Your Own Reality: A Seth Workbook,* by Nancy Ashley (Englewood Cliffs, New Jersey: Prentice-Hall, 1984), is a compendium of exercises in belief manipulation designed to improve quality of life. The book is based on the material channeled by the entity Seth through the late Jane Roberts.

The anonymously authored *A Course in Miracles,* 3 vols. (Tiburon, California: Foundation for Inner Peace, 1975) comprises a textbook, a workbook for students, and a guide for teachers—all channeled via a kind of mental dictation similar to what has generated my own trance-written sessions, but with a strong though unconventional Christian focus. The workbook contains an exercise for each day of the year designed to stimulate the ability to perceive, attract, or become the vehicle for miracles.

The New Diary: How to Use a Journal for Self-Guidance and Expanded Creativity, by Tristine Rainer (Los Angeles: Tarcher, 1978), provides a number of approaches to writing about oneself in a manner that enhances personal transformation.

The Possible Human: A Course in Enhancing your Physical, Mental, and Creative Abilities, by Jean Houston (Los Angeles: Tarcher, 1982), offers exercises in consciousness manipulation that start with the body's movement potential and progresses from sense perceptions, through brain-hemisphere interrelations and memory workings, to altered states of consciousness designed to release activities from usual time orientations or to generate a form for one's own internal teacher.

Charles's intention in recommending these works is not so much to encourage people to add them to their own Self-Awareness Menu but rather to define the kinds of activities appropriate for this menu. It just happens that I am familiar with all of these books, since my own developing self-awareness has drawn them to me at various times.

6. *Journeys Out of the Body,* by Robert A. Monroe (Garden City, New York: Doubleday, 1971), is probably the best guidebook available on out-of-body experiences.

Jon Klimo, in his book *Channeling: Investigations On Receiving Information from Paranormal Sources* (Los Angeles: Tarcher, 1987), defines channeling as "the communication of information to or through a physically embodied human being from a source that is said to exist on some other level or dimension of reality than the physical as we know it, and that is not from the normal mind (or self) of the channel." This book is an excellent introduction to the whole field of psychic phenomena associated with channeling, including a variety of theories about what is really going on when someone channels, and how to assess the quality or usefulness of the material thus received. There is a selected bibliography of writings by channels, as well as about them, and a glossary of terms people are likely to encounter both in the book itself, and in other related works. The author also includes a few exercises for people interested in developing their own channeling abilities.

7. There is a whole genre of fantastic fiction called "sword-and-sorcery" that deals with the archetypal-hero themes Charles mentions. Among the very best such tales are *The Lord of the Rings,* by J. R. R. Tolkien, 3 vols. *(The Fellowship of the Ring, The Two Towers,* and *The Return of the King;* 2nd ed., Boston: Houghton Mifflin, 1965); and *The Belgariad,* by David Eddings, 5 vols. *(Pawn of Prophecy, Queen of Sorcery, Magician's Gambit, Castle of Wizardry,* and *Enchanter's Endgame;* New York: Ballantine, 1982–84).

8. *The I Ching, or Book of Changes,* the Richard Wilhelm translation (from Chinese into German), rendered into English by Cary F. Baynes (3rd ed., Princeton, New Jersey: Princeton University Press, Bollingen Series XIX, 1967).

9. An excellent introduction to shamanism is provided by *The Way of the Shaman: A Guide to Power and Healing,* by Michael Harner (San Francisco: Harper and Row, 1980).

10. *Do What You Love and the Money Will Follow: Discovering Your Right Livelihood,* by Marsha Sinetar (Mahwah, New Jersey: Paulist Press, 1987).

APPENDIX

A Quick Reference Guide to the Menus System

The Seven Components of Life Purpose

Service to the Body

Anything done to enhance the body's ability to perform as a vehicle for the lessons of the soul.

Service to the Soul

Anything done to further the lessons the soul must learn in physical reality, usually by confronting every situation life has to offer without resistance.

Service to the Creator

Anything done to realize a creative project as a means of becoming aware of having been created oneself to fulfill some special function within the universe.

Service to the Personality

Anything done to realize within oneself as much as possible of the vast storehouse of human capability.

Service to Family

Anything done to help blood relatives or the spiritual family of one's closest friends to fulfill their individual life purposes, as well as allowing such persons to aid oneself in the same way.

Service to Humanity

Anything done to enhance the physical, emotional, intellectual, or spiritual well-being of mankind.

Service to All Life

Anything done to better the quality of life for other beings on the planet, animal or vegetable.

The Menus for Impulsive Living

Menu A—The Natural Schedule

Impulses that divide the day into flexible time units and signal the importance of shifting from one menu to another or from one project to another on the same menu. Service to the body.

Menu B—Physical Focus

Impulses that make you aware of, and help you overcome, inflexibility, coordination problems, and lack of presence in the body as you move toward realization of your ideal body. Service to the body.

Menu C—Self-Awareness

Impulses that make you aware of, and help you confront, the lessons of the soul and aid you to overcome problematic beliefs that block your ability to create your own reality in the manner most conducive to your growth. Service to the soul and/or service to family.

Menu D—Work

Impulses that allow you to increase your level of self-valuation, in terms of earning money or appreciation through career or volunteer work. Service to the body (preparing and shopping for food), service to the Creator, service to the personality, service to family, service to humanity, and/or service to all life.

Menu E—Play

Impulses that allow you to take a break from fulfilling your life purpose or to rehearse the vast storehouse of human potentialities to keep them from atrophying, often by playing games. Service to the Creator, service to the personality, and/or service to family.

Menu F—Cycles

Impulses that allow you to see how much you have matured—without symptoms of aging—and help you perceive the larger rhythms of psychological growth, built up from the flexible time units of Menu A into longer periods akin to days, weeks, months, and years. Service to the personality, service to family, service to humanity, and/or service to all life.

Menu G—Surprises

Impulses that redirect your projected course of action by interrupting your plans—leading to adventures or to warnings of the presence of damaging beliefs, attitudes, or behaviors—and preventing you from succumbing to routine and world-weariness. Impulses that shift you out of one menu and into another without the need to urinate. Service to the soul.

Functions of the Menu A Impulses

The Impulse to Urinate

Indicates the need for a change in focus of consciousness, divides the day into flexible time units akin to the hours, creates dedicated time slots within which activities of a certain menu may be pursued, and signals the need to shift from one menu to another.

The Impulse to Quench Thirst

Replenishes the water necessary to establish a new brain chemical balance (or state of consciousness) after urination; allows for smooth shifts between activities on the same menu within a single dedicated time slot.

The Impulse to Sleep

Allows the soul to convert the individual's experience in physical reality into the language of nonphysical reality (energy transformations); gives the soul an opportunity to assess the learning that has been accomplished in the course of a day and to provide recommendations—in the form of dreams—for how one's life force could be more appropriately managed; allows the soul to refuel the individual's life-force fuel tank for the upcoming day.

The Impulse to Awaken

Indicates that the soul's processing of the individual's experience has been completed, as well as the refueling of the life-force fuel tank; signals the appropriateness of beginning a new day.

The Impulse to Eat

Indicates the need to take time out from accumulating experience, in order to begin the process of digesting what has been learned from it and to fuel the process of experiential intake until the next meal.

The Impulse to Defecate

Signals the completion of a process or a stage in a process; allows one to monitor how efficiently one has been using his or her life force, through examination of the stool.

Principles of Efficient Life-Force Usage

1. When you leave behind a time slot dedicated to a particular menu at the point of urination, dedicate the next time slot as often as possible to a different menu.
2. Dedicate at least one time slot per day to each of the Menus B through F (the Once-a-Day Requirement).
3. Separate second- and third-time slots dedicated to a particular menu from each other by engaging in activities from at least one other menu.
4. When nearing exhaustion, shift into a menu that has thus far been neglected.
5. For maximum life-force availability in the course of a day, pursue impulses from all five menus as early as possible.

Rules That Guarantee an Impulsive Lifestyle

1. No menu shall be perceived as of greater value than any other.
2. No activity on any given menu shall be perceived as of greater value than any other.